Comparative Judicial Politics

★ ★ ★

Mary L. Volcansek
Texas Christian University

ROWMAN & LITTLEFIELD
Lanham • Boulder • New York • London

Executive Editor: Traci Crowell
Assistant Editor: Mary Malley
Senior Marketing Manager: Amy Whitaker
Interior Designer: Rosanne Schloss

Credits and acknowledgments for material borrowed from other sources, and reproduced with permission, appear on the appropriate page within the text.

Published by Rowman & Littlefield
An imprint of The Rowman & Littlefield Publishing Group, Inc.
4501 Forbes Boulevard, Suite 200, Lanham, Maryland 20706
www.rowman.com

6 Tinworth Street, London SE11 5AL, United Kingdom

Copyright © 2019 by The Rowman & Littlefield Publishing Group, Inc.

All rights reserved. No part of this book may be reproduced in any form or by any electronic or mechanical means, including information storage and retrieval systems, without written permission from the publisher, except by a reviewer who may quote passages in a review.

British Library Cataloguing in Publication Information Available

Library of Congress Cataloging-in-Publication Data
Names: Volcansek, Mary L., 1948– author.
Title: Comparative judicial politics / Mary L. Volcansek, Texas Christian University.
Description: Lanham : Rowman & Littlefield, 2019. | Includes bibliographical references and index.
Identifiers: LCCN 2018042005 (print) | LCCN 2018042862 (ebook) | ISBN 9781538104736 (electronic) | ISBN 9781538104712 (cloth : alk. paper) | ISBN 9781538104729 (pbk. : alk. paper)
Subjects: LCSH: Courts. | Political questions and judicial power. | Comparative law.
Classification: LCC K2100 (ebook) | LCC K2100 .V65 2019 (print) | DDC 347/.01—dc23
LC record available at https://lccn.loc.gov/2018042005

∞™ The paper used in this publication meets the minimum requirements of American National Standard for Information Sciences—Permanence of Paper for Printed Library Materials, ANSI/NISO Z39.48-1992.

Printed in the United States of America

For my four-legged editors:
Bianca, Grey, Red, and Micina

Contents

List of Figures, Tables, and Boxes   vii
Preface   ix
Acknowledgments   xi

1 **Law, Courts, and Politics**   1
   Judicial Empowerment   6
   Dispute Resolution   9
   Learning through Comparison   16
   What Follows   19

2 **Legal Traditions**   23
   Civil Law Tradition   27
   Common Law Tradition   30
   Islamic Law Tradition   33
   Customary Law Tradition   38
   Hierarchies of Courts   42
   Adversarial versus Investigatory   43
   Specialized Courts   45
   Conclusion   48

3 **Lawyers and Access to Justice**   51
   Legal Education   54
   Legal Profession   60
   Legal Mobilization   63
   Interest Group Litigation   66
   Conclusion   70

vi ★ Contents

4	**Judges**	71
	Judicial Independence	75
	Too Much Independence?	88
	Judicial Authority	90
	Judicial Decision Making	96
	Conclusion	100
5	**Constitutional Review**	101
	Constitutions and Constitutional Review	103
	Models of Constitutional Review	105
	Theories Explaining Constitutional Design	107
	Themes and Variations	111
	Strong or Weak Form	113
	Executive, Delegate, Guardian, or Political Courts	117
	Constitutional Review Viewed Pragmatically	121
	In New Democracies	123
	Conclusion	125
6	**International and Transnational Courts**	127
	Development and Evolution of International Courts	132
	International Courts	135
	Transnational Regional Courts	138
	Hybrid Courts	141
	Specialized and Administrative Tribunals	142
	Arbitration and the *Lex Mercatoria*	142
	Compliance and Enforcement	144
	Conclusion	148
7	**The Impact of Courts**	151
	Defining Impact	154
	Dispute Resolution (Micro Level)	159
	Policy and Institutional Change (Macro Level)	161
	Do Courts Matter?	165
8	**The Legitimacy of Courts**	169
	Defining and Recognizing Legitimacy	172
	Creating, Sustaining, and Forfeiting Legitimacy	175
	Conclusion	180

References 189
Index 225

Figures, Tables, and Boxes

★ ★ ★

FIGURES

4.1	Judicial authority and independence	74
5.1	Example of Kelsian model: German Federal Constitutional Court	106
6.1	Soft-hard legalism in international agreements	134
6.2	Sovereignty costs of international courts	146

TABLES

2.1	Legal Systems of the World	27
8.1	Confidence in Courts	180

BOXES

2.1	People's Republic of China's First Civil Code	29
2.2	Legal Pluralism in Sri Lanka	37
2.3	Conflicting Laws: Widows and Inheritance in Zimbabwe	39
2.4	Civilians in Military Courts in Venezuela	47
4.1	Politics and the Judiciary in Brazil	90
4.2	Curbing Judicial Authority in Turkey	93
4.3	Motives of Italian Judges	98
5.1	So Much for a Court Decision . . .	102
5.2	Pakistan President Musharraf versus the Supreme Court	111

5.3	Constitutional Hardball	115
6.1	The International Criminal Court Investigates a Mali Police Chief	137
6.2	Cuisine and the European Court of Justice	139
6.3	European Court of Human Rights and Political Expression	140
7.1	Potential Implementing Audiences for Court Decisions	156
7.2	Ripple Effects of Trial Court Decisions	160
7.3	Public Reaction to Sentences	164
7.4	Public Preferences in Bermuda Override Supreme Court Decision	167

Preface

WHEN I WAS a graduate student, Russell Wheeler first exposed me to pioneering forays into the study of foreign courts by luminaries including David Danielski, Donald Kommers, and Martin Shapiro, among others. I was captivated. I had barely ventured outside the confines of the United States, but the lure of the foreign and the exotic intrigued me. I started my professional life almost simultaneously with my travels around the world. The concept of comparative judicial politics traveled with me, but I could not discern how to actually compare judicial behavior when no two countries shared the same judicial processes or applied the same legal norms. Thankfully, the European Union—then the European Economic Community—presented itself as a possible laboratory, and the Visitors Information Program of that body graciously provided me with a grant, translators, and access to judicial officials in six member nations. My initial step into the field of comparative judicial politics and my first book resulted. I was hooked and have pursued a research agenda since then in the field of comparative judicial politics, even when the field was merely a stepchild in the political science discipline, owned neither by public law nor by comparative politics.

Times changed within the discipline of political science, and research into various aspects of comparative judicial politics burgeoned. I and many others wanted to teach this field, but no textbook was available. Indeed, no comprehensive or even semi-comprehensive theories, frameworks, or studies existed (and they still do not). One could manage a course at the graduate level by cobbling together a dozen books and multiple articles, but that was too cumbersome for the typical undergraduate class. Thus, I took on the project of writing a textbook to fill that gap. I make no pretense of being comprehensive, of offering overarching frameworks, or of generating a "theory" of judicial politics. What I intended was to take seven of the most salient aspects of judicial politics around the world and attempt to synthesize the scholarship in a fashion that would be accessible for upper-division undergraduates, graduate students, and law students. Perhaps even professionals in the legal field, comparative politics, and American judicial politics will find this text useful and possibly enlightening. At the very least, I want to offer a starting point on which others can improve, hone, and analyze our study of law, courts, and politics in various parts of the world. More ambitiously, I hope to enable others in the field to teach comparative judicial politics to a new generation.

The world has become smaller as we are progressively more interconnected via the Internet, commerce, human migration, and rapid transportation. My fascination with comparative judicial politics was born from a desire, perhaps a necessity, to break free of thinking only about how law, courts, and politics function in the United States. Law reflects culture, courts translate that culture, and politics shapes and is shaped by it. Understanding how other countries and other cultures confront and attempt to tame similar problems proves to be a powerful antidote to ethno- and geocentrism. Lessons can be gleaned from the experiences of other places for how we approach those in our own backyards.

—Mary L. Volcansek

Acknowledgments

I AM PARTICULARLY grateful to Russell Wheeler, who years ago introduced me to judicial politics and to comparative studies of the phenomenon. I also wish to thank TCU for providing me with a semester-long leave to complete this manuscript, as well as my wonderful cheerleaders in the process: Glen Hunt, Terry Leness, Carla Manley-Russock, Jerri Beth Palmer, Eric Peters, Connie Stevens, Lisa Stroud, and Patrick Walter. Their patience and encouragement were essential to the completion of this project.

I also wish to thank my editors at Rowman and Littlefield, Traci Crowell and Mary Malley. The thoughtful comments from reviewers of parts of this manuscript—Benjamin Bricker, Daniel M. Brinks, Mark C. Miller, Charles Anthony Smith, Michael C. Tolley, and Raul Sanchez Urribarri—served as sources of inspiration and of caution, both highly valuable.

1

Law, Courts, and Politics

ON MAY 5, 2015, the Constitutional Court of the Central African nation of Burundi announced a constitutional interpretation of presidential term limits that resulted almost immediately in at least nine deaths and scores of wounded people, and also sparked a much longer season of violence and civil unrest (Kushkush 2015). A month later the US Supreme Court ruled in *King v. Burwell* (2015) on a central plank of the highly controversial health-care law of 2010, known as the Affordable Care Act (ACA), but opponents of the court's decision did nothing more than mutter about judicial tyranny and pledge to repeal the law. Why such dramatic differences in how a judicial decision is received?

Both decisions required that a nation's highest judges interpret admittedly ambiguous legal language. Article 96 of the 2005 Burundi Constitution states: "The President of the Republic is elected by universal direct suffrage for a mandate of five years renewable once." However, sitting president Pierre Nkurunziza sought to seek a third term on the grounds that he was selected for his first term by parliament, not by "universal direct elections." The Burundi high court sided with President Nkurunziza, saying in its seven-page decision that "the only one and last renewal of the current presidential term, in direct universal franchise for five years, is not contrary to the Constitution" (Kushkush 2015). Six of the court's seven members signed the decision. Was that a plausible reading of the constitution?

Some six weeks later, Chief Justice John Roberts of the US Supreme Court, joined by four of the other eight justices, confronted verbal ambiguity in the ACA: Does the reference to "an Exchange established by the State" exclude exchanges established by the national government when a state failed to create one? Chief Justice Roberts concluded that instead of relying on the literal wording and plain meaning of the act's words, the context and structure of the law required reading the ambiguous passage as referring to *any* exchange or *an* exchange rather than strictly to exchanges created by the states. Was that a defensible interpretation of the law?

The Burundi jurists chose a literal interpretation of the words in the text, whereas the majority of the US justices decided based on the intent of the entire law, not on the precise words that were contested. Obviously political considerations played a role in how each court reached its decision, and the judges read the relevant laws through the prism of their own political lenses. Moreover, political reactions followed each court's decision, but they proved deadly in Burundi, while in the United States the decision merely gave pundits, observers, and politicians grounds for grumbling, critiquing, and speculating about what had motivated the pivotal vote, that of Chief Justice Roberts, to decide as he did. How can one explain how different courts choose to interpret all-too-frequently ambiguous or contradictory legal documents or to decipher what constitute credible facts in court cases? That is what this book explores.

Roughly two hundred nations were recognized in 2018, and each has some form of legal system or systems to enable resolution of disputes, not only concerning controversial laws and constitutional interpretation, but also between citizens and, of course, those adjudicating criminal violations. Sheer numbers and variations make generalizations hazardous, but some trends, theories, or at least tendencies can be discerned and to some extent explained. A complication exists for many nations that now fall under the jurisdiction of a growing web of international and transnational laws enforced by judicial bodies charged with policing a variety of human rights treaties, various international trade regimes, alleged war crimes, and even international investment and environmental protection agreements.

The type of law followed in each country, such as common law, civil law, Islamic law, and customary/traditional law, might suggest answers about how judges approach interpreting laws and constitutions. Burundi has a civil law system, adopted from the

Belgians, whereas the United States follows common law. However, in Burundi matters that generally could be labeled "family law"—inheritance, marital property, and gifts—remain largely governed by customary law (Bizimana, Burakarafitiva, and Ncanatwi 2012). At the abstract level, civil law systems are more restrictive of judicial discretion than are common law ones, in which much of the law is embodied in judicial decisions. That might explain the distinctive paths that each high court followed in these two decisions, but that explanation, though not totally without merit, seems superficial when looking at the totality of differences between the United States and Burundi. Legal systems do structure the range of possibilities available to judges, as discussed in detail in chapter 2, but they are not necessarily the determining factor.

Most judges are also trained in law, and the character of legal education and the practice of law may be reflected in how and why judges decide cases as they do. In the two cases from Burundi and the United States, some, but not a great deal, of variation can be observed. Judges on the Constitutional Court in Burundi must be "jurists," implying that they are judges and hence lawyers (Constituteproject.org. 2015, Art. 26). The US Constitution stipulates no requirements to serve on the US Supreme Court, but by tradition at least since the early twentieth century, all serving justices have been lawyers, and many have previously also served as judges. However, vast differences exist in the educational opportunities available in the two countries. Some two hundred law schools were approved by the American Bar Association in 2018, but Burundi has a single university, enrolling approximately thirty-three hundred students, with law constituting only one of several courses of study; the literacy rate in the country is only about 30 percent. Approximately two hundred lawyers serve a population of 8.5 million (eDiplomat 2005). Not surprisingly, the vice president of the court and lone dissenter in the presidential terms case, Sylvere Nimpagaritse, stated that most of his colleagues thought the decision violated the constitution, "but they were under pressure to change their minds" (BBC 2015). Nimpagaritse fled to neighboring Rwanda, along with about twenty thousand other Burundians, when the decision was announced (Ng'wanakilala 2015). The status and accessibility of the legal profession in various lands therefore provide insight into why and how judges behave as they do.

Judicial decisions form the core of what this book considers, making judges the primary focus of investigation. However, many different criteria drive the ways that judges view and approach their jobs. A variety of factors work to determine how judges conceive of their roles and appropriate modes of decision making, but the two most obvious and likely critical are the independence and the authority of the office. Independence is treated as protected (or not) by appointment, removal, and tenure requirements, whereas authority is determined by institutional design, but also through competition with other centers of power, both inside and outside of government. Article III of the US Constitution grants Supreme Court justices and indeed all judges at the federal level tenure "for life or good behavior." Only Supreme Court justice Samuel Chase was threatened with impeachment, in 1805, but the US Senate refused to convict him (Volcansek 1993). Constitutional Court judges in Burundi are appointed through a process that mirrors that employed in the United States: appointed by the president with Senate approval. The Burundi judges serve, however, only for one six-year, nonrenewable term (Constituteproject.org. 2015, Art. 226). The dissenting Burundi judge claimed that pressure was placed on his colleagues to rule in support of the president. Undoubtedly the US president was pleased with the Supreme Court for sustaining one of his signature legislative accomplishments, but no suggestion of inappropriate nudging of the US justices arose.

Constitutional provisions and institutional designs are necessarily shaped and changed by the political environment in which they operate. Most readers have likely surmised since the first page that the answer to why these two courts interpreted their respective constitutions and statutes as they did can be found in the history, politics, economics, and cultures of Burundi and the United States. The United States has been a stable democracy since 1787, with the exception of the Civil War in the mid-nineteenth century. Burundi, on the other hand, is heir to a vastly different legacy. Burundi was tacitly a German colony until after World War I, when it was passed to Belgium as an administrative protectorate until it gained independence in 1962. Ethnic competition among Hutus, Tutsis, and Batwa has characterized the land since the sixteenth century, and large-scale massacres, many ethnically based, occurred in 1965, 1972, 1988, and 1993. A fifteen-year civil war ensued after the assassination of one president and the death of his successor. The civil war ended with the Arusha Peace and Reconciliation agreement in 2000, which stipulated power sharing between the Hutus and Tutsis through a quota system in all governing bodies

(Bizimana, Burakarafitiva, and Ncanatwi 2012). A new constitution was passed by referendum in 2005, and President Nkurunziza was named by the Burundi parliament as the first president. Nkurunziza's desire to serve beyond his two-term, ten-year mandate was the catalyst for the Constitutional Court decision. Burundi is, moreover, an agricultural country, with only one-tenth of the population living in urban areas and more than half living below the poverty level. Not surprisingly, therefore, the political dynamics and hence the authority and independence of courts and the legal system have assumed different contours from those in the United States, despite somewhat parallel constitutional provisions in both countries.

Just as judicial decisions are not rendered in a political vacuum, they also often have an impact on society and the political system. The US Supreme Court decision in *King v. Burwell* (2015) to uphold the challenged ACA provision that sustained the health-care insurance system cast repeal or wholesale reform of the law as a major issue in the 2016 presidential election. The Burundi Constitutional Court decision permitted President Nkurunziza's bid for a third term in office, though violence erupted from the date of the decision and persisted at sufficiently high levels that the election was twice postponed. An unsuccessful coup attempt before the election and large protests were followed later by attacks at night, and most media outlets were muzzled (Santora 2015). Violence continued seven months after the court ruling and five months after the election that returned Nkurunziza to the presidency for a third term (Gettleman 2015). Three years later, Nkurunziza named himself "Supreme Eternal Guide" and staged a referendum that allowed him to remain in office until 2034 (*Economist* 2018b).

All court decisions affect someone, if only the parties to the dispute. Sometimes, however, decisions have far-reaching effects in the political, economic, and social worlds. Decisions having extensive consequences often create a form of feedback loop to the courts. That feedback may take the form of more litigation to test the limits of the decision or may be felt beyond the confines of the legal world. The Supreme Court decision in *King v. Burwell* essentially forced the appellants in the case to purchase health insurance or face a fine. However, it also led many in Congress who opposed the ACA to seek repeal and attempt to pass new legislation; health insurance companies that watched their profits fall pulled out of some programs and threatened to withdraw completely. In other words, ripple effects flowed from each decision, though the magnitude of those effects was vastly different.

In the case of *King v. Burwell* in the United States, the consequences were limited in scope and in geographic reach. No one outside the borders of the United States felt any impact. Not so in the Burundi case. Approximately a quarter of a million Burundians left the country, most to neighboring Rwanda (Crisis Group 2016). Though Burundi resided within two loose regional organizations, the African Union and the East Africa Community, neither had any legal basis for intervention in Burundi. Burundi had also accepted the jurisdiction of the International Criminal Court, which tries war crimes and crimes against humanity (CIA World Factbook 2016), but withdrew from the court's jurisdiction after a United Nations (UN) commission found evidence of extrajudicial killing, rape, and other atrocities two and a half years later (Moore 2017b).

JUDICIAL EMPOWERMENT

Courts, law, and judges were largely ignored in the treatment of comparative politics until recently, perhaps because judges were viewed as "independent neutral law appliers rather than policy-makers" and because law and courts function using a specialized, technical, and profession-specific language that differs from the common political one (Shapiro and Stone 1994, 398). However, scholars were unable to ignore an increase in levels of judicial empowerment in various places around the world (Ferejohn 2002). The phenomenon of the rising power of courts has been labeled *judicialization* (Tate and Vallinder 1995), *juridification* (Silverstein 2009), or *legalization* (Abbott et al. 2000). Subtle distinctions delineate these terms from one another, but they all aim to describe a form of increased judicial power. Judicialization was initially defined by Torbjörn Vallinder (1995) as occurring when decision-making authority moved from the traditional political agents to the courts or when judicial modes of characterizing issues spread to other political bodies. The nuanced variation of juridification refers to when legal language and processes replace ordinary politics (Silverstein 2009). The third variant, legalization, occurs when rules create legally binding commitments; legal and technical precision binds those rules; and third parties (most often courts) implement, interpret, and apply those rules (Abbott et al. 2000). At their core, all three characterizations imply that courts have supplanted the expected political decision makers in some aspects of their authority. Moreover, other political decision makers become more cognizant of judicial authority and prior judgments, because of the threat of future censure (Stone 1989). In short, more and more people rely on courts and judicial mechanisms to resolve "fundamental moral controversies and highly contentious political questions" (Hirschl 2008, 129).

How and why has the shift to an increased policy-making role for courts occurred? Usually the phenomenon occurs in tandem with the authority of courts to invalidate executive and legislative acts that they deem contrary to the constitution, constitutional review or, as it is known in the United States, judicial review. This authority was delegated to courts typically as part of the transition to democracy and, in the former eastern bloc nations, a market economy. In other cases, for example Canada (1982) and New Zealand (1990), the change was linked to the adoption of an enumeration of citizens' rights. Elsewhere, such as in Israel (1992), other forces drove the transition (Hirschl 2001; Meydani 2011). Circumstances have altered not only the environment in which courts operate, but also sometimes the attitudes of judges about their appropriate functions. Judges have largely demonstrated a willingness to regulate the reach of legislatures and executives, make substantive policy choices, and regulate political activity itself (Ferejohn 2002).

More and more political questions are also transformed into legal ones. But why has this trend seemingly become so pervasive? Explanations vary, but some common ones may be illustrative, though none may fully account for shifting power to courts. One recurring feature in the rise of judicial power lies in its link to the number of constitutional charters of rights that enumerate protections of minorities in the face of legislative or popular majorities. Courts are particularly well-positioned to arbitrate and guard those rights. Not surprisingly, therefore, political opposition groups find courts offer an alternative venue to legislative debate. Courts often also possess greater respect than do political elites, because of their procedural rules and ability to frame decisions in the context of law. In some cases, elected bodies have willingly delegated the resolution of issues to the courts rather than confront them themselves (Tate 1995).

The intentional delegation of authority to judiciaries by political officeholders might appear counterintuitive, since the essence of politics resides in obtaining and exercising power. Examining what has happened in some authoritarian or quasi-authoritarian regimes can shed light on the lure of delegation of authority to judges. In their collection of studies on authoritarian and semi-authoritarian governments across most continents, Moustafa and Ginsburg (2008) isolated five core functions that courts, including ones with constitutional review, serve in the context of a dictatorship: (1) social control, (2) "legal" legitimacy, (3) control of the bureaucracy and factions, (4) trade and investment credibility, and (5) implementation of controversial policies that offer political cover for those in office.

Social control flows from the criminal process that courts typically exercise but that can be diverted in cases involving political opponents to other forums if the regular courts are thought to be unreliably attached to the regime's values (Moustafa and Ginsburg 2008). Courts can also, if perceived as independent of the ruling party, cast an aura of legitimacy over an authoritarian government. Particularly in authoritarian states, "where the law supplants violence, it can allow an illegitimate government to appear more moderate, thereby augmenting its authority" (Massoud 2013, 14). Courts likewise provide a mechanism for citizens to litigate bureaucratic abuse or malfeasance and thereby mitigate the rise of factions or rogue elements in the government.

Courts also serve an economic function. Companies are unlikely to invest in or trade with countries in which no vehicle for protection of property and contract rights exists. The image, even an illusory one, of an independent judiciary offers a government's credible commitment to potential investors and trading partners that claims will be honored. Finally, many issues that cannot be resolved otherwise or are too divisive can be shifted to the courts. In that manner politicians do not have to share either credit or blame for controversial issues when the judges decide them (Moustafa and Ginsburg 2008). Authoritarian governments can use courts, in other words, to cloak their actions in the concept of the "rule of law" (Moustafa 2003a). The Burundi Constitutional Court's decision in the third-term eligibility controversy illustrates how President Nkurunziza used the courts, not the legislature or the public, to resolve the dispute, with the hope that a decision by a court would receive greater public acceptance. Public reaction to the decision belied that political calculation, as the court was not perceived, at least by the opposition, as able to act independently of the will of the presiding president. Similarly, when legislative stalemate prevented the US Congress from tackling the ACA, the issue was initially shuttled to the courts to resolve.

The reader may be asking, "How is the role of courts in authoritarian countries different in their functions from those in democratic nations?" This is precisely the point of this book: courts serve a number of very useful purposes for *any* government; that recognition has led to a progressively higher level of judicial authority. Law can be used and manipulated by any political system; "law is inherent in politics" (Massoud 2013, 5). Unlike their democratic counterparts, authoritarian governments may act to "judicialize repression" (Pereira 2005). The trend toward increased judicial empowerment has been observed in both countries that lack and have provisions for constitutional review (Gelber 2004). In fact, fear of enhancing the authority of unelected judges led Swiss voters to reject constitutional review in a 2000 national referendum (Rothmayr 2001). Even without the authority of constitutional review, courts at all levels in many places still make decisions about core political issues. A litmus test is lacking, however, for precisely how to distinguish between judicial questions and political ones (Edelman 1994).

DISPUTE RESOLUTION

Judicial empowerment cannot be viewed only as something that occurs solely at higher court levels and in major national political controversies. The core function of courts is to resolve disputes, and in most cases resolution means designating a winner and a loser and mandating some form of penalty on the losing party. Social, economic, and even political goods and values are regularly distributed in some fashion in the overwhelming majority of court decisions. Courts are universal because disputes are part of the fabric of human life, and conflicts are inevitable (Shapiro 1981). Conflicts rise to the level of disputes when competing claims are made public and a third party to whom the allegations are addressed intervenes to resolve them (Abel 1973). The natural inclination to resort to this process is aptly reflected in a description of a dispute within the West Bank Palestinian community:

> It is typical that many people, even anonymous bystanders, intercede in streetside quarrels and attempt to mediate between the disputants, who themselves seem to welcome the public hearing. Thus what may begin as a private confrontation often rapidly assumes the dimensions of a community event. Gratitude is showered on the mediator who can produce a resolution on the spot and a boost is given to his status in the community. (Starr 1992)

The Palestinian street mediator, however, had no authority to enforce his or her solution. Once acknowledged rules or norms begin to play a role in the resolution of a dispute, the intervenor gains authority to make a binding decision (Abel 1973). Hence the intervenor is transformed into a judge, adjudicating the rules. Crucial to the validity of the decision of the judge is the consent of the parties, and that implied consent in modern judicial systems comes with the assumption that those who hold judicial offices are not allies of one or the other parties (Shapiro 1981). The logic of "triadic dispute resolution" (Shapiro 1981, 3; Stone Sweet 2000, 12) provides the foundation for judges and courts. Two people engaged in a dispute turn to a presumably neutral third party for a solution, and that tripartite arrangement forms the universal forum for resolving conflicts. Triads are found in all political systems, and from "the simple invention of triads . . . [with their] appeal to common sense stems the basic political legitimacy of courts everywhere" (Shapiro 1981, 1).

Courts are called upon to resolve all manner of disputes involving family, property, commercial enterprises, labor, tenants, and contracts, among others, as well as to adjudicate criminal accusations. The laws that courts are expected to apply in these disputes have their origins in the traditional political sphere: legislative bodies, executives, and bureaucracies. Even where religious and customary courts are empowered to act, some political body granted them jurisdiction through a political act. Not surprisingly, therefore, similar disputes can lead to quite different results as distinct laws are applied. Laws vary from state to state within the United States; marriage laws and the legality of recreational or medicinal marijuana can be different in each state. The variations can be even more stark from country to country. The penalty for adultery in Saudi Arabia, though it is very difficult to prove, may be death by stoning, but in most Western nations adultery rarely merits mention in courts outside of divorce or child custody proceedings. In other words, law reflects culture, history, mores, politics, and power relationships. An expectation of consent in the dispute resolution process hinges on law. Therefore, judges can at the very least engage in interpretive policy making in their application of law to private disputes.

Sometimes judicial resolution of a private lawsuit carries no implications beyond the contesting parties, but at other times a decision in even the lowest levels of courts affects a larger swath of people. Governments also sometimes choose to delegate regulation of certain categories of contentious issues to courts rather than to bureaucracies. Little research exists on trial courts, where, even in highly developed nations, decisions are often not reported, nor are written explanations of decisions required. Moreover, litigation or criminal proceedings may be commenced, but cases are settled or dismissed without ever actually reaching a judge. One can assume, even so, that most of the settlements, dismissals, or guilty pleas are achieved because the parties or their lawyers attempted to predict what the outcome would be before a judge. Competent lawyers are aware of the propensities of judges or arbitrators and also of how similar cases have fared. Most scholarly studies of basic judicial resolution of disputes at the trial level focus on activities of specialized courts, on changes in the law, or on judicial reforms. Some case studies can nonetheless provide insights into how and why judicial dispute resolution can vary widely and have political implications.

Laws as applied reflect, even in the same legal system, the larger community culture. Indeed, culture provides a means for categorizing experiences that enable people to organize their lives and orient their actions in relation to others. Law constitutes one of the domains of culture (Rosen 2006), but whereas law often mirrors culture, it can also collide with it. Courts, even at the lowest echelons, can create and mold politics in ways that affect the larger political sphere and are in turn shaped by the culture surrounding them.

The interaction of law, courts, and politics at the initial dispute settlement level can be demonstrated by looking at the aftermath of the 1974 Marriage Law in Indonesia, which was designed to reduce the incidence of divorce. That law, despite its claim not to contradict Islamic doctrine, was immediately in tension with standard interpretations of Shar'ia law in Indonesia when it was passed. Common understanding of Muslim doctrine permitted a man to unilaterally divorce his wife, whereas a woman was allowed to seek dissolution of her marriage only in one of three specified ways and required appropriate approvals. Over the thirty years following passage of the Marriage Law, the courts gradually and subtly forced men, in accordance with the law, to prove in court sufficient grounds for divorce, but women's ability to obtain a divorce was not much affected by the law or the courts' application of it. The interesting twist in judicial treatment of divorce under the 1974 law was that, based on a survey twenty years after the law took effect, about half of Muslim divorces were effectuated "extrajudicially" or without a court proceeding because of cost, inconvenience, or ignorance (Cammack, Donovan, and Heaton 2007).

A different picture emerges, though, when looking at how Indonesia employs courts in the economic field. The Commercial Court was created in 1998 to handle bankruptcies and intellectual property laws that were enacted possibly under pressure from the International Monetary Fund (IMF). The court's handling of bankruptcy litigation in the aftermath of the Asian economic crisis in the 1990s was marred by allegations of judicial corruption, whereas its treatment of intellectual property—mainly trademark infringements—elicited praise. Corruption allegations in bankruptcy proceedings largely formed around treatment of domestic debtors pursued by foreign creditors. Cases were often decided in favor of the domestic entity through a complicated process of "voluntary debt compromise" proceedings. Allegedly fictitious domestic creditors were permitted to outvote foreign ones to accept compromise repayments at minimum levels. Why characterizations of actions by a single court vary so much can be attributed to the defendants or debtors involved in each type of litigation. In trademark cases the Indonesian defendants faced only small potential judgments, but in bankruptcy cases a whole business enterprise could be lost. In addition, in Indonesia criminal sanctions are filed in tandem with trademark violation cases, which adds incentives to defendants to settle and comply. Perhaps even more important, Indonesia has a strong and competent contingent of intellectual property lawyers. Many Asian countries have established some type of commercial court as part of economic development plans so as to provide a credible commitment to outside investors, but, at least in the Indonesian case, such courts serve more as levers to encourage dispute settlement outside of the judiciary (Linnan 2010). Not surprisingly, domestic courts, consciously or not, might favor domestic commercial enterprises.

Courts assumed roles in protection of intellectual property in Indonesia and elsewhere because of pressure from international nongovernmental donor agencies such as the IMF. Other countries, such as China and Japan, were prodded by requirements of the Agreement on Trade-Related Aspects of Intellectual Property Rights (TRIPs Agreement), which accompanies access to the World Trade Organization (WTO) and gives nations access to wider world markets. Japan established separate intellectual property courts in 2000, though regular courts had exercised jurisdiction over such cases since 1950. Whereas trademark infringement cases constitute the bulk of those heard in Indonesia, patent protection cases dominate in Japan. The new court in Japan has shortened the length of trials and pretrial delays, a particularly significant factor in patent cases since a patent is time limited. More important, it has provided predictability to resolution of patent disputes (Matsui 2010). Much of Japan's economy depends on technological innovation, which explains the governmental interest in protecting patent rights.

China, on the other hand, has became known as the "world's factory" and has gained a reputation for lax enforcement of patent, copyright, trademark, brand, logo, and domain name protection. Consequently, in 2006 the Chinese government announced creation of specialized intellectual property courts. The impetus for creation of specialized courts was to bring technical expertise and consistency to intellectual property law in China, but at least initially, few foreign companies sought protection in these Chinese courts. The courts had to overcome perceptions of close connections that might develop with repeat litigants to the disadvantage of one-time litigators. As China evolves into more of an innovator nation, greater incentives may drive judicial enforcement of intellectual property rights (Carter 2010). Then China, like Japan, may see a need for greater protection of intellectual property.

Examples of how trial courts can be drawn into deciding cases with political implications can be found outside of Asia. In urban areas of Egypt, for example, during the 1990s cases filed each year were so numerous that approximately one was filed per household. Though the situation may have altered in the aftermath of the Arab Spring in 2011, litigation was inexpensive and lawyers were abundant, about one for every four hundred Egyptians. A consequence of this litigiousness is that the backlog creates delays in reaching and enforcing decisions (Brown 1997). With so many cases and issues decided in courts, judges regularly allocate a variety of values, not solely economic ones, for Egyptian litigants.

Courts and their ability to successfully resolve disputes take on a different hue when more than one system of law operates despite the presence of a supposed national legal system (Engel 2009). The need for clear titles of ownership of property has arisen as central to the ability of countries to compete in the global marketplace. Land rights, however, particularly in formerly colonized countries, and the resilience of customary law have complicated establishing ownership (Gillespie 2011). In much of sub-Saharan Africa, multiple legal systems reside not side by side but rather superimposed upon one another. In Kenya, for example, customary law is recognized in courts, but the government has attempted to formalize and adjudicate land rights under a national system. Agricultural lands have constituted the major source of disputes. The collision between the government's goals and customary law can be clearly seen in the fates of women who have use rights to their husbands' land but cannot own land under the customary tenure system. Widows present a particular issue after their husbands die and their land becomes vulnerable to expropriation. Despite a 1981 national law that allows daughters to inherit land, customary law dictates that parental land must be divided only among sons. Presumably widows can also, under the national law, inherit their husbands' land. Since 1990 a government Land Tribunal has had jurisdiction over land disputes, but only after family, elders, and chiefs fail to find an accommodation. Courts are the last resort. Perceptions—and misperceptions—of costs associated with litigation deter most women from pursuing their claims higher than the mechanisms of customary law. Men, who face the same financial thresholds, do not fare as poorly because they possess autonomous, not mere use, rights to property. Therefore, women are disadvantaged by their reliance on customary dispute resolution mechanisms and tend to find the financial barriers to the formal court system prohibitive, even though their rights could be better protected in a formal judicial proceeding (Henrysson and Joireman 2009).

Vietnam also faced the need to clarify land titles, but with a growing middle class creating a thriving residential building boom, incentives for the government to intervene were stronger. During the early twenty-first century, the government established a system of compulsory pretrial mediation in land disputes, but most mediation proved unsuccessful, and cases reached the courts. Again a confluence of two traditions created difficulties. Land laws in Vietnam follow Western concepts of exclusive property rights, whereas most urban residents hold to a system of self-regulating traditions to govern land use. A consequence of state attempts to legislate titles to property and to foist resolution of disputed land claims onto courts led to a staggering increase in the number and complexity of cases, reaching approximately fifteen thousand in 2005. Judges notably blended the tradition of the self-regulating community with statutory requirements, except where the state was the party to benefit. Because of the nature of Vietnamese law and judges, little so-called legal doctrine is sought in or results from land dispute cases. Rather, judges seek on a case-by-case basis to find solutions that recognize community traditions over exclusive claim laws, a situation that bears implications for potential foreign investors (Gillespie 2011).

In rural Thailand in the early twenty-first century, geographical mobility, not laws or government actions, overcame the hold of some customary law, particularly that relating to compensation for injuries or torts. Household and village "guardian spirits" were traditionally seen as upholding customary laws of injury and required that injured parties be compensated appropriately. Those spirits are regarded, though, as geographically bound. Statutory law and customary law often functioned jointly, but the last decades of the twentieth century witnessed significant changes as geographic mobility replaced village-centered lives. This shift resulted in a surprising state of affairs. Although injuries caused primarily by motor vehicles rose dramatically, litigation for tort compensation claims actually dropped. Researchers' explanation for the failure to move disputes from village elders to courts when injured parties were dislocated from their native villages was that the Buddhist religion prioritized a generous act of forgiveness over the aggressive pursuit of restitution and loss of redemptive capacity when one was not resident near the "guardian spirits." Pursuit of retribution was viewed as potentially compounding, not remedying, the problem (Engel 2009). Religious precepts filled the vacuum created when customary law could no longer be applied.

The studies related above hardly represent the circumstances and conditions of most trial courts, particularly in advanced democracies, but they nonetheless point to some relevant themes regarding how courts, in their most basic role of dispute resolution, are political and have political consequences. Courts can block or moderate the goals of lawmakers. The case studies also illustrate, perhaps in the extreme, how courts are inevitably influenced and conditioned by their social, political, economic, and cultural environments. Courts affect culture and politics by allocating values, but culture and politics also mold judicial applications of the law.

LEARNING THROUGH COMPARISON

Why should one care about how courts, judges, or law operate in other corners of the world? The answer lies partially in our ability to see more clearly the systems with which we are most familiar. Description inevitably requires comparison: she is taller than, shorter than, or slimmer than someone else. Almond and Powell (1996) explain the logic of comparison by invoking Alexis de Tocqueville's acknowledgment that when he was writing *Democracy in America*, the contrast between the new republic and France was always in his mind. "Through comparison, we can learn that what works in one society may not work in another, *and why* [emphasis added]" (Wiarda 1993, 17).

Moreover, the world has shrunk, not geographically, but in immediacy. What happens elsewhere has become tied more closely together through a multitude of new developments. "[G]lobalization, mediazation and digitalization, increasing citizens' participatory demands, dissatisfaction with institutions of representative democracy, growing ethnic-cultural heterogeneity and social inequality, global financial turbulence and democratic malaises" (Geissel, Kneuer, and Lauth 2016, 572) flow across national borders in actuality and virtually through cyberconnectivity. Events within a single nation-state may be mirrored in others, such as the rise of anti-establishment populist movements and anti-immigrant attitudes across Europe and North America in the second decade of the twenty-first century (Friedman 2017). Comparison facilitates locating the commonalities, as well as the nationally idiosyncratic factors, that drive similar political phenomena. Quite simply, our understanding is enhanced when we are able to place our own national politics into a larger context. Within the realm of law, courts, and politics, for example, why are fewer and fewer legal cases reaching actual trials and instead being settled through negotiation, mediation, or the more formal process of arbitration? Why are high court decisions honored without question in some nations and seemingly ignored in others? Returning to our comparison of courts in Burundi and the United States, how is judicial independence ensured, particularly in politically charged cases?

The challenge of comparing judicial politics cross-nationally resides in the often striking and sometimes more subtle distinctions that pervade legal systems and discourses. Rarely is one norm applied across a number of nations such that its application can be traced and variations analyzed. Primarily for that reason, most scholarship on judicial politics takes the form of case studies focusing on a single or very few countries and typically on a narrow slice of the entire judicial process. Indeed, little comparative judicial politics scholarship actually compares. Yet that critique applies equally well to the whole of comparative politics, which "has been closely identified with [the case study] since its birth" (Gerring 2007, 93). Thus, comparative politics as a scholarly pursuit has constituted "the study of foreign countries, often in isolation from one another" (Mair 1996, 304) and comparison among countries to identify and explain differences among them. The so-called comparative method involves statistical analysis of differences among nations, but our inability to quantify human factors and inevitable variations among empirical indicators make quantitative precision difficult (Wiarda 1993).

Case studies are also time bound, as seen in those reported in the previous section, but their intent is not only to describe what happens in a given country at a given time, but rather to isolate patterns or trends. Chile now has a democratic government, but what occurred there under military rule in the 1970s and 1980s lends insights into how and why judicial institutions act as they do under repressive regimes. One-party rule no longer characterizes Mexican politics, but extrapolation about judicial behavior under that political condition can shed light on other nations' experiences with long-term one-party dominance. Once nations consolidate democracy, courts may not act as they did during the transition; nonetheless, their behavior instructs us about how transitions from authoritarian rule to democracy occur. Case studies, in other words, though "disrespected but nonetheless regularly employed" in comparative political inquiry (George and Bennett 2005, 19), allow scholars to overcome many of the difficulties inherent in cross-national work and to seek theories that may apply elsewhere under similar conditions.

Researchers who engage in case studies resemble ethnographers, as they tend to immerse themselves in the language and culture of a nation or a region, producing qualitative studies from which to derive or test hypotheses (Mahoney 2007). The case study strategy allows scholars to explore how informal rules (Helmke and Levitsky 2004) and intervening variables (George and Bennett 2005) shape political behavior. Indeed, sometimes "knowledge is expanded by the discovery of deviant cases" (Mayer 1989, 44), those cases "with outcomes that do not conform to theoretical predictions" (Mahoney 2007, 125). Thus, studies of the deviant cases often lead to better theoretical insights or may simply illuminate conditions that account for outliers.

Despite the proliferation of comparative judicial case studies and a growing number of cross-national statistical studies, both large and small, no unifying theories or comprehensive frameworks about the functioning of judicial politics have emerged, and they may not do so. Indeed, no overarching theory of how and why some democracies thrive and others flail exists, and the outliers, such as India in the case of an ongoing democracy, challenge our thinking about what conditions are essential to the maintenance of democracy. We know even less about what makes democratic regimes slip back into more authoritarian molds and why some never succeed in consolidating democratic norms. One should not be surprised, therefore, that a single theory cannot explain how judges make decisions, why prosecutors pursue some types of crimes more vigorously than others, or why some law enforcement agencies succumb to corruption or abuse and others do not.

Students of comparative judicial politics have applied theories and frameworks from studies of US courts, most commonly the US Supreme Court, to judicial systems elsewhere, and sometimes insights from US courts are useful. In other instances, such theories serve merely as "uncritical exports" (O'Donnell 2000, 3). Life tenure for judges beyond a mandatory retirement age and popular elections for judges, for example, have rarely been adopted beyond American shores. Likewise, having two alternating, stable political parties, each in turn naming judges to the courts, cannot be replicated in many other nations. Yet other aspects of the interplay of law, courts, and politics from the US tradition can be observed elsewhere. The multiple and disparate case studies that characterize judicial politics cannot, however, be ignored. Politics, and particularly democracies, must be studied with an eye toward the judicial system "insofar as the legal system enacts and backs fundamental aspects of both agency and democracy" (O'Donnell 2001, 8). The same appears to apply also to nondemocratic regimes. This book intends to explore some of the findings that can be gleaned from the now vast literature on courts in the United States and elsewhere.

WHAT FOLLOWS

The twin elements of judicial empowerment and judicial resolution of disputes drive the topics covered in this book, along with the essentially political nature of what courts and judges do. Courts are inextricably located in particular social, political, and economic environments, and in many places, whether by design or happenstance, they have increasingly gained authority in the political sphere.

The tradition of law, which is treated in chapter 2, necessarily conditions judicial empowerment. Even as judges in Indonesia attempted to reduce the incidence of unilateral divorces by men, traditional understandings, coupled with the cost of judicial proceedings, failed to alter the reality and frequency of how divorces occurred. Social norms and mores—a form of customary law— also blended with national law in urban land use cases in Vietnam. Religious law similarly can dictate different results from what can be achieved in secular courts. In the sphere of social control and criminal legal applications, inquisitorial systems can affect outcomes differently from what might happen in adversarial ones. Therefore, chapter 2 introduces the legal families—common law, civil law, Islamic law, and customary law—as well as the inquisitorial and adversarial approaches to adjudication of criminal allegations. That chapter also considers the hierarchy of courts and the role of appeals.

As the case studies on dispute resolution illustrate, resort to courts to resolve disputes hinges on access. Access may be barred by the absence of legal literacy, as seen in the Kenyan land cases, or by a belief in the demands of a higher power in the instances of injury claims in rural Thailand. Access may also be financially prohibitive, which explains the rise in extrajudicial divorces in Indonesia and the reluctance of rural Kenyan women to pursue their rightful land claims. Access depends, moreover, on the presence of a legal community that has sufficient numbers of lawyers and the expertise to adequately represent claimants. The meager legal profession in Burundi may have contributed to the constitutional court's decision to support President Nkurunziza's bid for a third term, whereas a vibrant intellectual property bar in Indonesia has clearly impacted the performance and results of cases before the Indonesian Commercial Court. Lawyers, the legal profession, and larger issues of access and legal mobilization are covered in chapter 3.

Judges constitute the focal point of judicial politics, either deciding cases or setting the parameters for out-of-court settlements that attempt to anticipate outcomes if cases were decided in court. How judges can decide cases depends on two crucial factors of institutional design: authority and independence. The Burundi judges presumably had the authority to decide against the sitting president, but apparently, if the lone dissenter is believed, lacked the independence to block the president's ambitions. The US Supreme Court clearly had the authority to determine the definitive statutory interpretation of the ACA and exercised complete independence in the close decision. Degrees of independence may, in other words, temper or enhance a court or a judge's authority. Judicial independence typically depends on how judges are selected, how they can be removed, and their tenure in office. Those features define the de jure or legal independence, but though the Burundi judges had constitutionally defined de jure independence, they lacked de facto independence. The authority of judges, on the other hand, depends also on other elements of institutional design, such as separation of powers and auxiliary functions that are delegated to them, for example, supervision of elections. Judges' independence and authority are explored in chapter 4.

The phenomenon of judicial empowerment tends to be linked to judicial authority to exercise constitutional review, but it has occurred in political systems that have denied courts that authority. Constitutional review, or the authority of a court or courts to invalidate legislative or executive actions and those of subnational governments, has emerged as almost ubiquitous, particularly among newly democratized countries, those rewriting their constitutions, and even authoritarian or quasi-authoritarian ones. Why would constitutional drafters grant a potential veto authority to typically nondemocratically selected judges? Moreover, can we expect judges on a constitutional court in Kuwait or Burundi to wield that authority in the same fashion as judges in Germany, Italy, or the United States? The array of potential configurations of constitutional review is vast—centralized or decentralized, concrete or abstract, limitations—and variations in those schemes can circumscribe or enhance a court's purview. Those questions, institutional design issues, and the effects of constitutional review decisions are considered in chapter 5.

An additional dimension of courts and legal rules emerged in the second half of the twentieth century as nations negotiated and signed numerous treaties. Many of these treaties provide for courts to enforce them. The International Court of Justice (ICJ), located in The Hague in the Netherlands, is the oldest of the international courts, but an ever-expanding number of others have been instituted to replace force and diplomacy to resolve disputes among nations with rules interpreted and applied by courts. These courts have jurisdictions limited by the provisions of the treaties creating them: trade for the WTO Standing Dispute Settlement mechanism, the European Union's (EU) European Court of Justice (ECJ), and panels for the North American Free Trade Association (NAFTA); protection of human rights for the European Court of Human Rights (ECtHR) and the Inter-American Court of Human Rights (IACtHR); and myriad others for environmental protection, financial and investment rules, and even the International Criminal Court (ICC) to prosecute and try allegations of genocide and crimes against humanity. The various international and transnational courts are considered in chapter 6, along with their efficacy for resolving disputes and altering national behaviors.

Courts make decisions, and the outcomes of those decisions presumably affect the parties to each case. Some judicial decisions, however, have a much broader impact. The US Supreme Court decision in *Bush v. Gore* (2000) essentially determined the outcome of a presidential election. The decision of the Constitutional Court in Burundi not only paved the way for President Nkurunziza to seek a third term, but also served as the catalyst for riots, deaths, and an exodus of Burundians to neighboring Rwanda. Yet decisions made by the UK Supreme Court, formerly the Judicial Committee of the House of Lords, that the government or its agents violated the Human Rights Act of 1998 are only declarations of "incompatibility" and require action by Parliament to have any binding force. High national courts may make decisions that are ignored, evaded, or avoided, such that they are rendered meaningless. Some trial court decisions also have ripple effects that extend far beyond the immediate parties to a particular case. The impact, particularly the political impact, of judicial decisions is the subject of chapter 7.

The International Court of Justice decided a dispute between China and the Philippines over the South China Sea in 2016 and one between the United States and Nicaragua regarding US activities to destabilize Nicaragua in 1986. In both cases, the larger and more powerful nations—China and the United States—refused to accept the jurisdiction of the international tribunal. Similar scenarios are played out following judicial decisions by all levels of courts and in many countries. The ability of courts to effectively and definitively resolve disputes relies on the legitimacy granted to the court, the trust that the triad's dispute intervenor is impartial, and the expectation that the court can compel compliance with its decisions. The efficacy of courts everywhere is grounded on a single concept and one of the slipperiest in political parlance: legitimacy. The book concludes in chapter 8 with a consideration of how the legitimacy of courts is achieved or forfeited. Legitimacy or the absence thereof bedevils and enhances the power of law and courts in the political process.

2

Legal Traditions

★ ★ ★

THE FRENCH MANAGING director of the IMF, Christine Lagarde, was investigated for an allegedly negligent act that occurred in 2007 while she served as the French minister of finance. Some eight years later in 2015, French prosecutors said that no case was warranted (Horobin 2015). Yet at the end of 2016 a French judge ordered the case to trial and convicted Ms. Lagarde of criminal charges for the misuse of public funds. More curiously, though, the judge imposed no fine or sentence on her (Thomas, Alderman, and Breeden 2016). How can a judge try someone when the prosecutors do not believe they have a credible case and then convict the accused? Perhaps, as one commentator noted, "It's all about French politics" (Thomas, Alderman, and Breeden 2016), but did something else—such as the nature of judicial discretion, or the definition of the judge's role in continental civil law countries, or the court in which the case was decided—enable that sequence of events?

A forty-five-year-old married woman from Sri Lanka, working as a maid in Saudi Arabia, was convicted of adultery and admitted four times to committing the act, as required by Shar'ia law. She was sentenced to death by stoning. The man with whom she was involved, single and also from Sri Lanka, was sentenced to one hundred lashes (Wheatstone 2015). Why the disparity? Why such a harsh punishment, while in European nations extramarital affairs are estimated to occur in upward of one-third of all marriages (Bartlett 2015), and in the United States, although twenty-three states consider adultery a minor crime (Murphy 2011), rarely is anyone prosecuted for the offense? Culture in some parts of Pakistan requires so-called honor killing when a female family member engages in extramarital sexual relations, but those murders are not sanctioned by law and in fact may well lead to criminal prosecution. Religion, culture, economic development, Westernization, and secularization are important factors woven into the fabric of a nation's legal and judicial traditions.

Legal *systems* tend to be nation specific and refer to institutions, rules, and procedures, whereas a legal *tradition* refers to a set of "deeply rooted, historically conditioned attitudes about the nature of law, about the role of law in the society and the polity" (Merryman and Pérez-Perdomo 2007, 2). The foundations of most national or subnational legal systems usually reside within one of the four loosely defined legal traditions: civil law, common law, Islamic law, or customary/traditional law. Considerable convergence and indeed mixing of traditions has occurred, but often one form of law has overlaid another such that layers more than mergers have resulted. Thus, *legal pluralism* best describes many, if not most, areas of the world.

Patterns of conquest and colonization imposed certain formal legal edifices on countries, and "'legal origin' [tradition] is almost perfectly congruent with 'colonial history'" (Klerman et al. 2011, 379). Some countries, such as Japan, Thailand, and Turkey, voluntarily adopted foreign legal practices totally (Klerman et al. 2011), but even they adapted them to the new environment, dominant culture, and changing attitudes and expectations, reflecting "the interaction of the legal tradition and of the new sensibilities" (Mattei 1997, 5). Legal transplants, wherein a practice from one legal tradition is metaphorically cross-fertilized with others, also characterize the landscape of law. Thus, we speak of the *ideal* legal tradition or family, recognizing that in each setting that ideal type has undergone a metamorphosis to accommodate the legacy and environment of the place where it currently resides.

Likewise, in criminal proceedings, judicial processes may be divided into rough ideal types of adversarial and inquisitorial (also known as investigative or nonadversarial), and the distinction between the two typically hinges on the role that the judge is expected to play in the proceedings. Overlays, transplants, and adaptations have diluted how strictly any nation's criminal process adheres to the dictates of the ideal type. Italy, for example, adopted a hybrid of the two in the 1980s and referred to the new system as

"Processo [trial] Perry Mason"—after an American television series in the late twentieth century that featured an aggressive advocate for criminal defendants (Volcansek 1990)—then later transitioned to a full adversarial scheme (Guarnieri 2015).

Courts in most nations are arranged hierarchically, with higher courts exercising some degree of control over lower courts. Specific contours and levels of authority and autonomy vary widely, but most places allow for an initial hearing and decision in a court of first instance and then permit some form of reconsideration of the first decision, usually within carefully defined parameters. Parallel court systems may also reside beside the strictly civilian ones, such as religious or customary courts. Often both types of courts function primarily to decide issues of family law, such as divorce, child custody, adoption, and inheritance, in conformity with religious or traditional dictates. Political and military courts may be created for a variety of purposes. Ms. Lagarde was tried, for example, in the Cour de Justice de la République, which exclusively decides cases against sitting and former government ministers. The United States has a separate system for adjudicating criminal acts allegedly committed by military service personnel, which intersects with the regular courts only at the higher levels of review. Some special military or political courts, however, are more sinister and aim to deflect certain cases and individuals from the standard legal system for overtly political reasons. Again, so much diversity exists that generalizations are virtually foreclosed, though specific examples can illuminate the processes and the motives behind them. Law is a political tool not only in blatant instances of political courts, but in every context (Hallaq 2009).

This chapter offers a description, not necessarily one that fits any, much less all, judicial systems, and rather focuses on models—those abstractions from reality that highlight only the most salient features—that can provide a vocabulary for considering how judges, law, and politics may interact and behave differently across multiple countries. So-called families of law or legal traditions display clusters of recognizable features but also harbor considerable diversity, much as human families do. Though some basic DNA may be shared, differences abound. And the quirky cousin always pops up, related somehow but sharing few readily discernible similarities. The four most readily identifiable legal traditions are civil law, common law, Islamic law, and customary law. Like many twenty-first-century human families, these four are often blended. Legal traditions have proven to offer little explanatory value for how society, economics, or politics manifest themselves, but the classification scheme does offer useful markers when one attempts to understand how and why different legal outcomes result in various settings. Moreover, law consists of classifications, and the families of law represent one more means to facilitate comparison of judicial politics cross-culturally.

Each of the four families of law has ancient roots: civil law dates from Roman times but was resurrected in the eleventh century, and codification was achieved by Napoleon in 1804; common law is traced to the Norman conquest of England in 1066; Islamic law emerged after the death of the Prophet Muhammad in the seventh century; and customary or traditional law has existed as long as people have lived together in communities and needed to resolve disputes (Glenn 2014). Some common elements can be discerned in each tradition, but the one feature that characterizes all four is that each has evolved far from its origins. Much of the evolution in each case derives from commerce, conquest, and colonization, but most profoundly from the rise of the modern nation-states in the seventeenth to nineteenth centuries. Politics has molded the law, and the law has reciprocally shaped politics both before the nation-state and within it. A kaleidoscope of variation can be observed within each tradition. Which tradition is preferable? That question should be posed as "preferable for whom?" A legal tradition ideally corresponds to the society that it serves, but what criteria should be employed to make that determination (Merryman and Pérez-Perdomo 2007)? No single tradition can be assessed outside of the context in which it has taken root.

Civil and common law are considered "Western" (Berman 1983), whereas the others are non-Western, but the reach of the two "Western" traditions is extensive. The civil law tradition accounts for half of the nations of the world (see table 2.1), but mixed traditions account for more than one-third. Even those classified as having civil law are often manifested in tandem with others. Bhutan, for example, has a civil law tradition, but one infused with Buddhism, and the Philippines has elements of civil, common, Islamic, and customary law. South Sudan and Libya are currently indecipherable due to political instability. One tiny nation-state, the Holy See (Vatican City), uses canon law. Only three nations can be classified as having purely Islamic law (Iran, Maldives, and Saudi Arabia), and only one, Togo, merits the label of having

Table 2.1 Legal Systems of the World

Legal Tradition	Number of Countries	Percent of Countries
Civil Law Tradition	98	50.0
Common Law Tradition	25	13.0
Islamic Legal Tradition	3	1.5
Customary Law Tradition	1	0.5
Mixed	69	35.0

Source: CIA World Factbook (2017).

totally customary law. Even so, customary and Islamic law traditions commonly mix with or reside side by side with civil or common law (CIA World Factbook 2016).

CIVIL LAW TRADITION

The civil law tradition can be traced to around 450 BC in Rome, when the Twelve Tables were written to prescribe how disputes should be decided, but can be more usefully tied to the Justinian Digest, compiled in AD 533 after the fall of Rome. Roman law thereafter entered a dormant period but returned in the eleventh to thirteenth centuries through the vehicle of the Roman Catholic Church's canon law and the rise of universities and a formalized legal profession across continental Europe. Over the next few centuries this revived Roman law began to spread across the continent, at different rates and with twists in various locales as political unification began to take hold. Simultaneously, an interest in national law sprouted. The Scandinavian countries were the first to produce national codes, in the seventeenth and eighteenth centuries, but the French Civil Code of 1804 and the German Civil Code of 1896 became the patriarchs of what we currently think of as modern code or civil law (Glendon, Carozza, and Picker 2014; Glenn 2014).

The essential elements of the civil law tradition were in place in the early 1800s. What were these distinguishing features? Three characteristics are most notable: codes of law, resident judges who controlled the procedures of settling disputes but lacked the discretionary authority to deviate from the written codes, and an ascendant class of academic lawyers who deciphered and interpreted the law (Glenn 2014). To examine those three features more closely, one must remember that these elements represent only ideal types, abstract from the day-to-day reality of dispute settlement. Such abstractions have often been taken so literally as to caricature aspects of the civil law tradition. Whereas each element describes the theory of civil law, these elements have often resulted in a type of folklore. Montesquieu famously wrote in his explication of separation of powers that judges were "la bouche . . . de la loi, de êtres inanimé, "the mouth of the law, dead beings" (Montesquieu [1748] 1949, bk. XI, 499). That statement is often cited as the ground for denying civil law judges any discretion in deciding cases. In fact most legal problems can be viewed from a variety of angles; moreover, laws are rarely complete and unambiguous. Thus, civil law judges have "a lot of interpreting to do" (Merryman and Pérez-Perdomo 2007, 83). The law of torts or injuries resulted almost entirely from the hands of judges in France, and precedents that epitomize the authority of judicial interpretation are regularly cited by lower courts there and elsewhere in civil law domains (Merryman and Pérez-Perdomo 2007). Resident judges may be the norm in civil law countries of Europe, but not necessarily in other nations following in the civil law tradition. The gloss that legal academics place on legal interpretation usually carries greater weight in the civil law tradition than elsewhere, but "legal science does not speak with one voice" (Merryman and Pérez-Perdomo 2007, 82), which further allows space for judges to exercise discretion with or without academic authority.

The civil law tradition is a bifurcated one, with two strands, the French and the Germanic. The French Civil Code preceded the first German one by almost a century, and the French code is simply written, whereas the German one is abstract and dense (Glenn 2014; Glendon, Cardozza, and Picker 2014). The German Civil Code required almost twenty years to write and is highly technical. Both codes nevertheless reflect the values of individual autonomy, freedom to contract, and private property, all concepts of the nineteenth-century liberal tradition. Not surprisingly, the two codes spawned two different sets of heirs as the civil law tradition spread across the world (Glendon, Cardozza, and Picker 2014).

The French model influenced Belgium, the Netherlands, Portugal, Spain, and Italy, though most of those countries' codes have been replaced by more modern versions. It also traveled with France to colonies in parts of the Middle East, Southeast Asia, Africa, and

> **BOX 2.1 | People's Republic of China's First Civil Code**
>
> The Chinese parliament passed "General Principles of Civil Law," an outline of legal precepts to drive a forthcoming civil code, in March 2017. The code that is intended to follow aims for the first time to regularize all noncriminal legal disputes. Though individual codes had been passed previously governing inheritance, contract, and property, many lacunae and contradictions left a muddled system for the Chinese highest court to try to sort out piecemeal. The new code, something first attempted in 1954, intends to clarify a host of rights and obligations, ranging from statutes of limitation to property ownership, and should make life somewhat less complicated for both users of the legal system and judges.
>
> *Source:* "Civil Law: Code Red," *Economist*, March 18, 2017, 42.

the French Caribbean. The French style was likewise imitated later in Central and South America, as former Spanish and Portuguese colonies gained their independence. After independence, many former French colonies in Africa maintained a formal edifice of the French civil law, but adapted it to the prevalent customary or Islamic legal traditions. The German version of civil law was quite nation specific, but its theory and doctrine influenced Austria, the former Czechoslovakia, Greece, Hungary, Italy, and the former Yugoslavia (Glendon, Cardozza, and Picker 2014).

The influences, particularly of the French model, traveled because of corporate and commercial intersections and were facilitated by a shared language. For example, "in Morocco, even corporate law treatises written in Arabic cite mostly French sources" (Spamann 2009). Indeed, French and German civil law focused primarily on private law, but changing political conditions in the twentieth century have given rise to public law as a concern. Civil law tradition did not traditionally carry public law components for labor, social security, and administrative law, and certainly not constitutional law, which largely emerged beyond US borders after World War II (Dam 2006). Economic, political, and social changes, together with regional integration, such as in the European Union, and transnational legal systems, as discussed in chapter 6, fostered and facilitated convergence between civil and common law.

COMMON LAW TRADITION

The origin of the common law dates from 1066, when the Normans under William the Conqueror successfully invaded England, but like the civil law tradition, it evolved in England to meet political exigencies and more as it traveled to future English colonies. The Norman roots persist in much of the language of the common law tradition. The victorious Normans, the elites, and the clergy spoke French, whereas English was the language of the lower classes. Hence, much legal terminology was in the French language: tort, acquit, voir dire, en banc (Schubert 2015). Those terms persist in some places where the common tradition is followed.

Although the Romans had at one point extended their law to England, after their departure little remained of it. It was replaced by a host of customary traditions, largely of the Teutonic tribal variety, which the Norman king left largely in place, with only a very few disputes reaching the king for resolution. Consequently, "administrative necessity rather than legislative design played the central role in fashioning the early structures of the post-conquest English legal system" (Glendon, Cardozza, and Picker 2014, 389).

Creation of a loyal group of royal judges, unlike the resident judges of the early civil law tradition, who could assert the king's authority in a uniform fashion across the country, was the most viable political solution (Glendon, Cardozza, and Picker 2014). Hence the term *common law*; it applies throughout the realm and is common to all (Dam 2006). At the same time, local conditions and customary norms were absorbed into the process through the use of a jury of local people who decided the dispute. The applicable law for the case was based on royal writs or royal instructions that usually defined a procedure for resolution of the case. Judges served to determine if the writ chosen by the complaining party was the appropriate one. In other words, judges arbitrated the procedures, while juries decided the cases. Writs limited the reach of the common law, depriving it of any moral quality. Ecclesiastical courts decided on so-called religious offenses or those that implicated morality (Glendon, Cardozza, and Picker 2014). The law grew through an accumulation of nonbinding precedents that offered the benefit of experience and reasoning. Substantive law was limited, as writs basically prescribed only a procedure. The shared experience of court decisions formed a substantive law.

Within the first two centuries after the Norman conquest, the outlines of the common law tradition were in place: a judge as the central figure, reliance on a prescribed procedure, shared case law, and a jury to make factual determinations. The jury has notably largely vanished from the landscape of the common law, not through repudiation, but rather because of irrelevance as the nature and means of settling disputes changed. By the end of the sixteenth century, parliament had replaced the monarch as the law-making body after a simmering tussle, finally resolved through a civil war (1625–1649). Parliament's role of writing laws has persisted. The common law's place was unaltered, and court decisions were collected in commentary form by Sir Edward Coke (1628) and later by William Blackstone (1765–1769).

Judicial reliance on precedents typically defines the common law tradition in popular parlance. Indeed, if common law is largely made by judges, then logic requires that the same "law" be applied in similar cases. In the formative years of the royal courts in England, decisions in prior cases were part of common knowledge among the judges, based on experience, and were useful for further reasoning. They were not binding, since the cadre of royal judges was small and all were colleagues—"Who could 'bind' a colleague of equal talent, equal authority?" (Glenn 2014, 250)—but objectivity in deciding cases required that "like cases should be decided alike" (Berman 1983, 479). However, this maxim was not equivalent to what normally comes to mind, because the system of precedent dates only from the sixteenth century. Earlier incarnations had relied on reasoning by analogy—by example—which seemed more fruitful than reasoning deductively from an abstract principle (Berman 1983).

To have a system of precedent requires first and foremost that prior decisions be available, that is, reported. Law reports were not formally published in England until 1865, though yearbooks containing notes on cases by lawyers emerged in the thirteenth century, followed by commentaries such as those by Coke and Blackstone (Glendon, Carozza, and Picker 2014). Stare decisis, often confused with precedent, refers to the rule requiring judges to follow precedent (Silverstein 2009) and functions within a hierarchy; lower courts are bound by the decisions of higher courts. But are higher courts bound by their own decisions? In 1889 the Law Lords (the highest court in England at that time) decided that it was bound by its own prior decisions, but that position was reversed in 1966 (Glendon, Carozza, and Picker 2014). In the United States the rule exists that the highest court is generally bound by its own precedents, at least in conventional wisdom, but between 1948 and 1991 the US Supreme Court overruled 115 of its previous decisions (Brenner and Spaeth 1995).

The common law tradition is also distinguished by the centrality of the judge in making/discerning/interpreting the law. If a lower court judge is bound by precedent (the rule of stare decisis), how much discretion can a judge exercise? Precedents largely remove some potential arguments from the table, but the judge still maintains the prerogative to "frame a set of facts within a particular line of precedents" (Silverstein 2009, 69); how the problem is presented drives the solution to be reached. Once a case is framed in a certain fashion, a legal path dependence formed by precedents then drives the outcome (Silverstein 2009).

Another essential feature of the common law tradition is reliance on procedure, which dates from the twelfth-century system of writs; if the proper procedure is followed, the result will be correct. "The process, rather than the application of a code or law, is intended to lead to justice" (Joireman 2004, 10). The nineteenth century in England witnessed significant parliamentary activity, but incremental changes ensued in procedures of the courts. Use of a jury, particularly in private actions, waned, and simultaneously the role of the judge as decider of law and fact was enhanced. The importance of procedure rose to counter, in part, the possibility of judicial error, but an appeals process was put in place as a secondary check (Glenn 2014).

Like the civil law tradition, the common law one was carried to British colonies, but the common law was more difficult to receive (Glendon, Carozza, and Picker 2014). It had to be nationalized for purposes of reception and for national identity, which means that it assumed many different forms as it was planted in British colonies (Glenn 2014). The process was easiest where no competing system of justice other than customary law was encountered, as in Australia, Canada, and the United States. India presented a special challenge, as a well-formed civilization was already in place when the British took over. Common law, judge centered and adhering to the persuasive authority of precedent, influenced English territories in Africa, the Middle East, and parts of Asia and the Caribbean.

Israel's law, especially in the early years, was significantly impacted by the common law (Glendon, Carozza, and Picker 2014). The common law tradition's influence was more diffuse in parts of Africa, but in some countries, like Sudan, the British criminal law went further and not only served for social control, but also embedded British norms in life and culture (Massoud 2013).

Language affected how deeply roots of the common law took hold in different settings. Even in Latin America, where the civil law tradition was exported via Spanish and Portuguese colonization, aspects of the common law tradition have been embraced partially because those colonies gained independence earlier, but more importantly because of their proximity and military and economic ties to the United States.

ISLAMIC LAW TRADITION

The rise of terrorism claimed by so-called jihadists and the mass migrations of people displaced by war or economic conditions from the Middle East and Africa have provoked interest in and even alarm about Islamic or Shar'ia law in the West. Islamic law, like civil and common law traditions, has taken many forms. Theoretically, since Islamic law all derives from the same source—the Quran and hadiths—it should be practiced the same way everywhere. That expectation falls into the same category as the belief that no civil law judge ever exercised discretion or that laws are not codified outside of the civil law tradition. Legal traditions adapt and bend to meet political conditions.

The Islamic law tradition does differ in some fundamental respects from the two Western legal traditions. First and foremost, Islamic law is unapologetically religious, whereas common and civil law traditions claim to be secular. Second, the Islamic law tradition possesses a much wider scope than Western traditions because—at least in theory—it reaches all human conduct; as a result, not all of it could ever be enforced in courts (Anderson 1959). Indeed, Islam is "sometimes described as theology in legal form" (Parsons and Makruf 2010, 308).

The Islamic law tradition dates from the death of the Prophet Muhammad in AD 632 and the two decades that followed, during which an authoritative version of what is known as the Quran or recitations was compiled. The Quran constitutes a collection of all of Muhammad's statements that had been transcribed to record the word of God spoken through Muhammad. Only a few of the verses in the Quran could be considered legal rules; the number varies from forty-nine to five hundred. Even these verses are not legal so much as discourses on ethical conduct (Janin and Kahlmeyer 2007). The Quran, like the Judeo-Christian scriptures, addresses a way of life, how humans should conduct themselves, rather than being a code of law. The Hebrew Torah can of course be viewed as more rule oriented than the Christian New Testament, but its authority is not expected to drive litigation outcomes in human courts (Glenn 2014). Similarly, the Quran as law binds all Muslims even without governmental authority.

Shar'ia law has two foundations: the Quran or Word of God and the sunna and hadith. Hadith records Muhammad's life and deeds, and the sunna collects the system of life derived from the hadith. *Shar'ia* means literally "way to water," but religiously it defines the sole path to a heavenly afterlife. Many people refer to *Shar'ia law*, but rather than being collected and codified, Shar'ia law represents systematic intellectual traditions. It is not a set of rules and regulations (Janin and Kahlmeyer 2007) and can best be understood as shared opinions among Muslims.

Both civil law with its roots in ancient Rome and common law with its original intent to extend a single law in England were devised with a purely secular intention of settling disputes. Shar'ia has a more lofty aim: "Shariah represents the idea that all human beings—and all human governments—are subject to justice under the law" (Feldman 2008, 2). The problem with this higher goal resides, of course, in the ambiguity of language in the Quran, sunna, and hadith. Even the validity of a particular hadith could only be established through its channel of transmission, and hadiths could be inconsistent. Consensus became an additional element of the law. More crucially, validating hadiths gave a place of importance to the scholar clerics, in the same sense that legal academic scholars gained prominence in the civil law tradition. A pluralism of thought and interpretation necessarily arose as the clerical scholars diverged and different doctrinal schools emerged (Hallaq 2009). Because no specific hadith was precisely applicable to solution of a concrete case, reasoning by analogy, akin to the logic of the common law tradition, came to characterize the Islamic legal tradition. This feature has facilitated a particular adaptability in Islamic law and enabled it to fit into various societies and to evolve over time.

Islam's early years survived in the absence of a modern nation-state structure. The caliphs (successors to Muhammad) were not involved in dispute resolution unless they were recognized as knowledgeable in Shar'ia law. The Islamic legal tradition was knowledge based, as distinguished from political, social, or even religious bases. Knowledge of the law was gained through study circles in which students would attach themselves to a scholar and debate religious questions. Because the "judges," those learned in the law, acted largely outside of government, dispute resolution was guided by Islamic ethics and focused on mediation without an externally imposed governmental disciplinarian. "AMICABLE SETTLEMENT is the best verdict" was the legal maxim (Hallaq 2009, 59).

Things changed under the Ottoman Empire, which emerged around 1300 and lasted until 1922. Especially during the sultanship of Süleyman (1520–1560), Islamic law also became positive, written law, although always supposed to be consistent with Shar'ia, and a hierarchical judiciary was established. Süleyman imposed a set of administrative laws on the empire that occasionally contradicted Shar'ia and extended to a range of topics for which the Shar'ia offered no guidance. The beauty of the Islamic legal tradition during the golden age of Süleyman was that it achieved uniformity across the empire (Janin and Kahlmeyer 2007).

Western influences and conquests had begun permeating Islamic lands as early as the sixteenth century, but Napoleon's victory in Egypt in 1798 heralded the first incursion of Western law and emboldened Muslim reformers. The most fundamental change was the separation of religious law from the secular and the placement of the latter under Western-style law, largely codes. The French and British left their marks on the legal traditions of much of the Middle East, the Eastern Mediterranean, and large swaths of Africa, and the Dutch left their imprint on Indonesia. The modern state came to overlay the Islamic legal tradition.

From Süleyman's time onward, man-made secular law began to take its place beside the conflict resolution mechanisms of the traditional scholar-cleric approach of the Islamic legal tradition. Indeed, many Shar'ia proscriptions were also formalized in statutes. The Ottoman Empire aspired to be Islam itself, and the Shar'ia was viewed as the basis of private and public life. Thus, Islamic judges and courts constituted the Ottoman courts (Starr 1992). The Islamic legal tradition was also faced with the implications of democratic Islam. What was the place of the Islamic legal tradition after the caliphate was replaced by the nation-state? Multiple interpretations of the role of clerics, democracy, and authoritarianism splintered any notion of a single contemporary Islamic legal tradition (Rahimi 2012). In the twenty-first century, most so-called Islamic countries are characterized politically by only a superficial embrace of Islam, to secure legitimacy. For these regimes, "Islamic law has meant little else . . . than chopping off hands, the stoning of victimized women, and public floggings . . . , harsh penalties [that] have come to embody and symbolize the vast entity that we call Islamic law" (Hallaq 2002, 1714).

Islamic courts are now generally recognized for settlement of religious issues—mainly those concerning family law—in many countries with sizable Muslim populations. Thus, the Islamic legal tradition, much like both the civil and common law traditions, has mixed with other traditions and has adapted to different political settings. To confuse matters for the non-Muslim, Sunni, Shi'a, and Wahhabism each form separate strands of contemporary Islamic legal traditions, with interesting configurations and a plurality of thought (Glenn 2014) and practice (Janin and Kahlmeyer 2007) resulting.

Moreover, as a consequence of the fracturing of traditional structures, different strains of Muslim discourse emerged: *secularists*, who fully embrace modernity and the West; *traditionalists*, who accept Islam as a way of life but also acknowledge the permanency of modern modes of life; *Islamists*, who advocate returning to a pure Islamic ideology; *Muslim liberals*, who accept the spirit rather than the letter of Islam and adapt that spirit to living in the contemporary world; and *modernists*, who live secular lives with a mere veneer of Muslim values (Hallaq 2002).

European colonization influenced or supplanted Islamic legal traditions, but some attempt was usually made to accommodate rather than undermine the Islamic tradition. In Sudan, for example, under British rule the legal department was divided, with the common law governing private and criminal law and Islamic law applying to family matters (Massoud 2013). A variety of stripes of Shar'ia coexist in different countries and even within countries. Modern Indonesia represents a good example of how variation occurs and the consequences. Almost one-third of the world's professed Muslim believers, some 225 million, reside in Indonesia and comprise almost 90 percent of the country's population. Islamic

> **BOX 2.2** | **Legal Pluralism in Sri Lanka**
>
> Sri Lanka's General Marriage Registration Ordinance sets the minimum age for marriage at eighteen, but Muslims in the nation are governed by the Muslim Marriage and Divorce Act, which allows for marriage of people at any age and only requires the approval of a Muslim family judge for marriages under age twelve. The Muslim law also permits men to have multiple wives without the consent or knowledge of other wives. The law governs only Muslims and those married to Muslims. Attempts have been made, beginning in 2009, to find a reconciliation between the two laws, but no one expects the divergent positions to reach consensus.
>
> *Source:* "Muslims in Sri Lanka: Doom and Groom," *Economist*, June 17, 2017, 37.

law there functions not through legislation, but rather through court decisions that, using a reasoning by analogy process, seek some level of consistency but remain case dependent. Decisions of Indonesia's religious courts are notably subject to state enforcement. Much Islamic law has nonetheless been codified in Indonesia (Ka'bah 2007). In the early 1990s Indonesia wrote a compilation of Islamic law and in 1991 designated it the sole source of law for Islamic courts (Bowen 2007). Indonesia has since 2008 sought to blend secular and Islamic law by bridging the gaps between more secular approaches to teaching law critically and unquestioning acceptance of Sha'ria, through "an orientation based on Islam, humanity, and the Indonesian context" (Parsons and Makruf 2010, 312). This has been accomplished by inclusion of courses in constitutional, public, and criminal law in the Islamic law curriculum and of Sha'ria legal topics in the regular law faculty (Parsons and Makruf 2010). Even so, Aceh, at the northern tip of the island of Sumatra, formally established Shar'ia law in 2001, the only province permitted to do so. Many Shar'ia-based local ordinances, however, have been passed nationwide. Most prescribe women's attire, regulate mixing of the sexes, and prohibit alcohol. Yet again, evidencing how the Islamic legal tradition can vary widely in practice, the Shar'ia law of Indonesia is viewed as a far softer version than that applied in, for example, Saudi Arabia (Emont 2017).

CUSTOMARY LAW TRADITION

Customary or traditional law presents a challenge to describe. It dates from when humans began living in communities and inevitably had disputes that required peaceful resolution. Hence, in the absence of a state, communities regulated themselves (Hallaq 2009), and Martin Shapiro's concepts of the triad, discussed in chapter 1, arose. Customary law persists in the world, but in the twenty-first century it typically resides alongside, fused with, or recognized by another form of modern national legal tradition. Consequently, generalizations can be hazardous (Woodman 2011). Customary law has been defined as a system of norms internal to itself (Glenn 2014) or as a set of interrelated rules that form "regular social behavior and . . . an accompanying sense of obligation" (Woodman 2011, 10). Such broad definitions could apply equally to how social clubs, neighborhoods, or commercial enterprises develop cultures with their own distinctive sets of expectations and taboos. What seems to set customary law apart from other social norms is that it tends to be rooted in long traditions and, although usually aimed at mediating conflicts, carries some authority of enforcement. As described by Englishman John Mensah Sarbah, traveling in the Gold Coast of Africa in the 1870s:

> There exists in such a community much of those positive rights and obligations . . . which may be called the Customary Law, and which each person can enforce against his neighbor, either by means of the village council sitting and acting judicially . . . or by invoking . . . the silent force of the popular sanctions according to an usage long established or well known. (Sarbah [1904] 2015)

Customary law dissipated somewhat through the processes of colonization and later urbanization and increased social and geographical mobility. Recall the examples of dispute resolution in Kenya, Vietnam, and Thailand from chapter 1. Customary law resided within and often prevailed over state-imposed regulations. Thus, customary law can most often be observed now in a hybrid or plural formation with national law (de Sousa Santos 2006). Yet types of customary law forming coherent sets of expectations for behavior have long been recognized and documented from at least the sixteenth century. Many nations, particularly those in sub-Saharan Africa, have legislatively recognized use of customary

> **BOX 2.3** | **Conflicting Laws: Widows and Inheritance in Zimbabwe**
>
> Former Zimbabwean opposition member of parliament and cabinet minister Priscilla Misihairabwi-Mushonga lost her husband and then most of her possessions. She and her late husband had owned three houses, several cars, and joint bank accounts, most of which were left to her by her husband's will. Yet upon her husband's death, most of the estate was awarded to her brother-in-law and her husband's children from an earlier marriage. This occurred, despite laws to the contrary, because of a tradition in customary law of *kugara nhaka* or "wife inheritance." Although wives are no longer physically passed to their husbands' brothers, their property often is.
>
> *Source:* "Inheritance in Zimbabwe: Why Widows Get Evicted," *Economist,* January 28, 2017, 42.

law. The British formally acknowledged "native" or customary law in India and the Gold Coast of Africa and imposed a duty on imperial courts to give effect to the customary law in certain categories of cases (Sarbah [1904] 2015). That trend persisted in parts of sub-Saharan Africa; for example, Zimbabwe has by statute applied customary law to private disputes when, according to the "nature of the case and surrounding circumstances, it appears just and proper, it should apply" (Rosen 2006, 36). Much previously regarded customary law has also been legislated into national law (Woodman 2011).

What distinguishes customary law, then, from the national law of whichever legal tradition a nation has adopted? First, customary legal traditions have been passed through generations orally and are consequently shared information within the community. That allows much of the customary law tradition, particularly with regard to family issues, to be informal and take the form of mediation or compromise in settling disputes and assessing reparations. Just as the Islamic tradition fosters mediation and views morality as central, so does customary law. Indeed, in most legal traditions law is indistinguishable from life (Glenn 2014). The customary legal tradition is also characterized by hierarchy—men usually over women, older over younger, some clans or lineages higher than others (Woodman 2011). Furthermore, some customary legal traditions rely on the supernatural and find applicability in concrete rather than abstract terms. Group responsibility and informal enforcement mechanisms are the norm (Oba 2011).

More than eight hundred ethnic or language groups exist in Africa, and each has its own customary legal tradition (Oba 2011). Multiply that number by indigenous peoples across the various continents and realize why describing customary law proves difficult, but also recognize why it needs to be understood. Some aspects of typical customary legal traditions have proved exceedingly useful, even though not likely transportable elsewhere. Reconciliation represents one of the foremost of these concepts, particularly in periods of transitional justice. Gacaca, named for the herb Umucaca, is a gathering of the men of the community to settle conflicts (Haveman 2011). After the genocide that began in Rwanda in 1994, the national courts were unable to cope with the volume of criminal prosecutions. Therefore, the Gacaca system was used to "try" low-level perpetrators and, though Western standards of legalism were not present, the results were largely consistent with the sense of justice of most Rwandans. The truth and reconciliation process employed in South Africa after the end of apartheid stands as the most well-known example of seeking reconciliation in lieu of retribution through a Gacaca-like process. Similarly, the Acholi people of Uganda require a wrongdoer to admit his trespass and seek forgiveness, after which the disputants and the rest of the community share a meal. Spiritual cleansing and purification rituals are also used in a number of places following conflict to cleanse the former combatants (Oba 2011).

Not all aspects of customary legal traditions serve the laudable purpose of achieving reconciliation, in large part because of the hierarchical nature of the tradition, particularly the treatment of women. Women typically lack legal capacity to contract, to sue, or to inherit under many customary legal traditions. Another point of discordance has been called "blood versus lifestyle" or kinship ties versus more metropolitan lifestyles, best epitomized by a 1987 case involving the burial of a prominent lawyer in Nairobi, Kenya. The widow of the lawyer wanted to bury the deceased in a cemetery outside of the capital, but his Luo clansmen filed suit to have the body buried in his birthplace in accordance with customary law. The case was ultimately decided by regular courts, but the judge gave preference to the customary law over the wishes of the widow (Widner 2001a).

Customary legal traditions can be found and legally recognized outside of the African continent. Indigenous peoples in the Philippines are granted state authority to resolve their own internal conflicts in accordance with their customary legal practices. The Philippines also, interestingly, recognize the personal law of Muslims (Agabin 2012). Similar legal arrangements for indigenous peoples, as well as a separate Islamic system, are found in Sri Lanka, resulting in a total of five systems of private law (Palmer 2012). In Pakistan, customary courts, *jirgas*, combine customary and Muslim law (*Economist* 2017d).

Customary legal traditions face considerable challenges in the twenty-first century, particularly because much of customary law allegedly conflicts with human rights, such as differential treatment of the sexes. Yet customary law possesses a fluid quality that enables it to change and adapt. Empirical studies in seven southern African countries, for example, found that inheritance laws have shifted away from an automatic preference for the male relation. Within the South African community of the Valoyi, a daughter was permitted to succeed her father as chief or *hosi*; that was a community decision subsequently validated by the South African Constitutional Court. Indeed, the interface between customary legal traditions and those of nation-states and their judiciaries is becoming commonplace. Access to national courts remains beyond the means of most people subject to customary law. The customary courts of Pakistan, *jirgas*, thrive because of the cost and slowness of formal courts. Although *jirgas* are best known for some bizarre misogynistic decisions, which are technically forbidden, they also offer speedy and often more satisfying results. A widow whose husband and son were murdered, for example, was compensated with $60,000 by a *jirga* decision. National courts can only punish, not order restitution (*Economist* 2017d). The judicial link between customary dispute resolution and national courts, however, potentially imperils the identities of individual ethnic communities if national courts apply the same standard to all even though their customary traditions vary (Himonga 2011). Twenty-first-century nations might, however, benefit or learn from much of the customary legal traditions, particularly the emphasis on reconciliation and rehabilitation back into the community (Oba 2011).

HIERARCHIES OF COURTS

The notion of taking an unsatisfactory decision by a court to a higher authority and thus creating a hierarchy of courts can be seen in the origins of the civil law during the late Roman Empire, though its very limited practice did not involve professional judges or even courts in the sense that we think of them today. Nobles decided conflicts, but many thought some decisions were corrupt. Therefore, a losing party could seek review by a higher noble, the praetor, who determined which types of cases could be heard and served primarily to formulate or set parameters on the case for the lower nobleperson to decide. Customary law traditions, until they were subsumed by the nation-state, were not conducive to complex institutions and sought only to resolve conflicts. Appeals proved unnecessary. Similarly, the Islamic tradition, until the overlay of the nation-state, considered that mistaken decisions would be rectified by God: "You can win, but still lose eventually" (Glenn 2014, 188–189). Likewise, early common law judges in England, all of whom rode circuit but were based together in London, had no superior judges to whom a dissatisfied litigant could appeal.

The canonical law of the Roman Catholic Church was written in the thirteenth century, but as judges became professionalized and societies became more complex, judicial structures were erected. Not surprisingly, the civil law was intertwined with canonical law, and European continental legal systems developed hierarchically. By contrast, the common law process that included the lay jury was organized horizontally (Damaška 1986). Yet common law also evolved a system of appeals, doing so through judicial decisions and legislative law until the nineteenth century (Glendon, Carozza, and Picker 2014). The need for appeals became apparent as juries became optional and judges decided cases. Then England created a court of appeal in 1875 (Glenn 2014). The nation-state necessitated adoption of some kind of supervisory authority within judiciaries and, hence, even the Ottoman Empire instituted a higher judicial body and began centralizing the Islamic judicial organization (Hallaq 2016). Where customary legal traditions persist and are recognized, an avenue to appeal to a national court is usually provided.

Though most courts have been organized hierarchically since the advent of the nation-state, not all higher courts hear appeals as they are thought of in common law countries like the United States.

Even so, the function of higher court review generally relates to guarantying consistency in application of the law (Guarnieri and Pederzoli 2002). As in Roman times, an appeal serves to provide a check on possible mistaken decisions by the court initially deciding the case. In the common law tradition, appeals typically are limited to review of errors in law. The French developed a more limited form of review—*cassation*—that has been imitated in much of the world that follows the civil law tradition. Cassation is from the French verb *casser*, to quash or void. This mechanism allows a higher court to eradicate incorrect judicial interpretations of legislation (Merryman and Pérez-Perdomo 2007). It is a more limited review than typically encountered in common law and is designed to curb individual judicial interpretation. Variations on the process of *cassation* may involve a higher court's completely retrying cases, including hearing witnesses, seeking expert knowledge, and even accepting new evidence (Glendon, Carozza, and Picker 2014).

The German version of *cassation* is revision, whereby the highest court of review considers what the first level of appeals court (a *cassation* court) decided. It is quite akin to appeals familiar in common law nations, but under revision the highest court can initiate its own review. The emphasis of the revision system is to maintain consistency within the case law (Geeroms 2014). Thus, common law appeals and German revisions accept some leeway in judicial interpretation but also aim to maintain consistency. The French *cassation* system was designed to curtail judicial discretion and uphold the intent of the legislator. In Japan, where the Supreme Court not only serves as the highest appellate court but also controls all appointments, assignments, and promotions for the judiciary, a lower court decision that is reversed on appeal can affect the future career of the lower court judges. Not surprisingly, a striking level of conformity prevails in Japanese court decisions (O'Brien 1996).

ADVERSARIAL VERSUS INVESTIGATORY

The civil and common law traditions typically are divided by the procedures that criminal trials assume. In both the Islamic and customary law traditions, compromise outweighs assignment of fault or reparations (Glenn 2014), making "trials" less necessary, or at least less constrained by procedural requirements. The adversarial form typically dominates in the common law tradition, whereas the investigatory, inquisitorial, or simply nonadversarial typifies most civil law traditions. Notably, as in the legal traditions themselves, convergence and the emergence of hybrids blur many of the distinctions. The investigative carries the more familiar label of "inquisitorial" from the notorious Inquisition, but that label is misleading.

"The adversarial and non-adversarial processes become fictitious creatures, seldom, if ever found in reality, but under certain conditions useful for analyzing it and making it intelligible" (Damaška 1986, 5). The adversarial arrangement replaced duels and trial by ordeal. The primary factor that distinguishes adversarial and investigative molds lies in the roles of the litigants and the judge. In the adversarial procedure, the contesting parties constitute the central actors, with a judge acting as the umpire who ensures that the rules are followed, much like a "judge in a debating society who, unconcerned about the issue under discussion, concentrates dispassionately on the display of forensic skills" (Damaška 1986, 101). Under the investigative system, judges hold the central focus and are supposed to represent higher interests than those of the litigants.

The judge in adversarial procedures has little involvement in the preliminary stages of a case, whether criminal or a private lawsuit, beyond possibly ruling on pretrial matters. The overwhelming number of both criminal and private law cases in the United States never reach a trial because of negotiated settlements in private cases or plea bargaining in criminal ones. The judge therefore plays little role in much litigation. In England, the process proceeds on a far more oral system than in the United States and is less procedurally restricted, particularly regarding evidence that may be presented. Objections are also less frequent (Glendon, Carozza, and Picker 2014). Nevertheless, in both countries the trial is the centerpiece, with judges and juries, if sitting, watching the disputing parties or their lawyers assume the active roles (Guarnieri and Pederzoli 2002). English judges, unlike their counterparts in the United States, may ask questions of witnesses and may inquire about evidence (Glendon, Carozza, and Picker 2014).

Judges in the investigative procedure assume a quite different role, in large part because in private litigation no "trial" takes place, and in criminal cases the judge takes an active role in the pretrial investigation as part defense attorney and part prosecutor. This is changing somewhat but still stands quite apart from the adversarial process. The procedure in private law cases involves the judge's participation in the pretrial phase, including questioning of witnesses and receiving evidence. However, the judge who formulates the summary record will not be the judge deciding the case. Witnesses are not cross-examined but are rather questioned by the judge, who poses questions submitted by the lawyers, and few limitations constrain what testimony can be elicited. Thus, the judge investigates the dispute and is quite restricted as to what awards can be made, usually only the amount required to compensate for any loss or damage (Merryman and Pérez-Perdomo 2007). The criminal process runs parallel in the civil law tradition, with a judge investigating charges brought by the prosecutor and, with the assistance of judicial police, gathering evidence. The investigating judge also examines the alleged criminal perpetrator. All of the material is collected into a dossier that undergoes review by a three-judge panel that determines if a formal charge is required. If a trial follows, the judge runs the proceedings except for closing arguments (Lerner 2001).

The civil and common law traditions diverged as they did largely because of the presence—or absence—of a single factor, the lay jury. The common law tradition was developed with the expectation that lay jurors would make the ultimate decision. Since the civil law tradition evolved with professional judges rendering decisions, a wholly different approach was devised. Even though the private law jury no longer exists in England and is rarely used in the United States, and the advent of guilty pleas now occurs more commonly in criminal trials in both countries, the jury system that has been in place for one thousand years seems impervious to change.

SPECIALIZED COURTS

Countries quite often partition judicial functions into separate judicial systems with distinct cadres of judges and sets of procedures. Most countries in the civil law tradition maintain an ordinary judicial system for criminal and private lawsuits but also have a separate administrative judicial system that hears cases involving administrative actions of the government or its employees (Merryman and Pérez-Perdomo 2007). Germany has supplemented ordinary and administrative judicial systems with specialized finance, labor, and social security courts (Guarnieri and Pederzoli 2002), and many countries, such as the United States, have created special judicial systems for offenses committed by those serving in the military. The creation of administrative courts in the civil law tradition resulted from a strict separation of powers, while other types of judiciaries were instituted in recognition of the specialized nature of the laws involved. Thus, the United States has a Court of Claims to adjudicate contract disputes with the national government, as well as family, juvenile, and immigration courts. However, two particular types of courts exist in various places whose functions cannot be tied to a separation of powers ideology or to specialization: religious courts and security courts, the latter of which are often military ones designed to consider criminal charges against military personnel.

Religious courts, specifically Islamic ones, can be found in Asia, Africa, and the Middle East and usually exercise authority that is typically sanctioned by the state over family issues: inheritance, marriage, divorce, and succession. Those issues have been discussed in the previous section on the Islamic legal tradition. In other nations with multiple religions, a different approach has been followed. India, for example, recognizes a host of personal status laws, largely based on religion and different schools within those sects. India adjudicates personal law questions, such as inheritance and divorce, in national courts. Those secular courts defer, however, to whether the parties involved are Hindu, Christian, Muslim, Buddhist, or another faith in rendering decisions. When disputes arise among people from different personal law communities, the secular courts apply conflict of law principles (Jambholkar 2007).

Israel encompasses a substantial number of religious communities and has created a mosaic of courts for fourteen recognized religious groups. Rabbinical courts, with authority over the personal status of Jewish people in Israel, date from the Ottoman Empire, were continued under the British Mandate, and became part of the modern State of Israel. The rabbinical court system governs marriage and divorce for Jewish people, but decisions must be consistent with what secular law requires for questions such as marriageable age. Islamic courts, on the other hand, have a broader jurisdiction than do the rabbinical courts on issues of personal status. The Druze constitute a group regarded by some as a heretical sect of Islam, but they view themselves as a distinct religion dating from the eleventh century and consist of a small, largely village-dwelling and secretive sect somewhat akin to what one might expect to find in a customary law setting. Druze courts exercise jurisdiction over not only marriage and divorce, but also

> **BOX 2.4** | **Civilians in Military Courts in Venezuela**
>
> Venezuela erupted in protests against President Nicolás Maduro in early 2017, with the demonstrators calling for new elections. In an attempt to hold his grip on power, Maduro ordered somewhere between 60 and 120—estimates vary—people arrested, most charged with inciting rebellion. For the first time outside of war, those arrested were taken to military jails to face military trials. "Military justice sows the greatest terror in our population," an opposition leader explained. Maduro claimed the authority to use the military under what he called "the Zamoro Plan," a set of decrees that shifted much law enforcement to the military and away from the police. The United Nations International Covenant on Civil and Political Rights, to which Venezuela is a signatory, advises against the use of military courts for civilian defendants.
>
> *Source:* Nicolas Casey, "Venezuela Tries Protesters in Military Courts," *New York Times*, May 14, 2017, A-1.

guardianship, maintenance, adoption, legitimation, inheritance, and succession (Edelman 1994).

Military courts' maintenance of discipline of the armed forces typically engenders little controversy. However, questions arise when civilians are tried in military courts or when special security courts are established. Use of military tribunals for nonmilitary personnel and security courts is typically linked to authoritarian regimes, but they have also been adopted in the post-9/11 era in the United States, most infamously at Guantanamo Bay, and in places like the Gaza Strip in Israel. Interestingly, when regimes choose trials rather than brute force in dealing with opponents, space is opened for defense lawyers to affect legal interpretations and to argue for rights. Indeed, defense lawyers were surprisingly successful in protecting defendants in Brazil during the authoritarian regime (1964–1983), much more so than in the neighboring countries under military rule, Chile (1973–1990) and Argentina (1976–1983) (Pereira 2005). "Legitimacy is important even for authoritarian regimes, if only to economize on the use of force" (Moustafa and Ginsburg 2008, 5). Certainly a legal structure can place an aura of legitimacy on repression that tactics like the Argentine "dirty war," in which dissidents were seized, tortured, and then "disappeared" without any record—totally extrajudicial proceedings—cannot (Pereira 2005). Ordinary courts cannot necessarily be relied upon to bend the judicial process to a regime's will; hence the choice of separate courts can provide the veneer of legality while simultaneously serving the regime. Normal courts in Uganda were not reliable when the primary political opponent of the incumbent president was charged with "seditious intent," but granted bail. Therefore the regime altered the charge to treason and transferred the case to the military court system (Gloppen et al. 2010).

Military courts can also be employed not only to divert politically inconvenient cases or defendants from civilian courts, but also as a mechanism of occupation. Control of a belligerent territory is recognized in international law (Kretzmer 2002), and one of the longest "benevolent" occupations has been that of Israel in the West Bank and Gaza Strip, occupied since 1967. According to Lisa Hajjar (2005), a very large proportion of the Palestinians residing in those territories have been arrested, though only about half of those arrested have been prosecuted in the military tribunals used there. The Israeli Supreme Court has been active in defining and protecting human rights, but it has adopted a largely hands-off policy with military courts, intervening only "in the event of a significant and salient error" (Meydani 2011, 88).

CONCLUSION

Courts across national boundaries share a number of attributes, in particular their hierarchical structure. Even the customary law, which is notably flat, has been overlaid with appeals and review by nation-states. Likewise, reliance on specialized courts is common both for efficiency and, particularly under authoritarian regimes, for more sinister motives.

The various legal traditions can easily be stereotyped, but that would be unfortunate. None of the legal traditions likely exists in an ideal type, as a consequence of legal pluralism, transplantation, imperialism, and adaptation. Different branches of law in a given nation may be more or less influenced by one tradition over another, and the particular dominant legal tradition in a country may not explain variations that inevitably arise. Yet different legal traditions are tied to some behaviors, one of which is the extent to which they accept and follow their international commitments (Powell and Mitchell 2007). More than that, however, law enables the formation of identity both for nations and for individuals. The nature or tradition of law offers a "legal identity (such as citizenship) [and as such] forms the basis for claiming rights and privileges" (Massoud 2013, 77–78). Legal traditions, modes of adjudication, and court structures create a legal vocabulary and define our ability to claim rights and privileges.

3

Lawyers and Access to Justice

★ ★ ★

THE FICTITIOUS CASE of Jarndyce and Jarndyce captures a common image of lawyers with a literary version of a lawsuit that proceeds through generations without resolution, in which "innumerable" people are born into it, more marry into it, and "old people have died out of it" (Dickens [1853] 1996, 16). No one understands or cares about it, and its final demise, some 972 pages later in Charles Dickens's *Bleak House*, serves as a cause of celebration. Lawyers filled with avarice or incompetence are depicted as the villains who have perpetuated the suit and drained the last material resources from the parties. Likewise, again in fiction, Franz Kafka derides "pettifoggying lawyers," bickering over trivia, in *The Trial*. William Shakespeare's Dick the Butcher in *Henry VI, Part II* advocates killing all lawyers. The Shakespearean character does not argue for slaying lawyers because they represent an evil, but rather because lawyers represent a potential barrier to overthrowing the monarch. The Shakespearean version invites us to wonder what situations might arise were there no lawyers or an insufficient number of them. Whereas many in the developed West of the world bemoan an excess of lawyers, in much of the world the supply is wholly inadequate. How has that occurred and what are the implications of being unable to secure legal counsel when one is criminally charged or in need of asserting legal rights?

Such is the case too often in Zimbabwe, where the courts are rarely staffed. In the nearby Central African Republic, UN peacekeepers complain that they cannot arrest criminals in the town of Kaga Bandoro because the jails, courtrooms, and judges to hold and try them are all but nonexistent. Whereas these may be extreme cases, much of the African continent suffers from insufficient legal resources, too often coupled with the risk of corruption. As a consequence, much potential investment in Africa goes unpursued by those from wealthier nations. Indeed, one businessman in Nigeria even evoked the metaphor of Dickens's *Bleak House* as postponement after postponement plagued his legal case (*Economist* 2017a). Such Dickensian conditions are not confined to Africa but are replicated in many parts of the world, particularly in more rural areas. Cases not only are not resolved, but people are unable to know their rights or engage competent legal counsel.

Mrs. Alice Sitali serves as a legal aid lawyer, one of twenty-four in the whole of Zambia, and in a single work hour meets with someone trying to gain help after borrowing from a loan shark, a man who lost one eye while working without the provision of protective eyewear, and a former police officer who was charged with attempted aggravated robbery but has already waited five years for a trial. Zambia has a population of approximately thirteen million, but only 731 lawyers work in private practice, or about one for every 175,000 people. Even those lawyers can only be found in one of three urban areas, and only 35 are available in the remainder of the country (Kahn-Fogel 2012).

Latin American constitutions written in the second half of the twentieth century cataloged lengthy lists of social rights, including rights of indigenous peoples, yet those rights largely remain illusory or perhaps merely aspirational for the poor whom they are supposed to protect and benefit, a situation described as the "Latin American legal paradox" (Gargarella 2004). In many places, the simple physical location of courts poses a barrier to vindication of legal rights. In Indonesia, for example, some communities are located a three-day trip by a combination of ferry and other transportation from the nearest courtroom (Gauri and Brinks 2008). Thus, whatever legal rights one might have as a consequence of constitutions, laws, or contracts are beyond the reach of many people. These people, mainly but not exclusively poor and rural, are effectively denied access to justice. Even in so-called developed nations, significant barriers prevent many people from having their legal claims adjudicated.

What makes the legal system inaccessible to such larger numbers of people? A variety of factors combine to create obstacles.

Absence of the knowledge of legal rights and responsibilities, also known as legal literacy, along with the costs entailed, block many. Perceptions of corruption and fear and mistrust also impede use of legal machinery. Similarly, the formalism employed by the legal process intimidates many potential claimants. Finally, the notorious slowness of the legal machinery deters others (Gargarella 2004). Yet one of the largest obstacles to accessing the legal system is the inability to obtain a lawyer, someone who can translate a dispute into legal terminology and navigate the system (Guarnieri and Pederzoli 2002).

Constitutions, laws, and treaties are meaningless without some mechanism to enforce them (Vermeulen 2016), and the necessity of access to the levers of the legal process has become even more pronounced in the twenty-first century with the rise of globalization, international trade, and rising economic commercialization. Contracts and the rights and obligations they entail proliferate with increased commercial activity and land development. Even more important, as society becomes more complex, advanced planning and negotiation of pacts and agreements become more necessary to prevent disputes from arising (Damaška 1986). Thus, the legal process now sits as central to much of twenty-first-century life, both to resolve and to forestall legal disputes.

Specialists—lawyers—have become progressively more essential for balancing rights and responsibilities and preventing disputes. Worldwide in 2010 some five million people were estimated to be lawyers, but more than one-fifth of them were in the United States and another 14 percent were found in Canada, the United Kingdom, Spain, Germany, and Italy—more than one-third of the total (Michelson 2013). In South Africa, one lawyer practices for every 2,273 people, and that ratio is better than in other African countries, except for Nigeria, where the economy is more developed (McQuoid 2013).

Lawyers constitute a necessary commodity, whether one seeks resolution in a single dispute or aims to achieve policy changes by harnessing judicial empowerment. Availability of legal education and both the quantity and quality of that education constitute the first link in the chain to make legal specialists available. That funnel directly connects the ability of people to claim rights via the legal process, as individuals or as groups. Legal mobilization to leverage judicial power to achieve policy changes for those lacking a voice in the political process requires legally trained people, and one's ability to utilize the legal process depends on this supply chain. If insufficient numbers of people can obtain legal education and certification, then the supply of legal advocates will be inadequate. Consequently, individual disputes will not be resolved and larger policy changes will not be achieved through the legal process. This chapter considers this supply chain by looking at, first, themes and variations in legal education, then the nature of the legal profession in various countries, and finally how the legal process can be yoked for service through legal mobilization to achieve social and economic change.

LEGAL EDUCATION

Countries' approaches to legal education have largely been shaped by colonization and geography. Just as the legal traditions of European colonial powers left their imprint, so did their modes of legal education. Of course legal education systems adapted in various countries to reflect economic, social, and political environments and continue to be modified to meet necessities that come with international trade and increasingly market-driven economies. The nature and quality of legal education impacts more than the availability of people to provide legal services. It also affects those who are educated for other positions in politics as well as creating a professional culture. Two basic models of legal education dominate: (1) the study of law as an undergraduate degree program, often followed by some form of practical apprenticeship, and (2) postgraduate legal studies, as in the United States. The variations on these models defy enumeration.

The earliest modern European university appeared in Bologna on the Italian peninsula in the late eleventh century and soon became the legal center of Europe. Those who came there to study returned to their homes and established more universities or schools of law (Merryman and Pérez-Perdomo 2007). Not surprisingly, therefore, a variation on that early approach persists in most countries of the civil law tradition, from Western Europe to Latin America, Southeast Asia, and parts of Africa. Law constitutes an undergraduate, interdisciplinary course of study taught as a science, complete with classification schemes. Differences arise from country to country, such as four-year programs of study in France and Germany but of varying lengths elsewhere. As is typical, an examination must be passed upon completion of one's formal studies. In both countries, a mandatory, formal practical training program—two years in France and eighteen months in Germany—follows passage of the exam. After that practical legal training, candidates face yet another examination, successful completion of which allows them formally to practice law (Glendon, Carozza, and Picker 2014).

Multiple variations on the French and German models are found across Western Europe. Finland, for example, sets a minimum age of twenty-five for one to be admitted to practice law, whereas Greece has a maximum age of thirty-five for admission to legal practice. Belgium's, Denmark's, and Italy's law programs take five years, whereas four years appears to be the most common. All require some type of formal examination, followed by a practical training requirement ranging from eighteen months in Greece and Portugal to five years in Finland (Carroll 2004).

Continental European students of law were attending universities before England was conquered by the Normans in 1066. As discussed in chapter 2, the genesis of the common law resides in a wholly different realm from that of continental civil law; hardly surprisingly, the teaching of the common law was consequently undertaken differently. Apprenticeships or "reading law" became the path to becoming a lawyer in England and later, the United States and other former English colonies. Law became a course of study at the university but was not the route to legal practice. Because law was learned "in chambers"—and specifically at the Inns of Court in London to become a trial advocate—the legal profession rather than universities governed legal education and entrance to the profession. Oxford and Cambridge did not offer degrees in law until the mid-nineteenth century.

In the United Kingdom today most aspiring lawyers pursue a three-year undergraduate curriculum for the LLB (bachelor of law) degree. Alternatively, a student could study, say, literature or history as an undergraduate and then take a one-year program leading to the postgraduate diploma in law. Whichever route a student selects, university studies are followed by another one-year course that is determined by the type of lawyer, solicitor or barrister, which is discussed in the next section; succinctly, barristers are trial advocates or litigators in US terminology, whereas solicitors provide all other legal services. Following the appropriate one-year course of study, aspiring barristers must engage in a one-year "pupilage," while those seeking to become solicitors contract for a two-year training program. Notably, after completion of the course to become a barrister, one must be "called" by the Bar to assume a pupilage. One is licensed thereafter, and no standardized examination is involved.

Neither of these models drove the system to obtain legal credentials in the United States, but "reading" law under the supervision of a licensed lawyer was the early practice and was permitted by most states until the mid-twentieth century, even though the college of William and Mary in Virginia created a law school in 1780. Today aspiring lawyers in the United States complete a four-year undergraduate education in any discipline and, depending on their undergraduate record and their scores on a standardized admissions test, enter one of the approximately two hundred law schools accredited by the American Bar Association. Unlike their continental European counterparts, US law schools rely largely on the case study method, whereby students learn the law by reading appellate court opinions, rather than studying law qua law. This practice is consistent with the emphasis in common law on judicial interpretation of law, but also supposedly enables teaching a style of reasoning and problem solving. After three years of study and successful completion of the juris doctor (JD) degree from a law school, the student must pass the requisite bar examination. States license lawyers, and each state administers and scores its own examination.

Changes are under way to massively overhaul legal education (and higher education generally) in Europe as a consequence of an agreement, the Sorbonne Declaration, signed by France, Germany, Italy, and the United Kingdom in 1998, which launched the Bologna Process. By 2016 the effort to reform and internationalize higher education involved forty-eight countries that had agreed on a common three-tiered approach: bachelor's, master's, and doctorate (EHEA 2016). The process could lead to the creation of a postgraduate master's in law, more akin to the US JD model, while retaining law as an undergraduate course of study. Whereas the advanced degree has not yet been adopted as an entry requirement to the legal profession, that may be on the horizon. At least some aspects of convergence across the twenty-seven countries of the EU in which legal certification in one nation must be recognized by other nations serve to achieve more homogenous quality among those in the legal profession (Terry 2010).

Latin American countries' legal education systems have been influenced by the legacies of Western European colonization and also by geographic proximity to the United States. Universities teaching law in Latin America date from the sixteenth century and even today replicate the European model of a three-year undergraduate curriculum that focuses on learning code law (Montoya 2010). A number of Latin American lawyers furthered their legal studies in the United States and returned to encourage the case method of study, public interest law, and clinical legal studies, through which law students gain practical experience while also providing legal services to those who cannot afford regular lawyers (Vermeulen 2016).

International trade and globalization have also pushed Latin American law schools to adapt, and the result has been the establishment of a number of "innovative" law schools, most of which are private. They challenge students to test empirical realities against abstract legal concepts and therefore focus on the context and practicality of law. Some incorporate a thesis and/or clerkship into requirements, as well as simulations and problem-solving activities. One older law school, Sonora in Mexico, reformed its curriculum in 2004 to a competencies-based system. All of the innovative law schools also place a premium on interdisciplinary studies. These law schools constitute, however, outliers, with most Latin American law schools hewing to traditional formalistic teaching of doctrine and codes, with little attention given to the efficacy of the laws and legal concepts for the world outside of law (Montoya 2010).

Most African countries also adopted the continental European model of law as an undergraduate degree. The distinction between how that works in Africa versus Latin America and Europe is the paucity of universities and therefore limited access to legal training. Indeed, after most sub-Saharan African countries gained independence in the 1960s, many aspiring lawyers studied in the United Kingdom. Though each African nation has its own individual story, most postindependence nations adopted the legal tradition and, hence legal education model, of the earlier colonizers. Thus, Tanzania followed the British common law and a three-year undergraduate course of study, followed by an examination (Widner 2001a). Zambia created a three-year undergraduate program, followed by one year of postgraduate training before one could sit for the exam to gain licensure. These imitations of European legal education suffered primarily because of a lack of resources, both teaching materials and teachers. Law teachers earned on average in 2012 between $400 and $1,000 per month and therefore supplemented their income with consulting and private legal practice (Kahn-Fogel, 2012).

South Africa has had a different experience, since it was hampered not by colonialism, but rather by the rigid system of apartheid until 1994. The nation has nineteen law schools that award the LLB degree after three years of undergraduate study, and one must serve a one- to two-year apprenticeship thereafter to qualify as a lawyer. Although approximately four thousand students each year earn the LLB, many forego the apprenticeship and enter government service or the private commercial sector (McQuoid 2013). Acceptance into an apprenticeship often carries cultural overtones that disadvantage particularly black graduates, who are blocked from fulfilling the requirements for entrance to the profession. Clinical programs in law schools have provided an avenue for those students to at least partially achieve their legal credentials (Maisel 2006).

Adoption of the European colonizers' system for legal education, that of an undergraduate degree, was prominent in Asia, but major regime changes, such as the 1970 Cambodian Communist coup, forced a complete reconceptualization of how lawyers should be trained (Kuong 2011), and the shifts from socialist economies to market ones necessitated other adaptations. Indeed, legal education was absent or stagnant in Cambodia, Laos, Myanmar, North Korea, and the Philippines for much of the late twentieth century. It revived in Vietnam subsequent to that nation's entry into the WTO in 2007 (Irish 2008). Low-quality education and minimal bar entrance requirements can still be observed in places such as Pakistan (Siddique 2014).

The economic powerhouses of Japan, China, and India capture both how the debate over which model of legal education—undergraduate versus postgraduate—is preferable and how the adjustment to the international market economy spurs introspection and innovation in how law is taught. India employs twin approaches, both undergraduate and graduate, to train lawyers, with newly created national law schools adopting the latter (Kumar 2013) and some requiring entrance exams. As in Vietnam, the shift coincided with India's decision to open its markets (Badrinarayana 2014). A similar approach can be seen in Japan and South Korea (Ginsburg 2004; Chen 2012). Japan, which has traditionally kept a tight grip on entrance to the legal profession by allowing fewer than

3 percent of those eligible to pass the bar exam (Matsui 2012), has loosened its standards, but still fewer than 40 percent pass and are certified (Chen 2012).

China exhibits the most dramatic evidence of change in its conduct of legal education; again, increased international trade and a market economy served as the catalysts. Following the Maoist revolution in China, in the 1950s legal education concentrated on Soviet law and aimed to eliminate "old" legal thinking. At the start of the Cultural Revolution in 1966, all law schools were shuttered, and they remained that way for a decade (Biddulph 2010). Law schools reopened in 1979, coincidentally the same year that the United States and China exchanged diplomatic recognition. Near the end of the twentieth century the juris master (JM) degree, a rough equivalent of the American JD, was launched (Eric 2009). Around one hundred universities now offer the JM degree, and by 2004 it had surpassed the MBA as the first choice of students for graduate education (Phan 2005).

Thus, one method of preparing lawyers, an imitation of that used in the United States, has gained popularity in the emerging economies of the Pacific, while the undergraduate route persists in most of the West. Governments often have motives extending beyond offering the best legal education to students. Sometimes the results achieved can best be characterized as unintended consequences, as single-party and authoritarian leaders have either adversely affected resources for legal education or have seen a way to capture it for their own ends. In Egypt under Gamal Abdel Nasser (1956–1970) and his successor, Anwar el-Sadat (1970–1981), every person was offered free advanced education, and between 1970 and 1980, university enrollments tripled to more than a half million students. Law faculties became among the least selective, and quality as well as prestige declined, but, inversely, litigiousness became the norm because the population of lawyers was large and consequently inexpensive. Yet as economic reforms ushered in economic growth and international trade grew in the 1980s, the legal profession rebounded and subsequently developed into a driving force for human rights (Moustafa 2007b).

The regime of Omar Hassan al-Bashir in Sudan that began in 1989 undertook a so-called educational revolution by focusing on law with the intention of fostering ideological indoctrination and forcing all law schools to focus on Shar'ia law, taught in Arabic. All twelve law schools in Sudan were established by nondemocratic governments. Only in 2005 was a first-year introduction to law class taught in English. The quality of legal education suffered, as elsewhere, because of an absence of adequate resources. The Bashir government intentionally overproduced lawyers, ones indoctrinated in Shar'ia, and dispersed graduates across the country in such a way as to prevent lawyers from coalescing in a single location and becoming an impediment to the regime's goals (Massoud 2013).

LEGAL PROFESSION

Legal education opportunities effectively limit the number of potential lawyers available to serve people's private legal needs, defend them in criminal cases, and seek review of court decisions on their behalf. Lawyers also form the pool from which many politicians are selected because of their experience, skills, and interests (Rincker, Aslam, and Isani 2017). Many of those completing their legal studies choose not to enter the practice of law or are not accepted because of examination results, as is common in Japan, or because of absence of apprenticeships due to cultural or social biases. Others are siphoned away into government or business. As noted previously, only five million lawyers serve a world population of around seven and a half billion, or about one lawyer for every fifteen hundred people, which might suggest more lawyers are available than are necessary. The problem, of course, is that a disproportionate number of lawyers are clustered in North America and Europe. Burundi and other Central and West African nations have one thousand or fewer lawyers for their entire countries, and many places have even fewer (Michelson 2013). In almost all countries the overwhelming majority of lawyers are concentrated in urban areas, leaving those living in rural settings either underserved or, worse, unserved. Moreover, lawyers' services typically are relatively expensive. People at the lower end of the socioeconomic continuum cannot afford lawyers and must rely on legal aid services, which are provided by governments or nonprofit organizations if at all. Therein lie perhaps the greatest obstacles to access to the legal system: the absence of lawyers or the inability to pay for them.

The legal profession also tends toward specialization. Often lines are formally drawn, such as between notaries and lawyers in many civil law jurisdictions. Notaries are specifically certified to draft certain documents, such as wills or marriage contracts; unlike other lawyers, they represent no side in the transaction but advise all parties (Glendon, Carozza, and Picker 2014). In England, Wales, and Northern Ireland the legal profession is divided into barristers and solicitors. Scotland has its own legal system, uses the terminology *advocates* and *solicitors*, and divides the legal profession into two distinct realms. Barristers and the Scottish advocates represent clients in court, whereas solicitors handle all of the noncourt needs of clients. The roles of the two are blurring, but generally barristers are solo practitioners, while solicitors usually work in law firms (Carter 2015). South Africa retained the barrister-solicitor bifurcation, but with the introduction of a common LLB degree for both branches of the profession in 1998, the two seem ultimately destined to fuse (McQuoid 2013). A similar trend may occur in other former British colonies.

The rise of multinational law firms has further altered the legal profession. In the late twentieth century the number of US law firms operating in Europe tripled, offering mega-lawyering techniques across jurisdictions (Kelemen 2011). The top two hundred law firms in the world had combined earnings of $100 billion in 2015 and include firms based in the United States, the United Kingdom, Asia, Canada, and Europe. Collectively, they operate in ninety-four countries. The largest law firm is Dentons, which was created by a Chinese-US merger in 2015 (American Lawyer 2015). These mega-law firms attest to both the growth and importance of international law and treaties and the commercial interconnectedness of countries, their economies, and their legal processes.

The concentration of lawyers varies vastly across countries. Countries with small populations of lawyers may yield a reasonable lawyer to population ratio, but legal professionals tend to locate in capital cities or commercial centers, with rural regions remaining unserved. This is the case in Pakistan (Siddique 2014), much of Latin America (Gargarella 2004), and sub-Saharan Africa (Kahn-Fogel 2012). Even in South Africa, where the population to lawyer ratio appears adequate, some 70 percent of the population cannot afford to pay for legal services (McQuoid 2013). The dilemmas of the inability to physically reach a lawyer and not having the financial wherewithal to pay for one have been compounded in multiethnic and multilinguistic countries, where significant numbers of people lack the linguistic or cultural skills to make use of the legal system. This can be observed, for example, in Ecuador, Peru, and Guatemala (Gargarella 2004). Thus, the spigot may have opened for production and certification of more lawyers in many places, but their services literally remain beyond the reach of large portions of people. One's financial capability clearly influences one's likelihood of even seeking legal advice (Huang, Lin, and Chen 2014).

Various forms of legal aid and even courses in legal literacy have been implemented to address issues of the affordability of lawyers and public awareness of legal rights and responsibilities. South Africa instituted a "Street Law" program using university students to teach primarily schoolchildren and prisoners how the legal system works, and legal clinics, pro bono, and legal aid offices have spread to alleviate the financial burden of the legal process for the poor. Because of the parallel customary law tribunals in some regions, those venues potentially offer forums for the rural poor, but with mixed results. South Africa requires that the tribal chiefs or headmen who preside in customary law tribunals be trained in constitutional guarantees (McQuoid 2013), but Zambia largely permits customary law to operate independently, with sometimes conflicting guidance from the highest national court (Kahn-Fogel 2012).

Clinical legal education, through which law students gain practical experience by assisting the poor, emerged as a staple of law school curricula outside of Western Europe (Wilson 2009). Clinical education aims to instill a social justice ethic in future lawyers (Maisel 2006), but sometimes that goal goes unrealized. Pamela Phan (2005) writes of watching two young women law students at Wuhan University in China try to counsel five older residents involved in a land dispute. The students had great difficulty understanding the heavy accents of their "clients" and complained about the daily calls they received from them on their cell phones. The experience was unlikely to have stirred a calling to a career focus on achieving social justice via the law. The experiences across Latin America (Vermeulen 2016) and Thailand (Bliss 2014), however, appear to be more promising.

Legal aid offices everywhere tend to be understaffed, underfunded, and overwhelmed, whether they are government-sponsored or created by nongovernmental organizations (NGOs) or other donor groups. These offices succeed in resolving many disputes but can only handle a small fraction of the poor who need legal assistance, and the staff usually are most useful with minor matters. Pro bono legal aid refers to lawyers in private practice taking on cases without compensation and is quite widespread, but again, the number of cases that can be served in this fashion is quite small and most likely, as in India, involve only those with high social resonance (Kumar 2013).

The entrance of women into the legal profession over the last few decades has also altered the practice of law, but though the phenomenon is widespread, it is hardly universal. Notably, despite the vast expansion of the ranks of lawyers around the world, India and China stand out as anomalies in that the number of women is not proportionate to the overall increase in the number of lawyers. Nevertheless, the rise in the number of women lawyers in much of the world has generally increased the access of women to legal resources (Michelson 2013). Though no data are available on India to explain why fewer women than elsewhere become lawyers there, a study on China concluded that a larger number of women enter law schools than ultimately become lawyers, choosing instead to become judges or enter the legal civil service, careers regarded as "more women-friendly workplaces" than law firms (Zheng, Ai, and Liu 2017). Women are also notably underrepresented in the legal profession in Indonesia and the Philippines (Michelson 2013).

Having access to a lawyer, however, may not be sufficient to achieve successful resolution of a dispute. Even legal aid lawyers in China, with no financial incentives to accept or reject cases, screen clients based on cultural stereotypes (Michelson 2006). Conversely, a study focused on legal aid clients in Shanghai concluded that those who had been involved with legal aid increased their sense of efficacy and competency in the use of the legal system (Gallagher 2006).

LEGAL MOBILIZATION

Most people enter the legal arena to win or at least to resolve a single dispute, without any consideration of consequences beyond the confines of their personal case. How then do major social and economic changes result through the legal process? Provisions for constitutional review and often lengthy catalogs of rights are ubiquitous in modern constitutions, and one would like to think that ideally, governments and political leaders are cognizant of and committed to translating those rights into reality. Experience has taught, however, that other actors—courts—are frequently the vehicles that render rights concrete and protect them from government encroachment. How does that happen, though, when lawyers are unreachable because of their limited numbers or because of the expense?

In theory, independent judges serve as a bulwark against rights abuses, but courts are passive institutions, and "cases do not arrive in supreme courts as if by magic" (Epp 1998, 18). A rights-conscious culture necessarily precedes rights adjudication, but legal literacy is woefully absent in much of the world. Most cases that change the course of rights litigation depend on legal mobilization, a process that requires sustained litigation and resources typically beyond the reach of a single litigant (Epp 1998). Difficult and expensive though legal mobilization may be, it offers a nonviolent and potentially sustainable avenue to achieve social change, more easily than organizing protests or attempting regime change. In other words, the legal forum can serve as another means for political participation (Zemans 1983).

People typically turn to the legal system for policy change when their voices cannot be heard in other institutions. That is why legal mobilization is usually, though not always, associated with securing the rights of the marginalized, those with insufficient voices to be heard through the ballot box in democracies or outside the favored circles of the ruling elites. One goes to the courts, in other words, because they are the only avenue available. Law can also offer a metaphorical verbal appeal or can be utilized concretely and pragmatically as a mechanism to assert one's rights (Zemans 1983). In democracies, in other words, litigation and elections provide vertical accountability for those in authority (Gloppen et al. 2010). Therefore, when other effective political vehicles for policy change are available, such as competitive elections, resort to courts for policy solutions is less common. Thus, in South Africa, Tanzania, and Uganda, where governments seem unresponsive to some social sectors, people are more likely to litigate for change. Even in Malawi, where party competition is more reliable, seeking redress via the courts remains easier than organizing collectively to push for change (Gloppen et al. 2010).

Legal mobilization occurs often in some countries, but not in all. Sometimes the mere threat of litigation proves sufficient to catalyze the political process to change policies. Health care in Brazil stands as an apt example. Courts there ruled on provision of hospital maintenance, and those decisions subsequently correlated with increased public spending on health care. Indeed, the prospect of litigation colors most interactions between dissatisfied patients and public health authorities there. A significant number of individuals, without organized support, drove the demand for policy change through judicial channels (Gauri and Brinks 2008).

On occasion a single decision can spark legal mobilization. One 1990 case decided by the Canadian Supreme Court on official minority language education under the 1988 Charter of Rights prompted a wave of litigation by Francophone groups that ultimately achieved funding for and forced implementation of language education (Riddell 2004). Legal mobilization can also create advocacy groups and make change at the agency level. The National Organization for Women in the United States emerged in reaction to unresponsiveness by the Equal Employment Opportunity Commission to claims of sex discrimination in the workplace, and that organization subsequently was at the forefront of many feminist causes (Woodward 2015).

Not all nations' political conditions, however, are conducive to legal mobilization, and therefore those lacking a political voice are denied any mechanism for assertion of rights. Lawyers, not government authorities, erected the barriers to workers bringing labor grievances in China. Their reluctance precluded many grievances from becoming legal complaints. All lawyers screen potential clients, but cultural stereotypes, more than the viability of the cases, colored the willingness of attorneys to take on the workers' cases. Ironically, the Chinese government had adopted legal reforms to enhance social stability, but the legal profession blocked access to legal remedies by many aggrieved workers (Michelson 2006). Few politically significant cases are litigated in Tanzania, likely because of shared expectations of judicial deference to the government and constraints on the legal culture. Yet when cases carry low political stakes, even the Tanzanian state sometimes loses (Gloppen et al. 2010).

An authoritarian regime may block legal mobilization, but "law"—so-called rights discourse—can be potent nonetheless, and the "law" emerges as a conceptual force. Homosexual conduct is illegal in Singapore, but gay rights activists adopted the rhetoric of rights. Their actions were limited, reflecting a careful awareness of Singapore's legal restrictions on dissent and political mobilization. The activists therefore remained on the side of what Singapore law permitted and utilized a larger conception of law and rights to quietly foster a campaign focused on how discrimination against gay and lesbian people "tarnishes the country's international legitimacy" and is "counter to a harmonious society that accepts differences" (Chua 2014, 161). The success of the gay activists cannot be predicted in Singapore, where dissent and legal remedies are foreclosed, but two court decisions in nearby countries in 2017, one in Taiwan and another in Hong Kong, upholding gay rights may yet impact the gay rights cause across Asia (*Economist* 2017c).

Indonesia and Nigeria possess the requisite components for legal mobilization, with sufficient lawyers and funds for rights campaigns, but rights groups doubt that courts would be sympathetic to their causes. Similarly, in India civil society groups have often eschewed litigation strategies, not because the courts are not receptive to their claims, but rather because implementation of judicial decisions is problematic (Gauri and Brinks 2008). Even in authoritarian regimes, such as the Hosni Mubarak regime in Egypt, litigation mobilization was possible, if only, to use Moustafa's (2007a) term, of the "small arms" variety.

When and where, therefore, can legal mobilization serve as an effective tool to achieve policy change? Charles Epp (1998) argued that in addition to constitutional or treaty guarantees and judicial independence and receptiveness, resources for sustained litigation are necessary. To counter that argument, Urribarri and his associates (2011) looked at cases over a thirty-five-year period in the United States, Canada, and England and found that judicial ideology and institutional arrangements, not mobilization, tended to determine the success of rights litigation. We know, if only intuitively, that institutions, including legal ones, produce different results in different contexts (Peerenboom 2006). Courts can achieve political reform only if political support for that change exists; "courts can *almost never* be producers of significant social reforms" (Rosenberg, 1991, 338; italics in original). That argument, based on US courts, may or may not be conclusive, but law as an idea carries significance among those who seek change, whether gay activists in Singapore or Egyptian rights advocates. Judicial institutions may afford more symbolic than tangible resources for those seeking change (Moustafa 2007a), but the symbolism of law and rights can be powerful.

INTEREST GROUP LITIGATION

Legal mobilization requires resources, first and foremost, and litigation, particularly sustained litigation, for success. And that requires money beyond the capacity of the average individual. Party capability theory (Galanter 1974) proposed that litigants can be classified as one-shotters (those involved in a single case) and repeat players, such as the government or a government agency or an industry or advocacy group that regularly participates in judicial proceedings. The repeat player, according to the theory, has the advantage because of experience, expertise, and a long-term strategy focused more on rules than on the outcome of any single case. That calculus changes, though, when two repeat players confront each other in court, such as an environmental protection group and a government regulatory agency. Although the repeat players—the "haves"—do not always prevail, the mission of a single person of average means to achieve a major change through the courts is typically quixotic.

Overcoming inequalities in expertise and resources in policy litigation usually depends on the services of a cause lawyer or the support of an interest group. Cause lawyers are those who have committed use of their legal abilities to achieving social good and refuse to act as "apolitical, value-neutral professional agents hired by their clients to foster the latter's interest" (Dotan 1999, 401). These lawyers usually share some of the resources of repeat players, even if they lack equivalent financial wherewithal. Indeed, in a study of house demolition orders before the Israeli High Court of Justice, cause lawyers were significantly more successful than their apolitical counterparts (Dotan 1999). Even in China, human rights lawyers have succeeded in focusing national attention on tainted milk and vaccines, police brutality, and illegal seizures of land. The success of those lawyers prompted a backlash in 2015, when more than 300 rights lawyers and activists were targeted; 27 were forbidden to leave the country, 255 were temporarily detained, and 28 were held in custody (Palmer 2017). One lawyer, Jiang Tianyong, was arrested in late 2016 and confessed to "inciting subversion" almost a year later. His trial and confession were broadcast and streamed on the Internet "to discredit human rights defenders" (Buckley 2017).

Class action suits can also change policy and can be directed at industries, corporations, or other nongovernmental groups as well as at governments. Class action lawsuits, whereby multiple complainants suffering the same injury at the hand of the same party join together in a suit, do not occur widely outside of the United States, and even there the requirements have tightened.

Many nations offer administrative remedies instead of enforcement via courts. Australia and Canada have some broadly similar provisions for group litigation, and in 1998 the EU directed member nations to devise mechanisms for something akin to class actions. Although collective action suits, such as those brought by state attorneys general in the United States against the tobacco companies, can accomplish significant change, they are more typically the product of entrepreneurial lawyers, who take a significant proportion of any monetary settlement. The lawyer's profit motive has been significantly restricted where collective suits have been allowed outside of the United States (Sherman 2002).

Most legal mobilization occurs, therefore, when civil society groups choose to become involved. When an interest group seeks to change a policy, it has a variety of political pressure points at which it may aim. Traditional lobbying in the legislative arena comes to mind immediately. One might target an agency of government charged with implementing the current policy or take one's case to the executive branch. Grassroots efforts can likewise be attempted. Generally speaking, policy change is thought of as occurring through campaign donations, legislative testimony, protests, or voter drives (Collins and McCarthy 2017), but in actuality multiple venues are open to lobbyists to make their case for policy change (Holyoke 2003). Why, then, would an interest group strategically choose to focus on the courts? The answer is simple: if the interest group represents marginalized people who lack clout at the ballot box, little realistic chance of change via the political process is likely. The idea aims to pool a collection of interests and strategically manage multiple cases through trials and appeals to achieve a breakthrough at the highest level of the judicial system.

Clement Vose (1959) meticulously detailed how the National Association for the Advancement of Colored People (NAACP) in the United States orchestrated a legal crusade to end racial discrimination in residential housing. That had been an NAACP goal since 1915 and culminated in the 1948 case *Shelley v. Kraemer*, in which the Supreme Court invalidated the use of racially restrictive covenants in residential housing. The process has been replicated in various parts of the world. An interest group identifies a number of people who have been denied a right, finances their litigation, and manages both trials and appeals so as to present the most compelling legal case to the highest court to achieve a change in policy.

Supreme Court justice Robert Jackson called the practice "government by lawsuit" (Hoover and den Dulk 2004, 11).

The strategy has been successfully employed by conservative Christians in Canada on issues ranging from abortion, to the right to die, to religion, to education (Hoover and den Dulk 2004), and the use of the public interest litigation mechanism in India enabled that nation's supreme court to make significant environmental quality decisions that led to reduced air pollution levels in Delhi (Faure and Raja 2010). The EU's legal system has enabled organizations in the United Kingdom to leverage EU law to combat gender discrimination in the workplace (Alter and Vargas 2003), and a group representing South African HIV-positive pregnant women won a case before the constitutional court for access to medication to prevent viral transmission to their unborn children (Gauri and Brinks 2008). Various NGOs have been active in litigation sponsorship in Asia (Peerenboom 2006); likewise, international NGOs assumed litigation sponsorship of rights cases in Egypt, particularly after 1997 (Moustafa 2007b), until the military assumed control in 2013.

Litigation sponsorship can be potent, but it is expensive, and little is known about cases or causes that never succeeded. Those numbers could be far larger than the reported victories. Years can easily be spent nurturing a case or cases through trial and subsequently through the appeals process. Many interest groups have resorted to a less onerous device, that of intervening as a third party in cases at the highest level. In the common law tradition, this process is known as amici curiae, but elsewhere it is referred to as intervenor. These legal briefs are intended to act as a written form of lobbying and provide appellate judges with additional information, alternative versions of the facts, legal arguments about cases and laws, and even information on the potential impact of a decision (Collins and McCarthy 2017). A good example is the "Linguists Brief" that was cited by the US Supreme Court in *D.C. v. Heller* (2008) to explain how a subordinate clause in the Second Amendment should be read when defining gun rights.

Since the passage of the Canadian Charter of Rights in 1988, the number of intervenors at that nation's supreme court has increased (Brodie 2002). How much influence do amicus or intervenor briefs exert in the outcome of a case? Imputing causation raises difficult problems, but the Treatment Action Campaign in South Africa has been credited with swaying the constitutional court to support a law making medications less expensive. We also know that success is more likely in places like Canada and the United States, where courts have the power of constitutional review and are supported by a bill of rights (Collins and McCarthy 2017).

Legal mobilization generally aims to give voice to those who lack a seat at the political table. But do the "haves" come out ahead? That has been more likely in the United States, but not necessarily in Australia (Smyth 2000), in Canada (Brodie 2002; Flemming and Krutz 2002), or the Philippines (Haynie 1994, 1995). Even with that recognition, legal mobilization has proved crucial to securing some groups' rights in various parts of the world. Without interest groups to provide financial support, legal talent, and management of litigation, even fewer changes would have been achieved.

CONCLUSION

Unraveling the tapestry that in the end makes courts an effective and efficacious route to resolution of private disputes or to unleash judicial empowerment for legal change leads back to economic development. It is the taproot of the supply chain. Wealthier countries offer more educational opportunities, which enhance legal literacy and open the door to those who seek to become lawyers. When more qualified lawyers are available, their services can be used to resolve disputes or mobilized for policy change. More economically developed nations are also more likely to provide for legal aid or alternative administrative mechanisms to remedy abuses. Legal literacy spreads more widely; consequently, people are more cognizant of their legal rights and responsibilities. Democracy and independent judges enhance the prospects for positive application of judicial authority. Without resources at the early stage of the supply chain—legal education—the ultimate outcome will inevitably be diminished.

4

Judges

★ ★ ★

THE TERM *JUDGE* conjures many different images, depending on where one resides, the legal tradition under which one lives, and one's position relative to the legal process. An accused criminal or a political prisoner has a very different image of judges than a tenant trying to obtain a refund on her rental apartment. Americans might picture former chief justice Warren Burger or his predecessor Earl Warren as the fitting stereotype of a judge: a tall, older white man in a black robe with a distinguished mane of snowy hair. A woman attempting to obtain child support in an Islamic court might think of an intimidating, older male cleric, while an Italian or Brazilian might envision a crusader intent on bringing organized crime or political corruption to heel. Someone with a land dispute in rural sub-Saharan Africa, on the other hand, might think of a tribal elder, most often male and perhaps adorned in traditional ceremonial robes. Judges rarely fit these stereotypes. In reality, they appear in all complexions, ages, genders, and attire. Most important, they vary widely in their independence and field of discretion. To some they are the faces of repression and to others the fonts of justice.

Martin Shapiro's (1981) triadic dispute resolution concept, introduced in chapter 1, refers to the almost universal idea that two people engaged in a dispute will turn to a third party, hopefully an impartial one, to decide who is right or who gets what. Not all third-party intervenors, however, are judges—not the parent arbitrating between siblings nor the instructor in a physical education class. Moreover, when someone informally decides a dispute, what motivates the loser to comply with the decision? The key element is consent; the result hinges on whether both parties consented to be bound by the decision. Shapiro argues that in complex societies, law and office have replaced specific consent to abide by the judgment of the intervenor. Consequently, anyone who is officially—legally—designated to decide disputes and criminality can rightly be called a judge (Shapiro 1981). The office and the law give that person the authority to make a binding decision.

Judges vary widely not only in their garb and their trappings, but also in more important ways. The Egyptian high court decided against the government of President Abdel-Fattah al Sisi in a lawsuit brought by Khaled Ali. Five months after that decision, in early 2017, the winner in court, Mr. Ali, was arrested for allegedly making an indecent hand gesture during a celebration following his victory before the Supreme Constitutional Court (*Economist* 2017e). Does winning and celebrating the outcome of a dispute protect one from reprisals when the loser is the government? Although the Egyptian government complied with the high court's decision in the original case, it still exacted retribution from the complainant who won the case.

Across the Atlantic, the US Supreme Court agreed in June 2017 to hear arguments some four months later on the constitutional validity of then newly elected president Donald Trump's order that banned people from entering the United States from six predominantly Muslim nations. Because lower court judges had blocked the ban, the nine justices on the highest court reinstated it pending a decision that would come months later. However, the justices imposed somewhat ambiguous restrictions on how the ban could be implemented before a formal hearing (*International Refugee Assistance Project v. Trump*, 2017). Though the justices clearly substituted their language for that contained in the president's order, the government implemented the plan in accordance with the court's instruction three days later.

Both governments complied with the letter of their respective high court's decisions, but differing outcomes awaited the legal opponents in each nation. Courts are usually passive institutions that must wait for cases to appear before them. They are likewise generally reliant on someone else to force compliance with their decisions. The element of consent that at least tacitly colors most disputes independently compels the losing parties to comply. But if they do not, someone other than the deciding judge must enforce the decision. Some courts, such as the US Supreme Court in the travel ban case, can usually expect their decisions to be followed, if only in the letter if not the spirit intended. Others, such as the Egyptian Supreme Constitutional Court, may succeed in the specific case but nevertheless have their intentions undermined.

Because the office of judge varies widely, a classification system for types of judges proves useful in attempting a description. Carlo Guarnieri and Patrizia Pederzoli (2002) have offered a classification scheme of ideal judicial types based on two of the most salient attributes of judges: the extent of their independence and limitations on their authority. Those two attributes set the legal parameters for what judges may do. *Judicial independence* has been defined variously, as discussed later in this chapter, but its essence in the Guarnieri and Pederzoli sense refers to independence from other political institutions. *Authority* subsumes the limits on judicial discretion or freedom to make creative decisions or ones not based strictly on preexisting law, but also includes courts' ability to have their decisions implemented (Linzer and Staton 2015). The latter may be dependent on specific cases or the context in which cases arise. The two elements of authority and independence tend to be more or less fixed in any setting and therefore allow for a fourfold scheme of classification and comparison.

With low independence and little political autonomy, the *executor* judge represents those who can only strictly apply the law as written, with virtually no variation or room for exception or discretion. Whereas Guarnieri and Pederzoli contended that such judges were unlikely to exist in reality, they were writing about judges in democracies and specifically about those in Europe. Reaching more broadly than Europe, however, allows one to envision judges with a tightly restricted range in authoritarian regimes or even in semiauthoritarian ones. The *delegate* judge has room for discretion but meager independence and remains subordinate to the political organs of government. In many hierarchically organized judicial systems, the disciplinary role of higher court judges could likewise serve to constrain autonomy of action. In other words, delegate judges have high discretion but limited independence, acting as delegates only of political organs. Interpretation and completion of gaps in legislative texts occur, but with deference to legislative intent as the overriding motivation. Where political autonomy— judicial independence—is high, judges can, however, decide against the legislator. If judicial discretion remains low, though, judges are necessarily limited in their ability to alter policy or even rigorously oppose prevailing legislative majorities. Judges so situated are *guardians*. The most potentially significant judges are those with both high autonomy and high discretion, the *political* judges who embody judicial empowerment. Such judges can most likely be found where they have been granted the power of constitutional review. The typology of judges is depicted in figure 4.1.

The axes of judicial independence and judicial authority are the aspects of judges considered in this chapter. Judicial independence can be viewed through two lenses: de jure (legal) and de facto (real). The legal guarantees (de jure) for judges on Burundi's highest court and that of the United States, as discussed in chapter 1, appear to grant strong political autonomy to judges on both axes. Yet allegations have been made that the Burundi judges were subjected to extralegal pressures to influence their decision. De facto, therefore, the Burundi judges may have lacked independence.

Judicial authority, like judicial independence, can be seen in different ways. *Institutional design* refers to how the judiciary has been organized, particularly in relation to other organs of government. That relational arrangement may limit or expand both

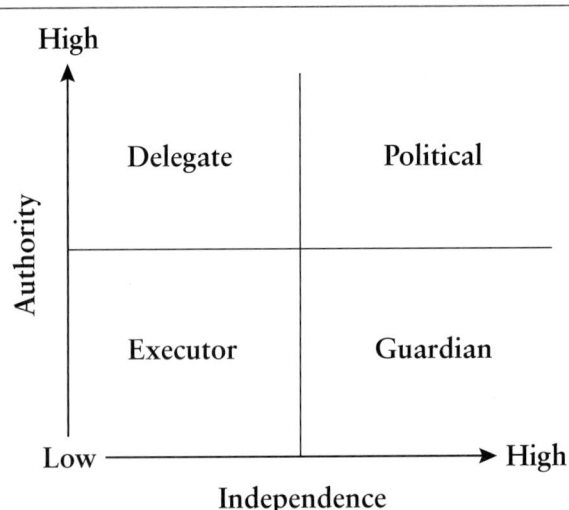

Figure 4.1 Judicial authority and independence

	Low Independence	High Independence
High Authority	Delegate	Political
Low Authority	Executor	Guardian

Source: Adapted from Carlo Guarnieri and Patrizia Pederzoli, *The Power of Judges: A Comparative Study of Courts and Democracy* (Oxford: Oxford University Press, 2002), 70.

judicial authority and discretion. Separation of powers can serve to enhance or circumvent judicial authority vis-à-vis other political institutions. The law as written does not, however, determine how all of the pieces of government will interact in reality. Extralegal factors also shape how institutions function. Some extralegal factors, such as public opinion or the practical consequences of a particular decision, may or may not emerge as benign considerations. Corruption, intimidation, and judges' personal or political ambitions are generally regarded as inappropriate influences.

Finally, once the factors that shape the political environment of judges are known, we are confronted with a more important question: How do judges in different contexts actually decide cases? We cannot get into the mind of a judge to know exactly why he or she decided a particular way in a given case, and very likely the judges themselves balance a variety of considerations, some consciously and some not, when making decisions. Researchers have nonetheless devised a number of theories about how judges decide based on inferences about patterns in outcomes of cases.

JUDICIAL INDEPENDENCE

Judicial independence developed as a value because of the logic of employing a detached third party to intervene and decide a dispute. The impartial intervenor stands as the fulcrum in that relationship, since the individual judge is expected to be indifferent to who wins. One would hope that most judges serving in all regime types decide most nonpolitically relevant cases impartially. The judiciary as an institution may not be positioned to act independently in all cases. Indeed, across 163 countries over a forty-year period at the close of the twentieth century, independent judiciaries provided a bulwark against democratic slippage into authoritarianism (Gibler and Randazzo 2011). Judicial independence has also been positively correlated with economic growth (Feld and Voigt 2003; Henisz 2000) and portfolio investment in developing countries (Staats and Biglaiser 2011).

Judicial independence should not be thought of as a dichotomy, either wholly subservient or totally unaccountable. Rather, as the Guarnieri and Pederzoli (2002) classifications acknowledge, judges are more or less independent. Think of points on a spectrum ranging from 100 percent independent to 100 percent dependent (Chavez 2003; Howard 2001). The independence of judges must be seen as instrumental—a means to an end—not an intrinsic good in and of itself (Geyh 2008). Indeed, a completely independent judge can also be a tyrant, ruling on personal whim and bias. The next questions are from whom is the judge supposed to be independent (Blondel 1995) and, beyond the goal of impartiality, is a completely independent judiciary really desirable? The answers to both questions presumably guide design of the mechanisms that locate the proper placement of judicial independence and its flip side, judicial accountability, on the continuum that runs from dependent to independent.

Judicial independence has been defined variously, predicated largely on the response to the inquiry independent from whom? Thus, the judiciary might need to be free from manipulation by politicians (Ramseyer 1994), insulated from retaliation by other political organs (Iaryczower, Spiller, and Tommasi 2002), able to decide without respect for the political preferences of other institutions (Rosenberg 1992) and other actors (Ferejohn, Rosenbluth, and Shipan 2007), or without "incentives and impediments" created extralegally (Howard and Carey 2004). The adage "without fear or favor" seems an apt summation. The difference among these various definitions rests on their emphasis; each at its core underscores that judges should not be compelled to decide cases on any grounds other than the law. Indeed, "legal norms [are] the only legitimate motive of judicial decisions" (Schedler 2004, 250).

The "law" in any specific case may be perfectly obvious or subject to differing interpretations, ambiguous, or even in conflict with another law. How much leeway a judge has in the latter situations depends on the authority of the judge. Delegate and political judges are expected to exercise discretion and even creativity when confronted with such cases. Guardian and executor judges, on the other hand, are granted less room for maneuver. Even so, judges with quite limited authority may find wiggle room in deciding cases in which the applicable law is not unequivocal. Since guardian judges are well insulated in their autonomy, their potential realm of creativity exceeds that of the executor judges, with only tenuous independence.

The laws that ideally bind judges necessarily reflect the political system in which they are embedded. Yet institutional insularity becomes even more important when the government is a party in a lawsuit, as judges should not be seen as biased in the government's favor (Larkins 1996). Repressive regimes may employ the law for different political ends than democratic ones. The apartheid government of South Africa, for example, completely complied with the governing law at that time (Haynie 1997).

Authoritarian regimes may not choose a repressive legal system, because judicial autonomy, at least in a limited sense, serves the regime's goals of, say, protection of private property. Therefore, authoritarian governments seek to structure judicial independence to support the government without helping the opposition (Moustafa and Ginsburg 2008). The generals under the Augusto Pinochet regime in Chile (1973–1990) left the mechanisms of de jure judicial independence intact and did not meddle in judicial decision making. In return the judges offered the regime a cloak of legitimacy while docilely accepting actions of the repressive regime as legal (Hilbink 2008). Similarly, in semidemocratic Uganda and Zimbabwe, courts were able to retain their independence if they had clear constituencies beyond lawyers or were able to attract international attention that could result in limitations on foreign aid (Widner and Scher 2008, 237). Also, in the autocratic nation of Singapore, although rarely ruling against the government, judges have maintained a reputation for independence (Silverstein 2008). The limits of judicial independence are consequently structured to serve the political system, usually through some system of reward or punishment (Melton and Ginsburg 2014).

Much of the ability of judges individually and collectively to act appropriately in their legally defined roles reaches back to long before a judge is selected for office. As discussed in chapter 3, many, if not most, countries in the world experience a shortage of people trained in the law. The supply chain of economic development to legal education directly impacts the pool of people eligible to be judges and, as their educational preparation varies, so does their ability to perform appropriately within their defined sphere of independence and authority.

De Jure Judicial Independence
De jure judicial independence can usually be located in the processes for judicial recruitment, tenure, promotion, and removal provisions. Those four elements locate the legal definition of where judges fit into one of the four ideal types. Depending on the amount of discretion permitted, judges with the longest tenure and most secure positions can be classified as political or guardian judges. On the other hand, judges with short terms of office and subject to

strict supervision for promotion and removal have, at least theoretically, the potential to serve as executor and delegate judges.

A seemingly endless number of selection mechanisms have been devised for naming judges, but they typically fall into one of the following four categories: (1) career service, (2) elective, (3) appointment by executive, and (4) judicial appointment commission (Malleson 2006). Of note, these categories may not fit comfortably for judges in the Islamic legal tradition or for customary law courts where judgeships are not always legally defined, but they most closely resemble executive appointments. The nature of the selection system generally also implicates tenure, promotion, and removal schemes. Federal judges in the United States, for example, are appointed by the president and confirmed by the Senate after having actively practiced law and have life tenure except in the case of unethical behavior. They can be promoted only through another executive appointment and can only be removed through legislative impeachment. Career service judges, on the other hand, enter the judiciary after some examination and/or apprenticeship system and, barring removal for cause, usually serve for life or until a mandatory retirement age. They are promoted up the system through some form of hierarchically supervised evaluation. The possible variations on those basic models are myriad, and they are multiplied for selection of judges exercising constitutional review, as discussed in the next chapter.

Those designing judicial selection systems tend to at least pay lip service to a goal of preserving judicial independence, but no consensus has been reached on which system best achieves that goal (Garoupa and Ginsburg 2008a). Moreover, those designing recruitment mechanisms for judges pay more attention to who will name and remove judges than to the grants of authority that will be made (Epstein et al. 2001). Selection systems are not created in a political vacuum (Tarr 2012), and perhaps most important, all are political both in design and in implementation. The political dimension is present "whether in terms of ideological politics, party politics, identity politics, regional politics, or institutional politics" (Gee et al. 2015, 159).

Career service judges are typical in civil law countries but can also now be found in China (Peerenboom 2008), Japan (Ramseyer and Rasmusen 2003; O'Brien 1996), and much of Southeast Asia (O'Brien 2006). Differences abound, but the stereotypical career judiciary begins with people who have completed their legal studies and passed a competitive examination. Some form of judicial education is then completed and followed by either formal studies or an apprenticeship. Ultimately qualified individuals receive a position on the lower rungs of the judicial ladder. Through some combination of seniority and merit, judges then climb the judicial hierarchy. Judges assume their first post not long after completion of their legal education, but more and more places are permitting lateral entry by experienced lawyers (Guarnieri and Pederzoli 2002). The Dutch, for example, permit both routes of entry to the judicial corps, but in addition to a test in law, candidates must also undergo a psychological exam and assessment, present letters of recommendation, and pass two or more interviews (DeGroot-Van Leeuwen 2006). Since 1995 China has required legal education and passage of an examination, but those holding judicial positions are also subject to annual performance evaluations. Thus, judges can be rather easily removed or transferred to nonadjudication positions, and positive evaluations drive promotions (Hawes 2006).

Many, but not all, career service models are paired with some type of judicial council that oversees judicial performance. These bodies are charged with overseeing selection, promotion, and discipline of judges. The French created the first one in 1946, but approximately 60 percent of countries now use some form of judicial council. These bodies tend to be dominated by sitting judges, usually elected by other judges, but most also include lay members or lawyers named by political organs, most often the legislature. Some councils, such as those in Germany, Austria, and the Netherlands, handle recruitment only and play no part in promotions and discipline (Garoupa and Ginsburg 2008a), whereas promotions in Italy under its council are determined solely by seniority (Guarnieri and Pederzoli 2002). Between those poles lie a variety of obligations falling under councils' prerogatives. All claim to protect judicial independence from political meddling while preserving some measure of accountability for sitting jurists (Garoupa and Ginsburg 2008a). Of course they do not always succeed. At the end of the twentieth century, twenty Latin American nations adopted judicial councils. Venezuela's was so politicized that it was eliminated in 2000, and others were of limited success in checking determined executives (Chavez 2007).

Most judges are technically appointed by the executive branch of government or, in the case of constitutional monarchies, by the crown. Countries with the common law tradition, such as the United

States, Canada, Australia, and New Zealand, follow the broad outlines of the historical process in England and Wales. Experienced lawyers are the ones who, at some point in their legal careers, make the transition to judgeships. The minister of justice or the attorney general normally serves to vet potential judges, usually with some specified obligation to consult with relevant parties. In the United States, the president formally nominates all federal judges who are subject to confirmation by the upper house—Senate—of the legislature. The attorney general's office investigates judicial candidates prior to nomination, and politics are an overt consideration. Judges so appointed in the United States and elsewhere hold their position for life or to a mandatory retirement age unless removed for misconduct. Promotions occur through the same process and are not necessarily expected during a judicial career. The process for all levels of judgeships tends to be secretive and informal (Gee et al. 2015), and many variations on the appointment model exist. Some Latin American courts posit appointment in the legislature and others, such as Paraguay, use courts to nominate with legislative approval (Driscoll and Nelson 2015).

Most people think of using popular elections to name judges as a peculiarity of some American states. Actually, the French flirted with the concept briefly after the revolution of 1789. The thinking was that justice should be common sense and not require a legal education. Only certain relatively low-level judges were elected, and only by "active citizens"; the practice lasted only until 1800 (Volcansek and Lafon 1988). Elections emerged in the United States, first in the state of Mississippi, in 1832 as a wave of populism spread under the presidency of Andrew Jackson. A similar, more recent populist tide influenced Bolivia to choose to elect its judges under a new 2009 constitution. The Bolivian wrinkle lies in the requirement that candidates for judgeships be evaluated for merit and preapproved by a supermajority of both chambers of the bicameral legislature before appearing on the ballot. The first elections in 2011 yielded the most diverse Bolivian judiciary in history (Driscoll and Nelson 2015).

In the United States, where judicial elections are ubiquitous in states in one form or another, the desirability of electing judges remains hotly contested almost two hundred years after it was first instituted (Geyh 2008). Elections may reflect the partisan attachment of candidates, be nonpartisan, or affect retention, in which voters indicate whether or not to retain a sitting judge in office.

Much recent scholarship has been favorable to the process. Indeed, campaign contributions have been found to have only a conditional influence on judicial decisions (Cann, Bonneau, and Boyea 2012), and despite the effects of campaign contributions and activities, the legitimacy-enhancing effects of elections outweigh concerns over the costs of campaigns (Gibson 2012). Nonpartisan elections actually cost more than partisan ones (Bonneau and Gann Hall 2009), and appointive systems are at least as partisan in outcome as partisan elections (Tarr 2012). A guiding assumption supporting electing judges is that voters, through the same democratic process applied to other officeholders, can hold judges accountable and oust them from office at the ballot box. Whatever legitimacy or democratic accountability electing judges may offer, however, detractors continue to argue that the potential taint of campaigns and contributions erodes judicial independence and impartiality.

Judicial appointment commissions "look likely to become the most popular selection system of the twenty-first century" (Malleson 2006, 6). Some version of appointment commissions can be found in Canada (Morton 2006); Norway (Grendstad, Shaffer, and Waltenburg 2015); England, Wales, Scotland, and Northern Ireland (Gee et al. 2015); South Africa (Haynie 1997); and Bulgaria (Melone 1996). Though details of operation differ from country to country, the system introduced for England and Wales by the Constitutional Reform Acts of 2005 is rather prototypical. The Judicial Appointments Commission (JAC) is staffed through an open competition for lawyers, judges, and laypeople, plus three senior judges named by other judges; a layperson serves as chair. The JAC employs a process of advertising, tests, interviews, and other screening mechanisms to nominate potential judges to the lord chancellor (equivalent to minister of justice or attorney general) in the executive arm of government. Fewer than 2 percent of the JAC's recommendations were not accepted between 2006 and 2013 (Gee et al. 2015). Similar to what resulted from the introduction of judicial elections in Bolivia (Driscoll and Nelson 2015), the bench in England and Wales was significantly more diverse as a consequence. The result of the new system turns on identity politics, if not partisan or ideological ones.

Is one system for selecting, disciplining, promoting, and removing judges preferable to the others? Has any been shown to produce more qualified or more independent judges? No. Those questions cannot be answered empirically, in part because no consensus has been reached on how to measure judicial competence or quality. Even stable political systems evolve and change in response to societal changes, and judicial systems and by whom and how they are staffed reflect some combination of societal norms and regime preferences. No single system could be implemented everywhere and achieve equal results. Yet the significance of an independent judiciary does not receive lip service only in Western democracies. In 2006 Chinese premier Wen Jiabao was quoted as describing the goal of a "socialist democracy" as consisting of three elements: "elections, judicial independence, and supervision based on checks and balances" (Thorton 2008, 4). The centrality of independent judges has achieved expansive recognition.

De Facto Independence
De facto judicial independence presumably results from all of the safeguards in place for selecting, promoting, rewarding, and sanctioning judges. Such measures are regularly enshrined in constitutions, something relatively rare even twenty-five years ago. Yet since 1985 two-thirds of newly written constitutions have contained explicit guarantees of judicial independence, protections for salaries and tenure, and limitations on the role of legislatures and executives in appointment and removal of judges (Melton and Ginsburg 2014). Can we assume, therefore, that all of the national constitutions that include such provisions have, in reality, ensured the impartiality of judicial decisions by insulating judges from extralegal influences and allowing only the guiding force of the law? Most people are not naïve enough to accept that assertion, but why do these parchment barriers not translate into de facto independence for courts? We are confronted with what Mark Ramseyer (1994) referred to as the "Puzzling (In)dependence" of courts. Of 177 nations from 1992 to 1994, only 40 percent had totally independent judiciaries, and almost the same number had the opposite (totally subservient); a mere one-eighth had partial independence (Howard and Carey 2004). The absence of congruence may reflect "an implementation gap between rules on the book and the rules in practice" (Mendelski 2012, 25), or it may result from something deeper, more suspect, even sinister.

The gap between de facto and de jure independence can be aptly illustrated by the case of Romania in the aftermath of its Communist era. Beginning in the 1990s the European Union adopted a goal of developing the rule of law in the new democracies of eastern and central Europe and appropriated substantial funds to that end (Piana 2010). By 2008 Romania had achieved 100 percent of the goals in judicial appointments, independence, and accountability, along with conflict of interest and asset disclosure requirements. Even so, while all of those reforms were present in the law, the fact remained that in practice—de facto—Romanian judicial activities reflected at best 50 percent achievement, according to a Global Integrity study (Mendelski 2012). Why the discrepancy? A number of resilient and powerful veto players, ranging from politicians, influential businesspeople, media moguls, and bureaucrats to the judges themselves, were able to corrupt, manipulate, or lobby to achieve their goals in the courts (Mendelski 2012). Parchment guarantees of judicial independence and impartiality were breached by entrenched political and judicial cultures.

De facto judicial independence depends not only on the procedures entailed in arriving at decisions, but also on perceptions that the formally prescribed processes have not been subverted by informal ones. Individual confidence that the judicial system is not rigged underlies the credibility of the judicial system and relies on trust in the impartiality, autonomy, and authority of the judiciary (Bühlmann and Kunz 2011). The absence of that confidence was illustrated in the response of an elderly aboriginal man who was called to testify in a coroner's court in Queensland, Australia, some few decades ago. The man was merely a witness to a traffic accident and not a party to the proceedings. Nevertheless, after being sworn in "this man looked slowly around at a sea of white faces and said simply, 'I plead guilty'" (Hulls 2017).

That example further points to the difficulty of measuring de facto judicial independence: we can see it only in its absence. "Judicial independence is not directly observable" (Linzer and Staton 2015). With few dissenters, most scholars conclude that formal indicators—de jure independence—"often did not conform to reality" (Larkins 1996, 615). Not only does judicial independence defy easy measurement, but those intent on subverting independence, within or outside of the political system, have proved crafty in their approaches. Judicial decisions respond to different incentives, as well as disincentives (Garoupa and Ginsburg 2008b). Therefore, assessing threats to judicial independence can be approached by looking at the types of potential menaces: those that are overt, those that are veiled or anticipated, and those that are structural to the system.

A blatant and deadly overt threat occurred in Colombia in 1985, when the M-19 guerrilla movement, possibly funded by drug cartels, attacked the Palace of Justice in Bogotá, killing some judges and burning the building (Uribe-Urán 2011). The judiciary in Poland emerged as a political prize in 2015, as the nationalist-populist Law and Justice Party (PiS) took control under Jaroslaw Kaczynski. The Civic Platform Party, which lost to the PiS, among its closing actions in power replaced three of the fifteen judges whose terms had expired, but then boldly appointed two additional replacements for those set to retire after the PiS took over. The PiS parliament invalidated all five appointments and named five new judges. Since the legitimacy of those five, one-third of the court, was not accepted by the remaining ten judges, parliament passed a law requiring most cases to be heard by at least thirteen judges. In short, the court was incapacitated (Kelemen and Orenstein 2016). Matters escalated thereafter. By mid-2017, the PiS parliament passed a law, one subsequently vetoed by the president (Lyman 2017b), to require the resignation of all judges on all courts that it had not appointed, and it had already legislated that all judicial appointments would require preapproval of the executive. The actions, according to the EU Commission vice president, "would abolish any remaining judicial independence and put the judiciary under full political control of the government" (Lyman 2017a). Recep Tayyip Erdogan in Turkey accomplished the same results in April 2017 via a constitutional referendum, which also essentially transferred control of the courts to the executive (Sezgin 2017).

The attack on the Colombian Supreme Court was intended to intimidate judges who might decide cases involving drug trafficking cartels, and the Polish and Turkish efforts were designed to transform courts into instruments of executive power. Overt threats to judicial independence can also take the form of removing courts' jurisdiction. Indian president Indira Gandhi declared a state of emergency in 1975 that lasted for two years, and during that time the ability of courts to hear certain fundamental rights cases was suspended. The declaration, according to the attorney general at the time, meant that "even if the executive shot a person dead or put him in prison, he could not invite a court to review the validity of such action" (Sathe 2002, 101). Another means to achieve similar ends can be to avoid the courts entirely, a process euphemistically called "extrajudicial executions." During the authoritarian regime in Brazil (1964–1985), of every twenty-three people tried for political offenses, one was executed extrajudicially. That ratio was far greater in Chile (1973–1984), where 1.5 people were tried for every one executed extrajudicially, and in Argentina (1976–1983), where the ratio was one trial for every seventy-one executions (Pereira 2005).

Judicial independence can also be infringed through veiled threats or anticipated reactions, which prompt judges to make decisions strategically. For example, whether or not actual threats were made to the Burundi high court judges discussed in chapter 1, the judges believed they were threatened and acted accordingly. Most validated the president's bid for another term, and the lone dissenter fled the country. Similarly, in Chile under General Augusto Pinochet (1973–1990), all judges on the supreme court claimed that their independence was fully respected, and the judiciary was not purged. Yet judges were cognizant of the wishes of the regime, and those on the highest court were enabled by legislation to dismiss potentially dissident lower court judges. The regime also deflected politically sensitive cases to military courts (Hilbink 2007).

Judges respond to threats and to incentives. Argentina had a history of political instability, which often meant the wholesale dismissal of judges on the highest courts when regimes changed (Brinks 2005). When Carlos Menem became president in 1989, many sitting judges were offered ambassadorships and other prestigious offices to induce their resignations, but only one judge took the bait. Menem was forced to act more transparently and enlarged the court to facilitate appointment of a majority of compliant judges (Larkins 1998).

Bulgarian judges in the 1990s were threatened with violence and subjected to "telephone justice," whereby a political functionary called to pressure them to make a decision (Melone 1996), but that gave way to pressures from other judges and threats of potential prosecutions of the judges. Whether or not the suspicions of the judges were well founded, a threat can nonetheless influence a judge's impartiality (Schönfelder 2005). The judiciary in Kenya under President Mzee Jomo Kenyatta (1966–1978) and his successor, President Daniel Arap Moi (1978–2008), was compliant to the executive in part because of "force of habit and the culture of officialdom that was too difficult to overcome" (Mutua 2001). In China judges face an unusual array of possible impediments in addition to the national standards, which protect judges from sanction for an unintentional legal error. Even so, many local "responsibility systems" designed by the Communist Party to evaluate, reward, and monitor bureaucrats regularly sanction local judges for accidental mistakes (Minzer 2009). In 2001, 995 Chinese judges were found to have violated rules, but that number represents less than 0.02 percent of the total Chinese judiciary (Peerenboom 2008).

The final category of breaches of de facto judicial independence is structural. These breaches occur in two primary forms: hierarchal supervision by higher courts and removal of cases from ordinary civilian courts. All judges have audiences (Baum 2006; Garoupa and Ginsburg 2008b), who evaluate them, some without material impact on judicial independence, such as legal academics who write critiques of judicial decisions. Other audiences, particularly in hierarchal judiciaries—where superior courts drive promotions, salaries, transfers, and discipline—the critiques of those audiences are significant. Wider audiences, particularly public opinion, can also be potent and sometimes to the advantage of the judges. For example, Ecuadorian president Lucio Guttiérrez attempted in 2004 to remove all of the supreme court judges. That action prompted protests and ultimately led to the president's removal (Pérez-Liñán, Ames, and Seligson 2006).

When superior courts, as in Japan, or judicial councils control promotions, discipline, and transfers, such as in Colombia, Ecuador, and Peru, the audiences to which judges are most attuned are internal to the judicial corps. Japanese judges are possibly the most rigidly governed by and subservient to higher courts (Ramseyer and Rasmusen 2001, 2003), and the Italian and Brazilian judges may be the least. In Brazil, though higher level judges may remove lower ones, lower court judges are not even bound by superior court decisions, particularly on constitutional issues (Santiso 2003). Seniority alone governs advancement in the Italian case. The judicial council can discipline judges (Guarnieri and Pederzoli 2002), but that occurs only in the rarest cases (de Franciscis 1996). Between those two extremes lie Chinese judges, whose promotions are merit based, but admittedly the merit criteria are not transparent. Higher court judges supervise the decisions of lower ones (Peerenboom 2008). Much of the merit evaluation apparently consists of measures such as the number of cases reversed on appeal. That has led lower court judges to use requests for advisory opinions (*qingshi*) before deciding cases, particularly in politically sensitive cases (Minzer 2009). The high courts in Mozambique hold administrative control over lower courts that can potentially infringe the independence of judges on the lower rungs of the judicial ladder, a practice that is even more pronounced in Chile (Gloppen et al. 2010). The judicial hierarchy in Bolivia before elections were introduced permitted hierarchal influences, but judges said that attempts at political pressure by public officials and politicians happened more often than interference by higher courts (Pérez-Liñán, Ames, and Seligson 2006).

Political officials are more likely to preserve the appearance and even the reality of independence for regular judges but steer politically sensitive cases to special courts, another structural impediment. Thus, the authority of judges becomes constrained when topics of law are carved out of the normal court portfolio, but the appearance of judicial independence is preserved. Judges who, at least on paper, have all of the trappings of guardians or political roles with high autonomy may have their authority redirected for some categories of cases. Not surprisingly, this strategy is a common ploy of authoritarian regimes. Spanish dictator Francisco Franco (1939–1975) allowed ideological diversity among the regular judges but created a parallel system of special courts to handle cases with potential political consequences, for which judges were appointed or removed by the executive (Toharia 1975). The military in Nigeria created special tribunals by decree and sometimes even gave them retroactive authority (Olowofoyeku 1989), and Burma under military control employed special criminal courts for which the decision to try whom and where was a matter of official discretion (Cheeseman 2011). Argentina, Brazil, and Chile while under military rule and under state-of-siege powers diverted cases to military courts with little objection from the ordinary civilian courts beyond an occasional habeas corpus petition addressing procedure (Pereira 2005). China has acted more subtly, steering certain types of cases to administrative review and prohibiting lawsuits by some groups, notably any brought by Falangon disciples (Peerenboom 2008).

The resort to special courts in authoritarian regimes may not surprise anyone. Nations continue to reap the benefits of reasonably independent courts to decide issues of contracts and property rights, which are important for international commerce, while also managing to quell dissent and dissenters. But what about the use of such tribunals in democratic nations? Following the attacks in the United States on September 11, 2001, and the US invasion of Afghanistan, military commissions, not US courts, were established under President George W. Bush. These courts were created under the executive branch to try "enemy combatants" held in Guantánamo Bay, Cuba. That group numbered around 775 initially (O'Brien 2011). The commissions have been likened to those in Brazil and Chile during the military dictatorships (Pereira 2005). Even though the US Supreme Court intervened in more than one instance to insist on procedural rights for those detained, the US military in Guantanamo continued to hold "enemy combatants" after President Bush's eight years in office and his successor's eight years ended.

Israel represents another democracy that has employed military commissions in the occupied territories of the West Bank, Gaza Strip, and East Jerusalem. These are basically lands that were seized by Israel in the Six-Day War with Egypt in 1967 and, with the exception of Gaza, from which Israel withdrew in 2005, have been occupied since then. This constitutes perhaps the longest military occupation in modern times. The high-ranking military officers who preside as judges in the military commissions are generally perceived as impartial, but even so approximately 813,000 Palestinians were arrested during the first sixteen years of the occupation (1967–1993). Intifada uprisings were admittedly national security threats, but crimes that came before the military commissions were not restricted to violent acts; rather, whatever authorities deemed menacing or disruptive to public order was included (Hajjar 2005). Just as the US Supreme Court intervened on some points affecting the military commissions in Guantanamo Bay, the Israeli Supreme Court acted in some instances to protect human rights, implicitly more often than overtly (Hofnung and Weinshall-Margel 2011).

TOO MUCH INDEPENDENCE?

The realization that governments or even higher courts act to rein in judicial independence points to the essential tension that exists between law and politics, between law and policy, and between independence and accountability. The normative value of judicial independence rests on the requirement that disputes, whether contracts, crimes, or executive actions, be decided impartially. Unfettered judicial power can be as dictatorial as unbridled executive or legislative power. "In a world of unchecked judicial authority, who guards the guardians?" (Clark 2011, 265).

Independent judges were crucial to the pursuit of corrupt politicians in Italy in the early 1990s and in Brazil, where former prime minister Luiz Inácio Lula da Silva received an almost ten-year prison sentence for corruption in 2017 (*Economist* 2017b). Italy and Brazil represent probably the most independent judges to be found. While too little time has lapsed since the Lula conviction to draw any conclusions, in Italy a backlash commenced in the early 2000s, with parliamentary attempts to curb judicial authority. When courts act too authoritatively and too independently, particularly on the hottest topics, they ironically become progressively enmeshed in politics (Russell 2001). "Striking the right balance between independence and accountability" presents a challenge (Russell 2006, 427).

The political cannot be fully displaced by the judicial, a phenomenon usually associated with the exercise of constitutional review (Ferejohn and Pasquino 2003), but it can also occur in the settlement of individual disputes and adjudication of criminal charges. In Indonesia, for example, a Christian former governor of Jakarta, Basuki Tjahaja Purnama, lost his reelection bid and was subsequently convicted of blasphemy and sentenced to two years' imprisonment. His crime resulted from statements he had made during the election campaign about whether the Quran prohibited Muslims from voting for a non-Muslim. Governor Basuki argued that such an interpretation was "misleading." This alleged insult to the Quran was adjudicated to constitute blasphemy (Cochrane 2017). Was that conviction judicial or political, and how can one disentangle the two when a politician faces a criminal trial?

Judges, like military officers and government bureaucrats, may be theoretically insulated from politics, but "judges enjoying a hefty measure of independence may be no more committed to the preservation of free and open debate" (Fiss 1993, 57) than the other two sets of unelected actors in the political system. Why would wholly unaccountable judges choose to be politically impartial and neutral (Maravall 2003)? Even in cases of political corruption in Italy in the 1990s, where judges were portrayed as crusaders against a venal and corrupt political class, some evidence suggests that judges colluded with politicians through informal contacts and that a professional culture drove some outcomes (Della Porta 2001).

> **BOX 4.1** | **Politics and the Judiciary in Brazil**
>
> A group of prosecutors and judges in Brazil, most in their twenties, thirties, and forties, launched a campaign championing transparency and responsiveness in government and waged their campaign on social media, as well as in courtrooms. Politicians of all ideological hues were investigated and charged. In 2017 former president Luiz Inácio Lula da Silva was convicted of corruption and money laundering, and his political rival, the sitting president Michel Temer, was targeted in an investigation, also for alleged corruption. The judges and prosecutors have denied any political motives, as politicians across all parties have been investigated, but those convicted have publicly challenged the legitimacy of the judicial actions. The investigations and trials could have a major impact on elections in 2018.
>
> *Source:* Ernesto Londoño and Shannon Sims, "Political Rivals Face a Common Threat: Brazil's Rising Judiciary," *New York Times*, July 14, 2017, A-1.

Outside of some US states and Bolivia, judges, like bureaucrats, are unelected and yet exercise political power. "Hence the problem posed by unchecked checkers" (Lane and Ersson 2000). In theory at least, courts are distinct from other unelected authorities because of their reliance on the law and procedures that are known (Vibert 2007). Yet are judges independent from "the latest political fashion [and] . . . popular feelings" (Koopmans 2003, 250), influenced by public opinion, or seeking public acquiescence with their decisions (Maravall 2003). Do judges, such as those deciding the Indonesian blasphemy case, have political interests of their own?

JUDICIAL AUTHORITY

Placement of judges into one of the four ideal types of executor, delegate, guardian, or political relies on two axes—independence and authority—but the two overlap and connect in a variety of ways. Does a judge with a highly restricted range of discretion require protection for her independence beyond what is required for impartiality? Most discussions of judicial independence focus on the de jure requirements for selection, promotion, tenure, discipline, and removal, but as the exploration of de facto independence indicates, those provisions can be and are breached in a variety of ways. Thus, both the authority and actual independence of courts are largely determined by the placement of courts in the larger political system.

Institutional design captures how all political actors are situated within a political scheme and how their relationships interconnect. It reflects all aspects of de jure judicial independence, but also defines interinstitutional accountability or insularity. Institutional design (and redesign) is always the product of politics. Some crafting designs may truly be motivated to create the most workable and enduring and perhaps even best political system for promotion of human rights and economic prosperity. However, politicians are by definition also driven by power. Ergo, the designs of institutions typically mirror politicians' calculations—sometimes miscalculations—about their chances of gaining and maintaining political power. "They will tend to make choices in ways that maximize their odds of winning elections" (Ramseyer and Rasmusen 2003, ix). Another calculation involves politicians' estimates of their and their party's staying power. If you assume that you will remain in power indefinitely, you want a different institutional arrangement than if you expect to be at least periodically outside of political power. Another estimate that enters the calculus is mistrust of those in power and those presumed to have authority to control them (O'Donnell 2001). A final consideration must be political culture, for law and culture are necessarily intertwined, and the former offers only a framework that needs to fit with other realms of citizens' or subjects' lives (Rosen 2006). This consideration constituted what was typically absent under much colonial rule, because the imposed political institutions did not mesh comfortably with existing cultures.

The calculations of authoritarian regimes differ from democratic ones because of the lack of legal competing political movements, but they still share the goals of protecting property rights for commerce and investment. That means that a role remains for courts that at least appear independent. Thus China, for example, has made an independent judiciary one of its goals (Minzer 2009). Authoritarian regimes must also devise institutional designs to deal with, among other things, succession and coup avoidance (Winthrobe 2007).

Democracies require more careful calibration, particularly with regard to courts, and judiciaries constitute but a single cog in most complex democratic mechanisms. The gear to one institution affects how all of the others move. Many terms have been adopted to describe the strategies employed in crafting constitutions that prescribe institutional design, but Tsebelis's (2002) concept of veto players may be most appropriate when considering the authority and independence of courts and allows inclusion of the concerns of even authoritarian regimes.

Veto players represent the actors in a political system who must agree for a change to occur in the status quo policy. Tsebelis (2002) identifies two categories of veto players: institutional and partisan. In the United States, the institutional veto players are the House of Representatives, Senate, president, and Supreme Court. Partisan veto players are those relevant political parties that result from the electoral system and are usually more relevant for multiparty systems that result in coalition governments, but also can apply in two-party systems. The numbers and types of veto players in a system affect policy stability. The more institutional veto players who must agree and, for partisan veto players, the less ideological distance separating them, the more stable a regime will be and the less policy change will occur.

Therefore, if you are designing an authoritarian government and expect to hold power indefinitely, how many veto players do you want? China, for example, has a single source of authority, the National People's Congress, a surrogate for the Communist Party. It chose to increase the independence of its courts, presumably for economic reasons, but does not permit courts to act as veto players. Even in dictatorships, courts offer investors credible commitments, monitor low-level bureaucrats, and lend an aura of legitimacy (Helmke and Rosenbluth 2009). In 2017 both Jaroslaw Kaczynski, head of Poland's Law and Justice Party, and Recep Erdogan in Turkey chose to reshuffle their respective institutional designs by eliminating as many veto players as possible, particularly the courts. Turkey's President Erdogan likely thought about being in power indefinitely; in the same referendum that weakened the courts, he extended his potential term in office. He now has the possibility of serving three additional five-year terms.

The number of institutional veto players in democracies tends to be contingent on two factors: (1) political compromise and (2) predictions of future election outcomes. The latter—future elections—has been called "political insurance." One wants to ensure the rules that will be applied will be applied when one is not in

> **BOX 4.2** | **Curbing Judicial Authority in Turkey**
>
> Following a failed military coup attempt in 2016, Turkish president Recep Tayyip Erdogan purged almost one-quarter of the Turkish judiciary, around four thousand people, alleging that they were linked to a secretive Islamic movement, the Gulenists, who were accused of leading the coup. Ironically, many of the purged judges had years earlier participated in a purge of military officials with the blessing of President Erdogan. Judges who defy the government, according to a Turkish bar association leader, face consequences. For example, when judges on one court decided in 2017 to release twenty-one journalists from pretrial detention, the judges were suspended and their ruling was overturned within twenty-four hours.
>
> Source: "Empty Benches: Purging Turkey's Judiciary," *Economist*, May 20, 2017.

office. The concept of political insurance takes the premise of the prisoner's dilemma as applied to the political sphere. In the prisoner's dilemma, one player can defect and implicate the other prisoner or cooperate in anticipation that the other prisoner will do the same. Prisoners expecting to play only once are more likely to defect. In the political realm, whether political actors will theoretically make judges independent depends on the twin expectations that elections will continue and that they will be won indefinitely. The insurance model has been used to explain judicial independence in Japan, where the Liberal Democratic Party won every election after World War II until the twenty-first century (Ramseyer 1994), and judicial reforms in Argentina, Mexico, and Peru in the 1990s (Finkel 2008), as well as in Taiwan, South Korea, and Mongolia (Ginsburg 2003). The rationale behind the argument is that if you expect your party to hold power indefinitely, judicial independence can protect the opposition and political adversaries. If, on the other hand, you anticipate being in the opposition in the future, you want autonomous courts to protect your and your party's interests.

The insurance theory implicates judicial authority as well as independence. Thus, an authoritarian regime may choose to grant courts significant independence but give them a limited range of authority (guardians) or, since Chinese judges can be relatively easily removed, give courts both low independence and little room for discretion (executors). Many democracies, particularly those in the civil law tradition, will select guardian mode judges, while other democratic systems may opt for delegate judges, with high levels of discretion but limited independence. Political judges, those with high authority and high independence, result primarily in systems with constitutional review, the subject of the next chapter. Tsebelis (2002) argues that courts, even those with the authority of constitutional review, cannot serve as veto players because they have been absorbed by the larger political system. That is, judges, through their professional training and selection processes, hold the same political values as do other political elites.

Separation of powers between the legislative and executive branches typically enables veto players and permits one of those organs to ally with or protect judicial independence, but only in majoritarian parliamentary systems. The objective of separation of powers can be found in pitting the ambitions of political institutions against one another (Calvert, McCubbins, and Weinghast 1989). Typically courts with the power of constitutional review are seen as players in separation of powers schemes, but the independence of the judiciary can be implicated even where it lacks that authority. Executive dominance threatens judicial independence and authority because courts often rely on the executive branch to enforce judicial decisions. Judicial independence arises as more crucial, but also tenuous when executive dominance becomes disproportionate: "hyper-presidentialism," a condition common in some Latin American and African nations (Gloppen et al. 2010). Whereas federalism offers another set of potential veto players that may in some ways limit executive power, a federal arrangement typically has little effect on either the independence or the authority of courts.

Tsebelis (2002) identified partisan veto players in addition to institutional ones. The number, viability, and ideological distances among partisan veto players are a function of electoral systems. The numbers and strength of parties, in turn, determine not only who dominates the legislative branch, but also the internal cohesion of the executive: majority, multiparty coalition, minority, or grand coalition (Lijphart 2012). Considerable research has found that electoral systems that foster partisan electoral competition and rotation in power may leave courts with their independence and authority less vulnerable to attack. Again, the logic of the insurance model applies: if your party may lose power in future elections, your political self-interest rests in unfettered courts to protect you when you are out of power. If one party controls the executive and a majority of the legislature, courts acting contrary to that unified opposition are more open to reprisal or override. In the opposite scenario, where the executive is multiparty or minority and the legislature is fragmented, courts are less likely to be at risk (Ferejohn, Rosenbluth, and Shipan 2007).

Chinese courts qualify as independent on, say, contract cases, so long as they remain consistent with higher court rulings. Since China is a one-party state, judges are not autonomous when the state or the state's interests are implicated (Minzer 2009). The same was true in Mexico from 1917 to 1994, when the Partido Revolucionario Institucional (PRI) dominated all elections (Domingo 2004), and in Japan since World War II, where the Liberal Democratic Party has held a monopoly on political power (Ramseyer 1994). Obviously, the same logic applies to one-party authoritarian nations, rendering state "commitments to judicial neutrality and the protection of rights of any kind . . . only contingent, not truly credible" (Helmke and Rosenbluth 2009).

The constraining force of a competitive electoral system, in which additional potential veto players come into play, has been found to determine levels of judicial independence in two adjacent provinces in Argentina, one with a competitive system and one without (Chavez 2003). A role for competitive elections in enhancing judicial independence was also observed in Mexican states, but international trade, poverty, and political participation were likewise factors (Beer 2006). However, one study of ninety-seven democracies introduced a caveat to the conclusion that electoral competition equals more independent judges. That conclusion holds for advanced democracies, whereas the reverse may result in developing democracies (Aydin 2013). That distinction was demonstrated in Ukraine (2002–2003), where courts acted less independently than in Russia, then an even less politically competitive electoral democracy, where courts behaved as though they were oblivious to partisan affiliations (Popova 2010).

Accepting the assumption that independent, impartial judges represent a value to be sought, how then is that goal best achieved? In the ratification debates over the US Constitution in the late eighteenth century, James Madison prescribed that "ambition must be made to counteract ambition" (*Federalist Papers* [1787] 1970, No. 51, 337). That axiom captures the essence of measures to maintain a rein on government authority and, incidentally, to preserve judicial independence and authority. Judicial independence stands as a value, though, first and foremost to ensure the impartiality of the judge. Thus, judges must be subject to accountability if they forfeit impartiality in settling disputes. The conundrum lies in locating the proper checks on both political and judicial power.

Multiple veto players, both institutional and partisan, with varying self-interests represent a starting point. Monolithic power will ultimately squash judicial impartiality when the interests of that single authority are jeopardized. In electoral democracies, the ultimate accountability resides with the electorate, vertical accountability. Outside of many American states and Bolivia, that form of accountability has no application to judges. Courts are by their nature passive institutions that must wait for cases to arise before them and are generally dependent on other institutions for enforcement of their decisions. They do not usually serve as veto players, except where they exercise constitutional review. Courts must therefore seek protection from other organs of government through the mutual competition of political institutions. Impartial and independent courts, when viewed as politicians' insurance when not in power, gain safe harbor from encroachment and interference. In other words, when competing partisan and institutional veto players see their political self-interests as protected by the empowerment of courts, independence and authority are enabled. Thus, reciprocal horizontal accountability among political organs and vertical accountability through electoral competition constitute the best guarantees for preservation of the judicial independence and authority that foster judicial impartiality.

JUDICIAL DECISION MAKING

Judges form the focus of the legal system because they, acting individually or collectively, decide disputes and adjudicate criminality or deflect conflicts from the legal forum. What then guides judges in making decisions? Obviously the law constitutes a significant, indeed, major factor, but depending on the range of authority and limits to independence, judges may and often do exercise discretion or creativity.

Chinese judges, particularly at the lower ranks, fit the mold of an executor judge, one with low autonomy and minimal discretion. Fearful of removal or sanction by either their local responsibility board or higher court judges, these judges employ the *qingshi* to request legal guidance from higher courts, even though reforms have attempted to limit this practice (Minzer 2009). We cannot know the various calculations that enter a Chinese judge's mind in the course of deciding a case, but we can reasonably infer that getting the law right in the eyes of superior judges constitutes a major, if not *the* major, consideration.

What drives decisions for judges in other systems, however, can be more difficult to discern. If the law is but one stimulus, to what other factors do judges respond, at least within the limits imposed on their offices? Again, explanations vary depending on the relative autonomy and authority of the judge and additionally on context. The motives behind judicial decisions can be personal gain—financial, career, reputation, prestige, or other benefits—or policy oriented, involving achievement of broad social goals or merely implementation of a preferred vision of the law in a specific case (Brinks 2005). Obviously fear, intimidation, and corruption, stimuli unfortunately influencing judges in many places, fall into the personal gain category. Policy preferences are typically thought to be factors at the highest levels of the judiciary, particularly when constitutional review is an option. Policy preferences can nonetheless color decisions of lower courts. The first injunctions against President Trump's travel bans were issued by US trial judges, who may have harbored a policy preference against the prohibition of visas into the United States from predominantly Muslim nations.

Alternatively, those initial trial judges may have had no interest beyond formalistically applying the law. It is likely that the formalistic approach of squaring the facts of the case with the applicable law explains how most judges decide most cases. That approach represents the professional training of judges (Moustafa 2007b), a tendency reinforced in court systems like those in China and Japan, with strong hierarchical supervision by higher court judges. What happens, though, when the facile formula of Law + Facts = Decision is not straightforward? In *International Refugee Assistance Project v. Trump* (2017), was the proper legal question one of the president's authority to protect national security in his role as commander-in-chief, or was it one of religious discrimination? The answer is both, and therefore, the trial judge necessarily must prefer one over the other or try to balance the two against one another. Formalism, unlike algebraic equations, does not always yield easy and consistently correct answers.

> **BOX 4.3** | **Motives of Italian Judges**
>
> Salvatore "Totò" Riina, also known as "the beast" and the former head of the Sicilian Mafia, was convicted and imprisoned for committing several hundred murders, including the particularly heinous killing of a fourteen-year-old boy. Riina reached the age of eighty-six in prison and was deemed close to the end of his life. A lower Italian court refused to grant him house arrest so that he could "die at home with dignity," but a higher court ruled instead that the lower judges had failed to prove that Riina still posed a threat that would justify his continued incarceration. The dilemma sparked outrage on all sides, from those who advocated compassion to those who believed that Riina, even while in prison, remained a formidable force in the Mafia. One anti-Mafia investigator remarked that "a boss like Riina can give orders with just his eyes" and could easily continue to direct Mafia activities. Compassion versus retribution drove the two courts.
>
> *Source:* "Italy's Mafia: The End of the Boss of Bosses," *Economist*, June 10, 2017, 53.

Many times judges confront cases in which the legal evidence and/or the applicable laws are unclear or contradictory. Judges are also presented with cases that involve new legal questions: How does the present law on libel (publication of false and injurious statements) apply to Instagram or Snapchat communications? Is a tablet a computer, and if so, does that categorization depend on the size of the tablet or on its computational capacity? Particularly in such instances, judges must draw on their experiences or other cues. For example, in 1984 the Dutch Supreme Court, a body without constitutional review authority, allowed that physicians can participate in euthanasia, although Dutch law at that time made the act a criminally punishable offense. The Dutch court simply determined that the physician in question made a reasonable choice under the specific circumstances of the case under a legal loophole for "emergency situations." That decision was consistent with Dutch public opinion and may have been in line with the sentiment of a majority in the legislature at that time (van Hees and Steunenberg 2000). Distinguishing whether the Dutch judges were deciding based on a pro-euthanasia policy preference, some religious or philosophical ground, their experiences watching a loved one die a particularly painful and demeaning death, or even having a relative who was a physician is complicated at best.

Attributing motives to judges can be tricky. Nevertheless, some cues may be more useful than others. Partisan affiliation, when known, usually communicates a signal about some of a judge's political values. Likewise, a number of studies in the United States have concluded that in some specific categories of cases women judges tend to rule differently than men. Race and ethnicity similarly have been correlated with decisional tendencies in some narrow types of cases. That does not mean that women judges always support female parties or that ethnic or racial minorities decide in favor of those sharing that attribute. Rather, in some subject areas, women judges may, because of their own values or experiences, see legal issues in a somewhat different light than men judges do. Therefore, the need to establish a more diverse set of people serving as judges has become a goal of some judicial selection mechanisms. Hence, identity politics has assumed ascendancy in some places. The ability to see the law through a variety of lenses, however, has little relevance when judges are executors, with minimal discretion or autonomy, or even guardian judges, whose independence is well-insulated but whose discretion or creative freedom is quite restricted. Only where political systems choose to institutionalize delegate or political judges does the judge have the authority to exercise much discretion.

Judges classified as executor, guardian, delegate, or political cannot be expected to act alike in all contexts. The national or even local environment in which a judge serves can influence judicial behavior. State judges in the United States "tend to be local folks—born, bred, educated, and socialized in the local culture in which they preside" (Carp, Stidham, and Manning 2014). Such localism cannot be totally filtered out of how a judge sees a case with ambiguous elements. A similar scenario can be replicated in various places, as the culture and values of a location temper judges' inclinations to decide in ways that comport with their environment. In Aceh, Indonesia, Islamic court judges evolved over the period of 1960 to 1994 in how they decided family property cases. Whereas they had initially tended to accept customary law solutions, they eventually imposed strictly Islamic ones, even though the governing laws were unchanged. Instead, the pervasiveness of

Muslim influences had grown (Bowen 2000). Informal institutions in adjudicating guilt and punishment for police involved in killings during the post-authoritarian period demonstrate the effects of local influences. In São Paulo, Brazil, for example, 94 percent of police involved in killings, which numbered more than the whole country under military rule, went unpunished (Brinks 2003). Despite untold sums spent by international and donor agencies in Guatemala since the 1996 peace accord, politicians have continued to be perceived as receiving preferential treatment by the courts, while only 6 percent of the population felt their rights could be protected by the courts (Sieder 2005). Local, regional, and national cultures seep into court activities and similarly can deter people from litigating to claim their rights.

CONCLUSION

No simple formula for the preferable type of judge in terms of autonomy and authority or the means of securing those parameters can appropriately apply everywhere. Each nation adjusts and adapts to its particular and peculiar history, culture, and economy in crafting institutional design. No one-size-fits-all solution exists. This is perhaps best illustrated in postconflict zones where the United Nations, national governments, or donor agencies try to achieve punishment for conflict-related crimes or to establish judicial structures. What succeeds and what fails in Guatemala (Sieder 2005) cannot be replicated in Uganda, Somalia, and Rwanda (Widner 2001b); Kosovo and East Timor (Strohmeyer 2001); and newly democratized Bulgaria (Frison-Roche and Sodev 2005). This applies equally when locating the delicate balance between judicial authority and autonomy and establishing an institutional design that will respect and preserve that balance.

5

Constitutional Review

★ ★ ★

POLAND EMERGED FROM Soviet domination in the last decade of the twentieth century and seemingly cemented a workable democracy with a constitutional court to referee the political rules enshrined in the new constitution. As might be expected in a new democracy, new political institutions tested, fumbled, and experimented, including the courts. Between 1993 and 2002, 258 cases challenging the constitutionality of legislative enactments reached the court, and 62 percent were struck down as violative of the constitution. Notably, a similar trend was observed in the neighboring new democracies of Latvia and Slovenia (Bricker 2016). At least one of those pronouncements left the Polish health-care system functioning with no legal structure for more than a year. In 2016 the court was the only bulwark standing between the Law and Justice Party's determination to enact laws to control the media, curtail civil liberties, and erode judicial independence (Kelemen and Orenstein 2016). The Law and Justice Party, with an overwhelming parliamentary majority, struck at the judges and determined to defang the constitutional court. Poland's largely ceremonial president, Andrzej Duda, refused to sign the proposed legislation. A year later, however, in 2017, President Duda did sign off on revised legislation that imposed age limits on judges and thereby created vacancies to be filled by a heavily stacked Law and Justice Party judicial council that appoints judges. In addition, a new "special extraordinary appeal" procedure was created whereby any case decided during the previous twenty years could

> **BOX 5.1** | **So Much for a Court Decision . . .**
>
> The Turkish Constitutional Court ordered the release of seventy-three-year-old Sahin Alpay, one of over one hundred journalists jailed in Turkey. Despite the decision of Turkey's highest court, when Alpay's family came to the prison to collect him, they were told that a lower court had rejected the decision. The lower court's decision had "no legal precedent, or indeed basis," but it did have the endorsement of Turkey's president, Recep Tayyip Erdogan, who accused the high court of violating the constitution. The sequence of a decision being made and then overruled was not an isolated event. The same had occurred to the head of a local chapter of Amnesty International and a group of nineteen journalists. Mr. Alpay and others then filed a case with the European Court of Human Rights, which has jurisdiction by virtue of a treaty to which Turkey is a signatory.
>
> *Source:* "Law of Rule: President Erdogan Snubs the Constitutional Court," *Economist*, February 17, 2018, 47.

be reopened (Santora and Berendt 2017). Thus, the Law and Justice Party positioned itself to capture the whole of the Polish judiciary and to undo all previous rulings of the constitutional court that had blocked Poland's shift to a "populist electoral autocracy" (Kelemen and Orenstein 2016).

The Turkish Constitutional Court dealt setbacks to the agenda of President Recep Erdogan when, in March 2016, it ordered the release of two Turkish journalists whose rights had been denied. The president publicly denounced the decision (Haimerl 2017). The Turkish court had in 2008 fined Erdogan's Justice and Development Party for undermining the secular foundation of the country (Shambayati and Kirdiş 2009). Not surprisingly, therefore, following a failed coup attempt and declaration of a state of emergency, Erdogan and the Justice and Development Party took aim at the Constitutional Court in a series of 2017 constitutional amendments that were approved in a national referendum. Though actual modifications to the court were minimal (reduction of the membership by two judges), it appeared to chasten itself. It removed two judges implicated in the coup attempt and refused to hear cases challenging the extended state of emergency. The court retreated into subservience (Haimerl 2017).

Courts exercising the power of constitutional review are presumed to operate at the apex of their authority. The Polish and Turkish examples illustrate, though, that courts can be contained and intimidated. Constitutional review, "the power to declare legislative enactments and administrative rules invalid on the grounds that they violate constitutional norms" (Shapiro and Stone 1994, 397), can serve to block executive or legislative excesses, such as those that occurred in neo-patrimonial Malawi and Zambia (Vondoepp 2005), but not always. It can also trigger potent backlashes, as in Poland and Turkey, among other places. Constitutional review may also serve as an instrument to move constitutional provisions closer into alignment with contemporary society, as was the case when the Indian Supreme Court agreed in 2018 to hear a case challenging the ban on homosexual acts (Schultz 2018).

Constitutional review was largely regarded as a peculiarity of the United States until after World War II, but its presence in constitutions subsequently burgeoned. Some 158 out of 191 constitutional documents included some form of it as of 2008 (Ginsburg 2008a). The nature of constitutionalism, motivations for adoption, forms and substance, and uses of constitutional review vary widely. Moreover, the implications of its use assume a kaleidoscope-like quality among different nations and over time. Comparisons can be tricky. The US Supreme Court is widely assumed to be a powerful court, but it invalidated only 182 national laws between 1789 and 2006. The Polish Constitutional Court, on the other hand, overturned 148 laws in the space of nine years (Bricker 2016). With that caution in mind, this chapter explores the multiplicity of forms that constitutional review can assume and theories proposed to explain its adoption and use.

CONSTITUTIONS AND CONSTITUTIONAL REVIEW

Constitutional review intrinsically presumes the existence of a constitution. Constitutions vary vastly, however. For example, the British constitution is said to be unwritten, but a more apt description is that it is flexible; that is, every parliamentary law becomes part of the constitution, along with unwritten traditions and some international norms (Leyland 2007). British courts cannot, therefore, invalidate parliamentary legislation. The converse, though, does not follow: a written constitution does not require that the authority for constitutional review be lodged in a judicial body.

Constitutions may be brief, like that of the United States (7,644 words), or lengthy. The average Latin American constitution written since 2000 has approximately 30,000 words, and European ones in the same period, more than 15,000 words (Versteeg and Zackin 2016). Longer constitutions typically include greater specificity but also include provisions for relatively easy revision. Constitutions also vary in their longevity, with that of the United States representing the most enduring (1787 to the present) and Sweden's in existence since 1814. On average, however, most of the world's constitutions last an average of nine to twenty years (Hirschl 2010).

Countries write constitutions to establish "the ground rules for organizing politics and governance" (Alberts 2009) and to demonstrate a credible commitment by the sovereign authority to honor the rights and responsibilities enshrined in the law (North and Weingast 1989). That is all well and good at the abstract level, but how does a polity decide if and when the constitutional commitments are honored? Ideally, constitutions create incentives by dispersing authority and generating competing power centers that can avoid winner-take-all outcomes and impose reciprocal self-restraint on officeholders (Alberts 2009), but auxiliary precautions may nonetheless be required. The logic behind empowering an independent court to referee whether laws comply with the constitution is that "if parliament itself is the judge of the constitutionality of its own laws, it can easily be tempted to resolve any doubts in its own favor" (Lijphart 2012, 212).

Conventional wisdom holds that courts exercising constitutional review are presumed to advance and promote democracy (Tolley 2018). Many observers of courts argue, however, that constitutional review merely represents an effort by political elites to preserve their interests without reliance on legislative majorities (Hilbink 2008) or, more aspirationally, to create a "state governed by law and respectful of its citizens" (Horowitz 2006, 126). Constitutional review arises also in states that practice federalism, as a strong umpire must be available to guarantee that all of the subnational units adhere to the rules and to protect the bargains struck between the national and subnational governments (Shapiro 2003).

Constitutional review also supposedly serves to protect the "religion of human rights"; for example, the Hungarian Constitutional Court abolished the death penalty and granted a privileged place to property rights (Scheppele 2003). Conversely, the Turkish Constitutional Court, in its pre-Erdogan era, assessed human rights in very restrictive terms (Belge 2006). Empirical studies have nevertheless linked constitutional review and independent judiciaries with greater freedoms (La Porta et al. 2004), and consequently some rights protections do matter, particularly requirements for fair and public trials (Keith 2002). That rights can flourish absent constitutional review is aptly demonstrated in Great Britain, where the newly instituted Supreme Court and its antecedent, the Law Lords, holds no authority to invalidate parliamentary enactments (Carnwath 2004). Likewise, the Netherlands grants the legislative body supremacy and prohibits constitutional review (de Poorter 2013), but neither the Dutch nor the British are noted for human rights violations. Furthermore, constitutional review cannot block or legitimate popular majorities over the long term, but it can alter "the balance of power between numerous political movements that struggle for power in a pluralist democracy" (Graber 2005). Indeed, although Singapore, for example, has empowered its courts with constitutional review, few rights cases brought against the government are won (Thio 2006). China, an authoritarian government, has refused to grant its highest court, the Supreme People's Court, that authority and specifically prohibits it from reviewing any laws passed by the National People's Congress (Fu 2017). Political context, though not an overall explanation, remains salient in assessing the successes and failures of constitutional review (Hirschl 2010).

MODELS OF CONSTITUTIONAL REVIEW

Two basic models for constitutional review dominate, that of the United States and the institution proposed by Austrian Hans Kelsen between the two twentieth-century world wars. The US model is decentralized, dispersing authority to exercise constitutional review across most courts. Thus, the range of litigants and types of cases that can trigger constitutional review vary widely. The Kelsian model concentrates constitutional review in a single, specialized tribunal, and the field of those who can invoke that court to review legislative or executive actions is limited (Tushnet 2014). Though many variations have developed, as discussed later in this chapter, the German Federal Constitutional Court typifies the Kelsian model.

As can be seen in figure 5.1, only very specific avenues are available to reach the constitutional court: other courts or institutions of government. Constitutional complaints (on the right side of the figure) offer the only means of access for individuals and nongovernmental entities, and those are tightly restricted. If particular rights have allegedly been violated and a party to a case has exhausted all other judicial options, litigants can seek relief from the constitutional court via the constitutional complaint avenue. Since 1969 local governments have also been permitted to use the constitutional complaint vehicle when alleging a public authority acted unconstitutionally. Some 188,000 such complaints reached the court between 1951 and 2011, and the overwhelming majority of them (more than 97 percent) were decided by three-judge panels, not the full court. Other challenges to constitutionality that arise in the course of normal litigation must be referred to the Federal Constitutional Court by another court and thus involve "collateral review." A mere 1,000 such referrals were decided by the court over the sixty-year period 1951–2011. All other challenges to constitutional validity must come from the specific institutions listed on the left side of the diagram (Kommers and Miller 2012). The Kelsian model, much more than the US decentralized one, limits who can challenge constitutionality. One should also note that not all courts bearing the title "supreme" hold the authority of constitutional review, as neither the British Supreme Court nor the Chinese Supreme People's Court do.

Figure 5.1 Example of Kelsian model: German Federal Constitutional Court

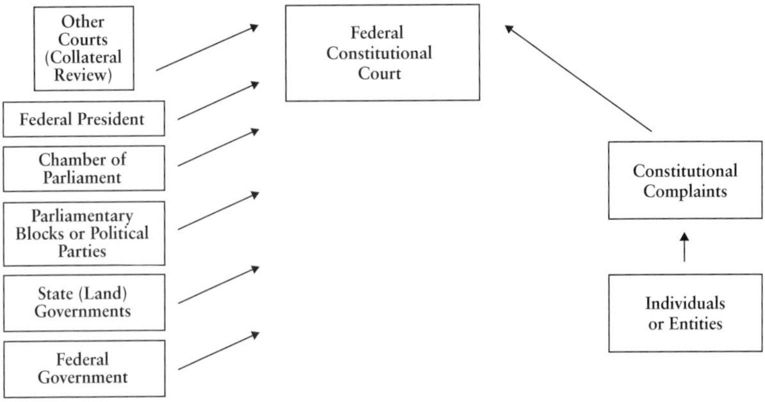

Source: Information in Kommers and Miller 2013, 11–13.

The US-style constitutional review, until after World War II, was seen as incompatible with parliamentary sovereignty and democratic values and also as inconsistent with the civil law tradition. The civil law tradition historically viewed judges, as discussed in chapter 2, as merely mouths of the law and not possessing the ability to develop legal rules. Thus, positing the power of constitutional review, with highly limited access, in a separate specialized court resolved the civil law dilemma. Constitutional courts were also conceived as exercising only a negative authority. Such a court could reject a law, but not positively create new law (Bricker 2016).

Neither model has gained dominance. Among the nations comprising the European Union, eighteen of twenty-seven have adopted constitutional courts along Kelsian lines (Comella 2011); Argentina follows the American decentralized version, but most other Latin American countries use mixed systems, with the two models operating in parallel or coexisting (Brewer-Carías 2009). The same configuration of mixed systems also characterizes the African continent. Despite variations in design, in most instances these courts have developed a human rights jurisprudence (Ferejohn, Rosenbluth, and Shipan 2007).

THEORIES EXPLAINING CONSTITUTIONAL DESIGN

Designing or redesigning constitutional arrangements occurs usually at some critical moment in a nation's life and crucially institutes rules for subsequent political contests. Decisions are always made in situations of some uncertainty (Jung and Deering 2013). Even so, those writing constitutions seek to anchor some principles firmly, such as the provision in the Chinese constitution that places the Supreme People's Court squarely under the supervision of the National People's Congress, an arm of the ruling Communist Party (Fu 2017). Others place their emphasis on achieving consensus to ensure that no faction, by virtue of exclusion, views itself as not bound by the constitutional bargain. That often necessitates a final document that is ambiguous and kicks the most contentious issues down the road for future resolution. Thus, for example, those writing the Iraqi Constitution of 2005 included a Kelsian-style constitutional court, but agreement on much else was elusive because of secular and religious divisions. The constitution therefore provides (only and ambiguously) that the court will be staffed by "judges, specialists in Islamic jurisprudence, and legal experts" (Hamoudi

2014, 96). Similarly, Israel's quasi-constitution (two Basic Laws) granted its Supreme Court rather modest authority, but that court claimed the power of constitutional review in a 1967 case (Woods 2009) and solidified that claim in a 1995 case (Reichman 2013). Most nations, however, explicitly granted constitutional review in post–World War II constitutions.

The intentions of the constitutional draftsmen in the United States regarding constitutional review are unclear, but a specific grant of that authority is not stated in the Constitution. Europeans largely rejected constitutional review until the second half of the twentieth century, on the grounds that it violated parliamentary sovereignty or the will of the people expressed through their elected representatives. Through whatever lens one views constitutional review, whether positively or negatively, it clearly serves as a potential check, perhaps a veto, on democratic will. Why then would those writing or revising constitutions choose to grant a court or courts the power to overturn legislative and executive actions? More to the point, most who were involved in writing constitutions were politicians who presumably expected to play a role in their newly revised political systems, so why would they create a system whereby their future actions could be blocked?

Four primary theories have been proposed to explain this apparent paradoxical situation: (1) credibility, (2) co-optation, (3) delegation, and (4) insurance. As noted previously, the purpose of a constitution can be located in a regime's desire to demonstrate a credible commitment to honor rights, particularly property rights (North and Weingast 1989). Without an enforcement mechanism, however, commitments are hollow, subject to revision or revocation. Hence, constitutional review serves to demonstrate a regime's commitment. Evidence of this motivation was seen when Egypt's authoritarian regime chose to create its autonomous Supreme Constitutional Court in 1979 to secure private investment as the government sought to move to a market economy (Moustafa 2003b). Similarly, Russia also implemented a powerful constitutional court to signal to both its citizenry and the international community that its commitment to the rule of law was genuine (Thorson 2004). On the other hand, the State of Israel refrained in 1948 from institutionalizing constitutional review precisely because its political economy at that time did not require foreign investment; when it did, investors saw their direct access to political elites as a better guarantee of their economic rights than an independent judicial body (Reichman 2013).

The co-optation theory to explain adoption of constitutional review was initially articulated by American political scientist Robert Dahl decades ago; one can hardly suppose that "a court whose members are recruited in the fashion of Supreme Court justices would long hold to norms . . . that are substantially at odds with the rest of the political elite" (1957, 291). Courts exercising the power of constitutional review can be expected to share and therefore protect the values and interests of others in political authority. Rather than acting independently and contrary to other political power centers, co-opted courts could be relied upon to reinforce the regime. Thus, the Turkish Constitutional Court could accurately be expected to reflect the interests of the military establishment in the pre-Erdogan era (Shambayati and Kirdiş 2009), as could the court in Chile under military rule from 1973 to 1990 (Hilbink 2007). Similarly, Hirschl (2000) argues that so-called constitutional revolutions in Israel (1992), Canada (1982), New Zealand (1990), and South Africa (1993) demonstrated attempts by the ruling elites to protect their interests in culturally divided contexts via constitutional review rather than relying on democratic majorities. Also, a number of Russian regions instituted constitutional review in the 1990s in an attempt to legitimate the authority of their political elites. By the beginning of the twenty-first century, however, only fifteen of eighty-nine regions still had functioning constitutional courts (Trochev 2004).

The delegation theory of constitutional review resembles that of co-optation, but presumes that principals delegate authority to agents who are likely to hold a preference for values similar to theirs. Who, though, are the principals making the delegation? Are the people the principals, at least in democratic systems? The concept of constitutional review represents a means to prevent politicians from violating constitutional bargains. The fallacy of that assertion lies in the inability of "the people" to monitor constitutional design and its implementation. We are thus left with the view that self-interested politicians are the principals (Ginsburg 2001). This is where the delegation theory most overlaps that of co-optation: the constitutional designers delegate authority to a court or courts to invalidate the work of legislative majorities that runs counter to their interests. Constitutional framers must therefore trust that the judges' choices will always be consistent with theirs. Some prefer the metaphor of "trusteeship" over agency in recognition of the absence of principal control once the authority has been delegated (Stone Sweet 2002; Dyevre 2015). But the distinction between the two is thin, resting on preservation of the values of the constitutional designers versus the "best" legislative outcomes (Dyevre 2015). Ideally, the two should most often coincide and not diverge significantly. The delegation thesis differs from the co-optation one in the explicit role of politics in the act of delegation (Hilbink 2008). The Israeli case is frequently cited as a clear example of delegation, but other nations with significant divisions over such issues as secular versus religious preferences have also delegated authority to courts with constitutional review. By delegating resolution of questions such as religion or even languages where consensus is elusive, the conflict becomes a legal rather than a political problem (Hirschl 2004b). One can observe in the Indonesian case, for example, that the delegation does not consistently develop as anticipated (Horowitz 2013).

The insurance theory proposed to explain the creation of constitutional review likely achieves greater currency for the largest number of countries. The insurance model functions much as automobile or life insurance works: since we cannot predict when an accident or death might happen, we purchase a product to help mitigate the loss should it occur. The key element is uncertainty. Therefore, when constitutional designers cannot reliably predict that they will win in future elections and remain in power, they insure that the bargains and rules will be enforced when they are not in power. When a party dominates the constitutional design process and can confidently presume remaining in power, constitutional review is less likely. That presumably explains why authoritarian governments are less likely than democratic ones to adopt constitutional review, except when they need to demonstrate a credible commitment to constitutionally enshrined values (Ginsburg 2003). The insurance theory has successfully explained the rise in constitutional review in new or reinstated democracies in Asia (Ginsburg 2003), Colombia (Uprimny 2003), Italy (Volcansek 2010), Mexico (Oseguera 2009), and Argentina and Peru (Finkel 2008). Yet as seen in the performance of the Serbian Constitutional Court in the post-Milošević era, constitutional review may not offer any insurance if the judges' past habits and ideology induce passivity (Beširević 2015).

> **BOX 5.2** | **Pakistan President Musharraf versus the Supreme Court**
>
> Pervez Musharraf, as head of the Pakistan military, seized power in a coup in 1999. Though popular for a time, he ultimately lost public support. In 2007 President Musharraf sought a third term in office, which the Supreme Court was expected to block. Musharraf declared a state of emergency, suspended the constitution, and placed thirteen of the seventeen judges on the Supreme Court under house arrest. He had previously suspended the chief justice of the court, Iftikhar Muhammad Chaudhry, on ethics charges and briefly arrested Aitzaz Ahsan, the leader of the Pakistan lawyers' movement, then rearrested him, placing him under house arrest and prohibiting him from giving interviews. Ultimately, Musharraf sought a third term and lost power in elections in February 2008. Musharraf then left the country and remained in exile.
>
> *Sources:* Reuters, "Pakistan's Pervez Musharraf to 'Join Politics': TV Report," May 21, 2010, https://www.reuters.com/article/us-pakistran-musharraf/pakistans-pervez-musharraf-to-join-politics-tv-report-idUSTRE64K1TP20100521 (accessed 2/26/2018); and David Rohde, "Anti-Musharraf Lawyer Is Suddenly Freed, Then Abruptly Arrested Again," *New York Times*, December 22, 2007, A-8.

THEMES AND VARIATIONS

Two basic models of constitutional review dominate, but the possible variations are vast. Those familiar with US-style constitutional review have likely simply accepted that all courts hear concrete cases in which constitutional issues arise that are central to the outcome of the case. To those versed in different systems, the US practice is decentralized (almost any court), concrete (involves litigants presenting a real, not hypothetical, conflict), and review is a posteriori (after the challenged law has taken effect). Not all or even most countries where constitutional review exists follow the US model.

Constitutional review may be exercised by a single court (centralized) that may or may not be attached to the larger judicial system (Kelsian style) and may be abstract (hypothetical) as opposed to concrete. Abstract review, unlike concrete review, does not arise from an actual controversy in litigation, but rather asks if the law in question, divorced from a specific set of facts, is constitutional on its face. Usually, where abstract review is possible, only specific, institutional actors (those on the left side of figure 5.1) can initiate review, and generally a court cannot refuse to decide the case. In addition, one of those institutional actors typically will include access by a specified percentage or number of parliamentarians, which allows the opposition party or parties to effectively challenge a law passed by the majority. Thus, the threat of constitutional review can act indirectly by encouraging the majority party to compromise to avoid review. That may not occur, however, if the reviewing court generally defers to the legislative branch or if future electoral outcomes appear favorable to the majority party (Vanberg 1998). If, as is required in many countries, most notably France, the constitutional validity of the law is determined by a court before it takes effect, the review is a priori or ex ante, before the law is promulgated (Epstein, Knight, and Shvetsova 2001).

The United States is not the only place where laws or official actions can be challenged in a concrete case, but Kelsian-style courts usually employ avenues distinct from those with decentralized review. The Italian system, for example, allows a judge at any level who presides over a legal dispute to conclude that the outcome of the case hinges on the constitutional validity of the law driving the case. When that occurs, the judge can halt the proceedings and refer the question of constitutionality to the constitutional court for a definitive ruling (Barsotti et al. 2016). In France since a 2008 reform, a similar process has been followed, except that the legal dispute must be considered in the hierarchy of regular courts and can only be referred by the highest court in the hierarchy, such as the Court of Cassation or the Council of State, depending on the law in question. The German constitutional complaint process also permits concrete review of laws, but only after all other possible judicial remedies have been exhausted (Comella 2011).

Importantly, the various types of constitutional review can be mixed and matched by constitutional draftsmen in a multiplicity of fashions. Some systems embody both abstract and concrete review and/or permit both a priori and a posteriori review. None of the labels should necessarily be viewed as absolute, but rather as relative, with numerous potential plot marks along a continuum. The rigidity of the categories often depends on who has access or standing to raise the constitutional question. Determination of who properly has standing usually rests with the relevant constitutional tribunal. The South African Constitutional Court, for example, has interpreted standing to challenge the constitutionality of violations of some provisions broadly: "anyone acting in the public interest" (Amar and Tushnet 2009). Such a sweeping grant would not be expected from, say, the US Supreme Court, which has narrowly defined who may and who may not bring or defend a case.

The reach of constitutional review is confined to who has access to bring a case, which court or courts may adjudicate constitutional validity, when cases may be brought (a priori or a posteriori), and whether cases must be concrete legal controversies or abstract challenges prima facie to a challenged law. The restrictions or openings permitted channel how robustly or deferentially constitutional review can be used.

STRONG OR WEAK FORM

The contours drawn by those writing constitutions define the limits of the exercise of constitutional review, but once a court with such authority begins functioning, it may further restrict or, conversely, push the limits of that authority. Judicial power is often conceived as definitive because a constitutional ruling presumably happens as the final act in the sequence, but that may be based on faulty assumptions. Even in the United States, where the Supreme Court exerts considerable power, the high court's actions are in many ways dependent on choices made by other actors (Lemieux 2017). Courts in different political contexts may likewise be constrained not only by the choices of other political actors, but also by their own reading of the political temperature and the range of cases presented. Thus, for example, the Serbian Constitutional Court has chosen a passive approach to controversial political cases (Beširević 2015), while the short-lived first Russian Constitutional Court acted boldly and was subsequently abolished (Epstein, Knight, and Shvetsova 2001).

Mark Tushnet (2014) identified two strategies that new constitutional courts might follow. First is "one and done," whereby a constitutional court asserts its authority in a politically important case and decides against the dominant party or coalition and thus has its *Marbury* moment, a reference to the landmark decision in the United States that claimed the power of constitutional review for the Supreme Court. Then the court recedes, having established its authority but also protecting itself from potential backlash. The US Supreme Court acted decisively in *Marbury v. Madison* in 1803 but did not invalidate another act of Congress for half a century. An alternative approach is "incremental and relatively continuous," in which a court consistently overturns minor legislation and accustoms other political actors to the practice (Tushnet 2014, 42–43).

Scholars recognize variations in the potency of constitutional review, but describe it differently and, indeed, ascribe different labels to it. How one defines and measures the strength of constitutional review authority drives the ultimate conclusions. Lijphart (2012) classifies constitutional review by the frequency and vigor of its use and finds only six democracies (Germany, India, the United States, Argentina, Canada, and Costa Rica) where it is exercised strongly. Notably, eight of the thirty-six democracies he studied do not permit any kind of constitutional review. Lane and Ersson (2000) looked at 146 countries and found a strong version of constitutional review practiced in 60 of them. They, unlike Lijphart, define "weak form" constitutional review as "relying on procedural fairness and public accountability" instead of by how frequently legislation is struck down.

Mark Tushnet (2008) employs yet another metric for measuring the strength of constitutional review. He categorizes constitutional review used to invalidate laws passed by legislative bodies as "strong form," citing the United States as the exemplar of this style. "Weak form" contrasts with the more muscular version by allowing courts only *provisionally* to identify and enforce particular social and political rights and subsequently permit legislatures to respond. This form preserves the democratic authority of the legislative bodies and simultaneously places legislatures in a dialogue with the courts. The logic behind weak form review, as Tushnet defines it, lies in the recognition that "reasonable judicial interpretations have no intrinsic superiority to reasonable legislative and executive interpretation" (Tushnet 2008, 79). In certain types of legal cases, the Brazilian Federal Supreme Court, though endowed with strong form review, follows the path of weak form by transferring the final word on some constitutional issues back to the legislature (Leme de Barros 2017). Conversely, in the United Kingdom a variation on weak form constitutional review was instituted with the passage of the Human Rights Act of 1998, but it may arguably act in practice as strong form (Kavanagh 2015). Tushnet acknowledges that his "weak form" of constitutional review may not be constitutional review at all, but rather an interpretative method. In

> **BOX 5.3** | **Constitutional Hardball**
>
> *Constitutional hardball* refers to using the letter of the law to undermine its spirit and is a common phenomenon in failing democracies. Thus, when Argentine president Juan Perón encountered opposition from the country's supreme court, he initiated impeachment procedures in congress against three of the five justices on that court for "malfeasance." They were replaced by Perón supporters. Likewise, in 2004 congressional allies of Venezuela's president Hugo Chávez added twelve seats to the twenty-person supreme court, to which Chávez supporters were appointed. "Both Perón's and Chavez's court-packing schemes were legal but they nevertheless destroyed judicial independence."
>
> *Source:* Steven Levitsky and Daniel Ziblatt, "Is Our Democracy Wobbly?," *New York Times*, January 28, 2018, SR-5.

Canada, New Zealand, and Great Britain a mechanism was placed on courts' reviewing authority that enables a legislature to respond to constitutional difficulties identified by courts, such as the legislative override Canada adopted (Tushnet 2007).

Even if a constitutional document empowers a court or courts with constitutional review, other factors may temper the vigor with which review is exerted. One moderating factor lies in the collegial nature of decision making on multiple-member courts; all constitutional or supreme courts use more than one judge to reach decisions. The moderating influence of group decision making is often overlooked but becomes particularly salient for legal questions, which are almost always binary choices—yes or no answers—to legal questions, winners and losers (Kornhauser 1992). Making collective decisions necessitates aggregation of judgments and of preferences (Kornhauser and Sager 1986). Judicial choices are likewise constricted by legal doctrine, and judges are less able to ignore those strictures when acting on courts with others. Thus, collegial decision making encourages strategic voting (Lax 2011). Of course, constitutional courts do more than apply legal rules; they can also create new rules and modify existing ones. Thus, in a collegial court setting, each judge's individual preferences and rules are molded by the necessity of achieving consensus or at least a majority vote (Landa and Lax 2009). A study of the Australian High Court from 1940 to 2002 that isolated cohesion and collaboration in decisions involving at least three judges added the person serving as chief justice into the equation. Levels of cohesion and collaboration varied under different chief justices and their apparent leadership styles (Pierce 2008). In Canada, scholarship has also traced how long-term societal attitude shifts have impacted decisions of its Supreme Court judges, emphasizing the role that public opinion plays in judicial decision making (Wetstein and Ostberg 2017).

Grants of constitutional review authority do not predict or ensure how that power will be wielded. Informal factors also shape the contours of judicial action, particularly the strength of other political actors and economic conditions, but also the legal issues presented and the identities of the litigants (Herron and Randazzo 2003). Thus, judicial power and the exercise of constitutional review can be fragile and reflective of the interests of other political actors (Lemieux 2017).

Constitutional courts consequently may serve as veto players in political systems. George Tsebelis (1999) proposed that the variations in politics that occur in different systems depend on the number of veto players—actors who must agree to alter the status quo—that exist in a system. He initially conceived of veto players as parliaments, executives, and political parties, but not the courts. He later conceded, however, that if a court may interpret a nation's constitution, then it also becomes a veto player (Tsebelis 2000). Because actions by a constitutional court are usually the last in the sequence of changing policies, and because judicial rulings are presumably regarded as binding, courts may be less sensitive to the policy preferences of other veto players (Epstein, Knight, and Shvetsova 2001). Nonetheless, as explained later in this chapter, such is not always the case. Recall the decision of the Burundi Constitutional Court discussed in chapter 1. That has led some to characterize courts with constitutional review authority as "conditional veto players," whose ability to effectively assert constitutional review depends on the ideological leanings of the court, patterns of government control, and the limits of postdecision legislative procedures (Brouard and Hönnige 2017). In other contexts, specifically those like the Brazilian Supreme Federal Tribunal (Brazilian Federal Supreme Court), the presence of expedited access by opposition political parties also enables the parties outside of power to exert a veto, even though this is successful only about one-fourth of the time (Taylor 2006).

The French Constitutional Council is often cited as the ultimate judicial veto player, but the council may also be unique in its design and function. Created in 1958, its powers were expanded in 1974 to allow it to hear challenges to legislation brought by a minimum of sixty members of parliament, essentially meaning those in opposition. What distinguishes the French Constitutional Council from most other constitutional tribunals is that it can act on constitutional challenges a priori or before the questioned legislation is signed into law. Moreover, the council has a number of decidedly nonjudicial characteristics. Foremost among these is who can be appointed and how they attain positions on the council. The fifteen-person body is selected by the president of the republic, the president of the Senate, and the president of the lower legislative chamber. Every three years, each of these politicians names a council member for a nine-year term, and no qualifications are prescribed. One need not have legal training or judicial experience. Thus, from 1959 to 2007 two-thirds of the appointees were politicians with strong, public, partisan positions. Not surprisingly, the council actively and regularly vetoed legislation, an average of 16.5 percent of the time over the 1959–2007 period, a higher rate than for any other similar court (Brouard 2009a). The Italian Constitutional Court has also acted as a veto player, but often only indirectly and in concert with another veto player (Volcansek 2001). The Italian court has been described, consequently, as never singing solo, but always "as a member of the choir" (Barsotti et al. 2016, 235). That role is in keeping with findings that constitutional review may not always represent an autonomous power, but rather one that can be utilized by legislatures to affect policy outcomes (Shipan 2000), or more likely, as in the French case, as a tool of the opposition (Brouard 2009b).

EXECUTIVE, DELEGATE, GUARDIAN, OR POLITICAL COURTS

Courts with constitutional review authority hold a place in political systems distinct from other judicial bodies and potentially possess significant clout. Using that authority effectively does not always follow, in part because a risk is usually confronted when declaring winners and losers among other political actors (Tushnet 2014). Intuitively, one might extrapolate that constitutional review courts would be classified, according to the Guarnieri and Pederzoli (2002) typology described in chapter 4 (figure 4.1), as either guardian or political, based on their autonomy and authority. That intuitive assumption often rings hollow. The exercise of constitutional review varies, as seen previously, and the extent of its variance defines the authority axis of the Guarnieri and Pederzoli matrix. The independence axis, moreover, often limits or unleashes the authority of the judges.

Courts with limited independence are unlikely to wield the authority of constitutional review vigorously and typically fall into the executor or delegate category. For a court to achieve guardian or political designations, sufficient insularity or independence must be assured. Constitutional designers focus on methods of appointment and removal, tenure in office, and placement of countervailing powers to create what they hope is the appropriate measure of judicial independence. Notably, complete or significant independence is not necessarily the goal. Where constitutional review serves only to present a credible commitment, independence may intentionally be restrained. Methods of selection can also be adopted to ensure a co-opted or delegate court that will reflect the values and goals of the dominant political elite. Constitutional designers adopting constitutional review as a form of political insurance tend to favor more independent, but not necessarily totally independent, courts.

Thus, in many respects the French Constitutional Council might be seen as an example of a co-opted or delegate court because of the free range of options of appointing authorities—the president of the republic and the president of each chamber of parliament—who act unilaterally, with no hearings and no confirmation votes. The factors that moderate the co-opted or delegate courts are the possibilities that the three appointing authorities have divergent partisan or ideological allegiances and the fact that one-third of the council's membership rotates every three years, thereby permitting additions or subtractions to its dominant partisan bent (Brouard 2009a). Similarly, until 2010 in Turkey, the president of the country appointed the eleven justices from among nominees recommended by the civil and military courts and institutions, who were all presumed to be "Kemalists," meaning secularists and nationalists. Moreover, all judges served until the mandatory retirement age (Moral and Tokdemir 2017).

Ríos-Figueroa (2016) distinguishes two mechanisms for naming constitutional judges: veto players and quota systems. Veto players, in his terminology, refer to appointment schemes that require the concurrence of at least two actors. In the United States, for example, the president nominates, but the upper legislative house must confirm. In theory, though not an unchallenged one, that leads presidents to nominate Supreme Court justices whose ideologies match that of the median senator. However, presidents have often been more aggressive than that theory would predict (Cameron and Kastellec 2016). A similar process occurs in Mexico (Volcansek 2007). According to Ríos-Figueroa (2016), the system produces more centrist judges *if* the ideological preferences of the different actors are at odds. The quota system, on the other hand, gives different institutional actors a specified number of judgeships to fill, as on the French Constitutional Council. Individual judges may sit at ideological extremes, but the tendency is to produce more moderate positions for the court as a whole. In some countries, such as Germany, quotas can be found within quotas, usually prompted by a supermajority requirement for selection. Thus, the German Federal Constitutional Court is staffed by sixteen judges, eight named by each chamber of parliament. A two-thirds majority vote requirement virtually guarantees a stalemate. The two major parties, by mutual agreement, divide the appointments evenly. Each major party typically also has a smaller coalition partner; consequently, the major party shares one or more of its quota of appointments with the junior party (Volcansek 2007). This system typically ensures balanced ideology on the court, which in turn necessitates compromise and moderation.

How judges secure positions on constitutional tribunals may, however, be rendered meaningless if the judges' tenure is too limited or too insecure because of the ease of removing them. Despite the existence of legal means to protect it, independence may be compromised when other political institutions are armed with potent weapons to attack constitutional courts. When a judge's tenure is short, future employment concerns may sway her (Ríos-Figueroa 2016). Thus, the Egyptian Supreme Constitutional Court embodied independence provisions prohibiting removal of judges until a mandatory retirement age of sixty-six (Moustafa 2007b). Insecurity of tenure has been linked with strategic, rather than law- or policy-driven, voting by judges in Latin America (Basabe-Serrano 2014; Tiede and Ponce 2014).

New democracies and politically fragmented societies place constitutional courts in contexts in which judicial independence can prove precarious. Political fragmentation opens a wider space for a judiciary to act independently (Ferejohn, Rosenbluth, and Shipan 2007) but can also lead to political stalemate that can threaten the political system. Likewise, in divided societies, judicial independence may not overcome deep-seated social cleavages. In Bosnia-Herzegovina, for example, not even firm protection for judicial independence could surmount ethnonationalist voting by the constitutional jurists (Schwartz and Murchison 2016). Generally speaking, however, judicial autonomy can be preserved by assuring judicial tenure that exceeds that of the appointer and procedures for removal of judges that require a supermajority vote in the legislature (Ríos-Figueroa 2016).

Whatever institutional provisions are designed to insulate courts' use of constitutional review may not protect courts from all political manipulation. Courts function and exercise their review authority in broader political and institutional settings (Ferejohn, Rosenbluth, and Shipan 2007). Thus, the Constitutional Court in Burundi possessed all of the trappings of an independent court, capable of acting as a guardian or even a political body, but allegedly fell victim to other pressures in deciding the constitutionality of a third presidential term. In Honduras, President Juan Orlando Hernandez was inaugurated in early 2018 to a second term, which was enabled by a decision of that nation's supreme court, to which Hernandez had appointed five judges (Ernst and Malkin 2018). A similar result occurred in Bolivia, where President Evo Morales sought a fourth term in contradiction of the constitution, but was affirmed by the country's highest court. That court ruled that term limits were unfair and in violation of a half-century-old treaty. Again, the judges had all been named by Morales (Casey 2018). Threats to judicial independence for those exercising constitutional review can also come from outside the political sphere. In 1985 the Colombian Supreme Court building was attacked by guerrillas allegedly funded by narco-trafficking cartels aiming to block extraditions to the United States. In that instance, several justices were killed, and the building was burned down (Uribe-Urán 2011).

In other words, courts exercising constitutional review may act as executor or delegate courts, despite legal provisions to empower and protect them. Some, more likely in mature democracies, act as guardians to protect rights from government abuse or may insinuate themselves into political controversies and overstep the bounds of traditional judging. Total independence of the kind represented by political judges is not a quality that attaches easily to any political institution; executives should encounter checks and legislatures should answer to voters. Indeed, "a judge cannot be too capable, honest, or impartial, but can be too independent" (Geyh 2016, 128). The parchment provision of constitutional review—even strong form review—may, however, be wielded so timidly as to be no more than an annoyance, not an instrument of control. Yet when constitutional courts enter the political fray as guardians or political players, they inevitably invite politicization, particularly in the appointment process.

CONSTITUTIONAL REVIEW VIEWED PRAGMATICALLY

Judges presumably encounter constraints of law, because the law and legal maxims form the core of their professional training and lives. Yet as study after study has demonstrated, judges on some constitutional courts vote in accordance with their policy preferences, in what is called the "attitudinal model," and those preferences are typically reflective of their partisan allegiances or those of their appointing authority. Often, of course, constitutional provisions are readily susceptible to various interpretations, and judges, like all people, see those provisions through the prisms of their partisan and ideological inclinations. Difficulties consequently arise in inferences about motivations and goals from decisions that judges make. Some justices undoubtedly seek to achieve good legal policy, legal accuracy, and legal clarity. Pursuit of those goals may coincidentally lead to conclusions consistent with a judge's ideological and partisan persuasion. Judges on constitutional courts may also, however, seek to affect broader public policies, and their votes can be naked assertions of their policy preferences (Baum 1997). The difficulty lies in disentangling the threads of those motivations.

Even so, the attitudinal model of judicial decision making cannot be discounted. Partisan or ideological decisions have been documented across a number of constitutional courts for which the individual votes of judges are reported. The ideological position of a judge has been shown to explain dissenting opinions on the Ecuadorian Constitutional Court (Basabe-Serrano 2014); overall judicial votes in Portugal (Amaral-Garcia, Garoup, and Grembi 2009), Canada (Ostberg and Wetstein 2007), and the United States

(Clark 2008); and the ideology of the pivotal or median judge in France and Germany (Hönnige 2009). That pattern can also be discerned in ethnonationalist rather than ideological proclivities in Bosnia-Herzegovina (Schwartz and Murchison 2016) and secularist versus Hindu religious biases in India (Jacobsohn 2003). As pervasive as that trend may be, it cannot explain all judicial decisions by all constitutional courts. For example, procedural devices, such as a court's ability to control its own docket, alter the effects of ideological voting on state supreme courts in the United States (Brace, Yates, and Boyea 2012). On the Brazilian Supreme Federal Tribunal, ideological leanings of the judges arise as but one of a series of factors that judges appear to balance tactically when making decisions, at least on economic policy questions (Kapiszewski 2011). Sociopolitical alliances formed at times of dominant coalition shifts, instead of partisan ties, tended to drive decisions of the pre-Erdogan Turkish Constitutional Court (Belge 2006), but no correlation was found between the party sponsoring an Irish Supreme Court judge's nomination and voting patterns of the judges on that court (MacCormaic 2016). In other words, judges' ideologies or partisanship are undeniably a factor driving decisions on constitutional issues, but often they are but two factors among others.

In addition to reflecting fidelity to the law and judicial attitudes, constitutional review often is wielded strategically, that is, with an eye on the practical or political consequences of a given decision. Indeed, strategic choice in judicial decisions has been proposed as a moderating influence on judges' inclinations to follow only their policy or ideological preferences. Judges "are not unsophisticated actors"; rather, they consider "the preferences of others, the choices they expect others to make, and the institutional context in which they act" (Epstein and Knight 1998, xiii). All people who make decisions that ripple beyond themselves calculate strategically, sometimes consciously, but most times not. If I buy an expensive dress, what else will I be willing to give up to pay for it? Johnny hit me, but if I strike him back, will I be punished, will others think ill of me, will Johnny and his friends include me in future activities? Thus, judges may seek to achieve goals of legal accuracy or partisan ends, but what are the potential ramifications of acting on those goals? Notably, judges, like all of us, may also miscalculate on occasion. The first Russian Constitutional Court was created in 1991 when Russia had little experience with democracy,

Russians exhibited little trust in courts based on their Soviet experiences, and the new institution had no reservoir of goodwill with the Russian public. Shortly thereafter, in 1992, the new court invalidated a referendum question posed in the Russian Republic of Tatarstan. Tatarstan persisted with the referendum. The same year, the court invalidated a presidential decree. In October of the next year, President Boris Yeltsin closed the new constitutional court pending the writing of a new constitution (Epstein, Knight, and Shvetsova 2001).

The Argentine Supreme Court was more savvy in the era 1976–1989, recognizing the limits of its efficacy. That court chose to "strategically defect" and based its decisions on the political climate, particularly as a presidential term was nearing its conclusion. If the dominant faction in the current regime was likely to remain in power, the courts would defer to the dominant faction. Similar trends were identified in Venezuela, Chile, and Mexico (Helmke 2005). The Peruvian Constitutional Tribunal also reacted to a challenged law deferentially if the enacting authority remained in power (Tiede and Ponce 2014). Even in more mature democracies, constitutional courts often make calculations that are predicated more on strategy than on legal or partisan grounds. The Italian Constitutional Court made strategic choices in its treatment of divorce and decree laws (Volcansek 2001), and the German Federal Constitutional Court gauged the political environment, particularly public opinion and the interests of the dominant parties in parliament, when deciding constitutional review cases (Vanberg 2001).

IN NEW DEMOCRACIES

Scholars typically accept that established judicial bodies can and frequently do employ constitutional review in an unfettered or at least unrestrained fashion. Established courts can more safely make decisions contrary to the goals of other political actors, because they have the benefit of public support that comes with age and familiarity (Epstein, Knight, and Shvetsova 2001). That assumption may or may not be accurate across most countries and political eras, but clearly new judicial bodies exercising constitutional review are well-advised to use caution in confronting elected political actors. Despite multiple and viable defenses of and arguments for constitutional review, the reality persists that constitutional courts are "unelected and largely unaccountable actors in democratic government" (Bricker 2016, 87). No direct tie exists between the voting public and a constitutional court. Only two indirect links exist: (1) when public opinion confers legitimacy or acceptance on a court or a policy choice and (2) where those charged with naming judges can be politically held to account for their choices (Epperly and Lineberger 2018). The latter connection, however, is tenuous, since it relies on an assumption that the voting public can and does monitor the activities of judicial appointees and connect those activities to the appointing authority.

Constitutional courts sit at the pinnacle of judicial authority and often have the final say on the validity of legislative and executive actions. That image was well-captured in a statement by Irish Supreme Court justice Cecil Lavery: "We are the Supreme Court, and under God we can do anything" (MacCormaic 2016, 9). That sentiment may ring true in some, most likely mature, democracies, but cannot be extrapolated across all countries' courts. Many courts are unable to secure compliance with or enforcement of their decisions and are incapable of motivating legislatures to alter or amend invalid laws (Bricker 2016). Courts, particularly those in new democracies, might do well to heed the admonition of former chief justice Francis Nyalali of Tanzania, who, recognizing the potential embarrassment to political actors whose actions were overruled by the court, practiced his "four r's: respect, restraint, responsibility, and reciprocity" (Widner 2001a, 191). Most of the cases reaching constitutional courts in new democracies involve intense political consequences as ground rules are defined during transitions from one type of governing system to another. Each case carries the potential for resentment and hostility (Schwartz 2000).

Courts in mature democracies can likewise provoke the ire of significant political actors. Between 1877 and 2008, 897 separate statutes or amendments were introduced in the US Congress to curb the power of the Supreme Court, even if they were proposed with no expectation of ultimate enactment (Clark 2011). Exertion of judicial power via the instrument of constitutional review can serve positive ends by breaking through barriers, but it can also derail political momentum and work counter to legislative initiatives intended to support judicial directions (Silverstein 2009). Unintended negative consequences can litter the wake of well-intended judicial work. That can lead to undermining perceptions of the foundations underlying the rule of law. Geyh refers to the "acceptable hypocrisy" that judges are subject to the same host of influences from life experiences, backgrounds, partisanship, and emotion that all other people are. This runs counter to the rule of law, which requires "independent and impartial judges [to] apply pertinent law to relevant facts—period" (2016, 3). Those risks or miscalculations raised in the context of the United States can be exponentially greater when applied to a transitional or new democracy. Creating a new constitutional court, as Indonesia did in 2001, may be relatively easy, but making one function effectively presents a challenge. Indeed, the Indonesian Constitutional Court early in its life thwarted opportunities for useful dialogue with the legislature (Horowitz 2013).

The limits of constitutional review are apparent in mature democracies such as Germany, where the Federal Constitutional Court holds considerable power, but even that court is constrained and attentive to likely reactions of other political actors (Vanberg 2008). Public support for constitutional courts is paramount. High levels of public support for the Polish Constitutional Court from 2003 to 2010 correlated with the likelihood that the court would overturn legislation (Bricker 2016). Conversely, the most active periods for court-curbing legislation in the United States coincided with the Supreme Court's loss of popularity in the court of public opinion (Clark 2011).

Constitutional courts must establish reputations for probity and ability through honest adjudication, transparency, openness to criticism, and rights consciousness (Horowitz 2013). And those qualities need to be perceived by the public, for public support ultimately buttresses and protects a constitutional court. Constitutional courts are well-advised to act as mediators among conflicting parties (Ríos-Figueroa 2016) and to seek to join in the choir and sing in harmony with the other institutional and political actors (Barsotti et al. 2016).

CONCLUSION

Constitutional review gained popularity in the second half of the twentieth and the early twenty-first centuries as a means to render government commitments credible and ostensibly to protect human rights. The mechanism may have accomplished those goals in some places, but hardly in all. Those writing or rewriting constitutions—all politicians—responded to different motivations when choosing to include constitutional review and configured the new courts that were designed to achieve their political goals. Thus, virtually no two constitutional courts are identical, nor are they vested with exactly the same authority, the same access, and the same insularity.

Not surprisingly, therefore, some courts have emerged as bold and enduring, whereas others have acted timidly. Some lived only briefly, and others were emasculated when their actions ran counter to the wishes of the ruling elites. Constitutional review has not proved to be a panacea for rights protections or for regime credibility. De jure guarantees to insulate constitutional courts have easily been breached, particularly in new or transitioning democracies as well as in autocracies. Pragmatic, tactical use of constitutional review most likely ensures the efficacy of the authority and the longevity and viability of the court empowered with it. Courts function in political environments and cannot be divorced from the social, economic, historical, and political contexts in which they operate.

6

International and Transnational Courts

★ ★ ★

COSTA RICA PROHIBITED in vitro fertilization, a medical infertility treatment, and thus denied Daniel Gerardo Gómez Murillo and his wife the ability to seek that means of reproductive assistance. The Constitutional Chamber of the Costa Rican Supreme Court upheld the prohibition. The Gómez Murillos and five other couples subsequently took their case before the IACtHR, where the Costa Rican law was declared to violate personal integrity, personal liberty, and the right to form a family (*Gómez Murillo y Otros v. Costa Rica*, 2016). A year later and an ocean away, the ECtHR sustained a decision by a German court that prohibited the far right, anti-immigrant German National Democratic Party from publishing a press release (*Nationaldemokratische Partei Deutschlands v. Germany*, 2017). Also in Europe, but before a different court, the ECJ of the EU, the German producer of Tofutown, a dairy alternative to animal products for vegetarians, was told that it could not legally market its products using the terms "Soyotoo tofu butter" and "veggie cheese" (Kanter 2017). The ICC acknowledged that it was investigating Philippine president Rodrigo Duterte in 2018 for crimes against humanity committed in the course of his "war on drugs." A Filipino lawyer had filed a seventy-seven-page application with the court two years earlier, based on his representation of two men who claimed to have previously served as assassins for Duterte. Duterte shortly thereafter withdrew the Philippines from the jurisdiction of the ICC (Villamor 2018). Also in 2018, US president Donald Trump announced his intention to dramatically increase tariffs on imported steel and aluminum, which prompted speculation about how that violation of the WTO's rules would fare in its dispute settlement procedure (Swanson 2018).

Who are these courts—IACtHR, ECtHR, ECJ, ICC, and WTO—that arbitrate across national borders and regularly tell sovereign nations to change their domestic policies and laws? The post–World War II era witnessed an explosion of international and transnational treaties to regulate and police international transactions, norms, and even crimes. A proliferation of international adjudicatory bodies accompanied the growth of international treaties and signaled a willingness of nations to employ litigation across an expanded range of legal and procedural issues. The webs of global governance have led to a phenomenon called "ruling the world," as international rules have expanded across more and more issue areas (Dunoff and Trachtman 2009). Enforcement of international treaties has always proved problematic, since diplomacy, threats, and force had been the only tools available to coerce compliance. The last half of the twentieth century saw countries embrace an alternative mechanism for enforcement and choose judicial bodies in lieu of saber-rattling. Though no definitive listing or even count of these courts exists, litigation clearly emerged as the preferred method of settling international conflicts. Some of the dispute settlement systems rely on courts with permanent judges, whereas others use ad hoc jurists; some employ arbitration rather than straight litigation; some are hybrids, being empaneled for a single situation such as prosecuting war crimes in Rwanda or the former Yugoslavia; some endure and others are dismantled or wither for lack of use. As of 2004, eighty-two judicial or quasi-judicial ones existed, but twelve of these were dormant, having received no applications for several years, and another seventeen were either extinct or had been aborted (PICT 2004).

These courts are in some way emblematic of the process of globalization. Prior to the rise of "ruling the world," only customary international law had governed relations between nations; by definition, those rules were not definitively collected in any document and included only those accepted in practice (Wheatley 2010). However, nations have subsequently become so interconnected through trade, communications, investments, human mobility, and a post–World War II belief in human rights that only through rule-bound cooperation—written and agreed upon rules—might some semblance of order and fair play be achieved. Diplomats and politicians also acknowledged that certain conditions that required regulation were not contained by national borders, such as the oceans, environmental conditions, criminal cartels, and climate. Thus, treaties and agreements were negotiated to secure or limit national actions and to curtail detrimental transnational effects. Courts, again, became an often preferred vehicle to secure compliance with those negotiated agreements. Thereby, governments forfeited both autonomy and authority and empowered third parties to resolve issues critical to international relations (Katzenstein 2014). Thus, triadic dispute resolution assumed a place in international politics. Many of these arrangements also entail considerable coercive mechanisms—with some nations agreeing to implement sentences imposed by the ICC and the potential for WTO members to legally engage in trade retaliation once their claims have been sustained through the organization's dispute resolution system (von Bogdandy and Venzke 2012).

In the first decades of the twenty-first century, a countermovement gained momentum in a number of countries. Nationalism and protectionism, not globalization, were embraced in both the developed and developing worlds. The strength of that countervailing force may conceivably lead to more extinct and abortive enforcement mechanisms, including international and transnational courts. Or maybe not. Lacking a crystal ball and recognizing that concepts like "rule of law" tend to be resilient, the existing transnational judicial entities will likely continue their work so long as petitions for relief continue to reach them. At the same time, little is actually clearly understood about global governance and its levers, influences, and channels (Kennedy 2009). What alternatives might replace courts to resolve nation-to-nation conflicts?

International rules now often dominate instead of "self-interested, coercive and power politics" (Hurd 2017, 11). The various treaties and rules that stretch across the world and constrain nation-states generally result from the artificiality of national borders. Geographic lines drawn on maps cannot contain problems, commerce, moral sensibilities, and communication. Stone Sweet and Sandholtz (1998) offer a paradigm to explain the extraordinary shift of power from nation-states to the EU, and their proposed explanation, with some modifications, also sheds light on the rise of the international and transnational tribunals that currently exist. The basic question they attempt to answer is: Why would sovereign nation-states willingly surrender authority to supranational governance? Transactions form the basis of their theory to explain cross-border integration. Non-state actors conduct transactions and communicate across international borders, and transnational rules and regulations facilitate those transactions by making them easier and less costly. "Separate national legal regimes constitute the crucial source of transaction costs," they claim, "for those who want to engage in exchange across borders" (Stone Sweet and Sandholtz 1998, 11). The possible transaction costs are numerous, but a major one is the absence of a means to authoritatively settle disputes. Thus, if transactions—commercial, communications, mobility, pollution, or moral sensibilities—occur across national borders, some dispute settlement mechanism arises as an imperative. As nations confronted progressively more transactions, more rules—treaties—became essential. Many, if not most, treaties rely on diplomacy, goodwill, threats of retaliation, or loss of international reputation to settle disputes. Certain types of conflicts cannot, however, be effectively enforced through those avenues. Laws and courts are best placed to resolve those and hence were built into at least some international agreements.

The range and reach of international and transnational agreements and tribunals are varied, and each has a charge to police a single sliver of human activity, within a carefully defined geographical sphere. The variety of arrangements challenges any meaningful synthesis. Conclusions about the effectiveness or efficacy of so many diverse courts also defy coherent analysis. They vary in geographic limits, subject matter, longevity, membership, and number of binding rulings (Alter 2014). Some of these courts are "old-style," lack compulsory jurisdiction, and prohibit individual access, whereas others are "new style," including both of those features absent in the older tribunals. Nineteen of the twenty international or transnational courts were created in the 1990s (Alter 2006). Thus, the proverbial apples and oranges dilemma arises. Because of the multiplicity of international and transnational courts, this chapter discusses five categories of transnational courts and, rather than tediously explaining the intricacies of each, focuses on exemplars of each type.

The first category, actual international courts with potentially global jurisdiction, includes only four courts: the ICJ, the International Tribunal for the Law of the Sea (ITLOS), the ICC, and the dispute settlement mechanism of the WTO. Notably, the last three, as is generally true of all transnational courts, have no jurisdiction to settle disputes unless a nation is a signatory of the treaty and in some cases has accepted the compulsory jurisdiction of the specific court. For example, the United States withdrew its signature from the treaty creating the ICC and therefore is not subject to any of its rules. The WTO similarly represents an organization to which countries must apply and meet certain criteria. Countries that are not WTO members consequently are not bound by its rules.

The second category comprises transnational (regional) courts, such as the IACtHR and the ECJ. Again, only nations in specific geographic regions that have signed the applicable treaty are subject to the rules. The United States is a member of the Organization of American States (OAS), the parent body of the IACtHR, but the United States has not agreed to accept the compulsory jurisdiction of the court. Switzerland lies in the geographic center of Europe but is not a member of the EU, parent to the ECJ, and the ECJ has no authority over transactions taken by the Swiss government or by businesses or individuals within Switzerland.

Hybrid courts, those created for a single situation, such as that instituted in 2003 in response to humanitarian violations in Sierra Leone, make up the third quite distinct category. Usually, jurisdiction is not contingent on signing a treaty or accepting compulsory jurisdiction. The fourth type of courts includes highly specialized ones, often called administrative tribunals. Many of these conduct only appellate work, such as the Appeals Board of the European Space Agency. Permanent tribunals for transnational arbitration constitute the fifth category and include such courts as the International Center for the Settlement of Investment Disputes and the Court of Arbitration for Sport.

International agreements are bedeviled by problems of enforcement and compliance, and obviously those concerns apply equally to decisions of international and regional courts. All courts, even domestic ones, potentially suffer from the inability to enforce their rulings, but those difficulties increase exponentially for international and transnational courts that typically lack an executive arm carrying coercive clout. No discussion of transnational judicial bodies would be complete without a consideration of what is and what is not known about transnational judicial enforcement.

Of note, none of these courts decides, either because of jurisdictional limitations or because of the delicacy of the conflict, the most potentially damaging international disputes, the most important issues: those relating to use of force. When the courts have addressed those questions, their success in achieving resolutions has been modest (Shany 2009). Even so, international relations has evolved as more of a legal process now than a diplomatic one (Johns 2009).

DEVELOPMENT AND EVOLUTION OF INTERNATIONAL COURTS

The work of international/transnational courts, in all of their facets of effectiveness and ability to achieve compliance, depends on international law. The existence of a semblance of an international rule of law alone can sometimes tame the anarchy of some approximately two hundred sovereign nations, unaccountable otherwise to any higher authority in dealings with other sovereign nations. International law has evolved over centuries, but the contemporary conception is typically dated from the Peace of Westphalia in 1648, which established the modern nation-state and recognized the unimpeded authority of the government of each nation-state over its inhabitants. Some rules were necessary to govern relationships among these nations and their conduct toward one another. The difficulty with applying international law lies in the reality that unlike domestic law, it is not readily "accessible, coherent, or certain" (Aust 2010, 5). Much of international law was once customary and therefore challenging to locate, interpret, or apply, but now much of it is codified in the form of treaties. These treaties may be bilateral (between two nations) or multilateral, and those considered in this chapter fall into the latter category. Some five hundred multilateral treaties were signed between 1900 and 1925, but the post–World War II era (1951–1975) saw the greatest number, another two thousand, and the trend toward more multinational agreements continued through the end of the twentieth century, albeit at a slower pace (Simmons 2008).

More and more multilateral treaties seek to institute an enforcement mechanism, and, as noted previously, a number have adopted a legal mechanism: a court or quasi-court. Generally, an international or transnational court can be defined as an independent judicial body, created by treaty and authorized to apply the relevant international law to cases brought before it (Shany 2015). Such courts had issued some thirty-three thousand rulings as of 2007, three-quarters of those after 1990 (Alter 2008). Why would courts be the vehicles selected? A number of theories have been proposed to clarify why nations choose to bind themselves by willingly accepting the terms of a treaty and, more specifically, to subject their actions to scrutiny by an international tribunal. Why a binding court decision instead of old-fashioned diplomacy and bargaining? Indeed, the existence of a legal institution can potentially impede international cooperation by lessening the information available in settlement negotiations, reducing the likelihood that pretrial settlements will be successful, and increasing the level of brinksmanship over high-value assets (Gilligan, Johns, and Rosendorff 2010). Kono (2007) found that at least in the area of free trade, strong, more legalized dispute settlement mechanisms did not achieve their intended ends. What international judicial rulings do offer is domestic political cover for politicians, who can alter policies in an unpopular direction by claiming that their action was necessitated by an international court decision (Allee and Huth 2006). The primary tool of these courts, beyond sanctions that may or may not be imposed, is the threat of damage to a country's international reputation.

A number of theories have been proposed to explain why countries sign onto treaties that make them subject to a judicial tribunal outside of their boundaries. One theory holds that international crises spur a move to establish an arbiter for international disputes, whereas others focus on information sharing and transaction cost reduction or a state's desire to signal its credible commitment (Katzenstein 2014). Goals and incentives behind the implementation of international tribunals to resolve conflicts also shape the contours of treaties and of the adjudicating bodies that enforce them. For example, agreements can be deep—that is, well-developed with apparently effective adjudication—or shallow (Carrubba 2006). Another way of phrasing that is soft versus hard law. *Hard law* describes international agreements that create legally binding commitments that are precise in their requirements and contain institutions for interpretation and implementation. *Soft law*, on the other hand, refers to treaties that are less binding, less precise, and lacking in effective adjudication features (see figure 6.1). One means of understanding the distinction is by comparing covenants and contracts. A covenant represents a normative commitment (soft), whereas a contract is binding (hard) (Abbott and Snidal 2000).

An early attempt to create hard international law, at least in the sense of establishing an international court, followed World

Figure 6.1 Soft-hard legalism in international agreements

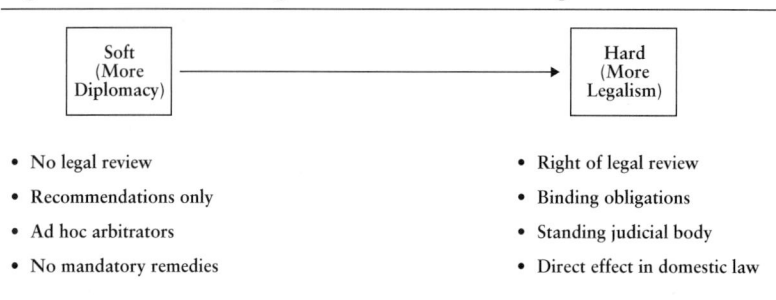

```
   ┌─────────┐                                    ┌─────────┐
   │  Soft   │                                    │  Hard   │
   │ (More   │  ─────────────────────────────▶    │ (More   │
   │Diplomacy)│                                   │Legalism)│
   └─────────┘                                    └─────────┘
```

- No legal review
- Recommendations only
- Ad hoc arbitrators
- No mandatory remedies

- Right of legal review
- Binding obligations
- Standing judicial body
- Direct effect in domestic law

Source: Adapted from James McCall Smith, "The Politics of Dispute Settlement Design: Explaining Legalism in Regional Trade Pacts," *International Organization* 54 (2000): 143.

War I: the Permanent Court of International Justice (PCIJ). That court ultimately died without support from Great Britain and with opposition from the United States over sovereignty concerns. The PCIJ met for the last time in 1939 as World War II commenced in Europe (Katzenstein 2014; MacKenzie, Romano, et al. 2010). Prior to or contemporaneous with the first world court, another four courts were attempted, but they failed to be implemented (Katzenstein 2014). At the conclusion of World War II, at the urging of the United States, the International Military Tribunal, commonly known as the Nuremberg Tribunal, was created by the victorious Allies to try the principal Nazi war criminals; that court sat from November 1945 until October 1946. At the time, no nation had obligated itself to a legally binding agreement that called for prosecution. Indeed, the crimes prosecuted were subsumed under "crimes against peace," a crime not previously recognized by customary international law. In fact, resort to war was not unlawful until the Nuremberg Tribunal. Similar trials were also held in Tokyo. Both sets of trials held individuals, not nations, accountable, and their perceived success provided the impetus to establish the ICJ (Alter 2014). Only after the International Military Tribunal and its counterpart in Japan shuttered their doors did the United Nations General Assembly approve the Convention on the Prevention and Punishment of the Crime of Genocide, in 1948 (Tucker 2001).

Perhaps the experience with so-called victors' justice or simply a recognition of the increasing interconnectivity of the world led to the writing of more international treaties in the aftermath of World War II. The absence of precision was eventually addressed for all international agreements in the Vienna Convention on the Law of Treaties in 1969, which purportedly applied to interpretation and application of all treaties (Pauwelyn and Elsig 2018). As of 2009, however, only 109 nations had signed as parties to that convention (Aust 2010).

INTERNATIONAL COURTS

Only four courts can be characterized as both "international" and a "court": the ICJ in The Hague, the ITLOS, the WTO standing dispute settlement system, and the ICC. Each of these judicial bodies is unique, and each has its genesis in a different era and a distinct context. Consequently, each is considered individually here, because they represent the vastly varying ways that diplomats negotiating the respective treaties sought to constrain behavior—national, commercial, and individual—that extends across national boundaries.

The oldest of these courts is the ICJ, designed after and almost copied from the pre–World War II PCIJ, which dates from 1946 and serves as the principal judicial body of the United Nations (MacKenzie, Malleson, et al. 2010). The ICJ's jurisdiction extends to treaty interpretation, general international law, and breaches and reparations for violations, but as widely as it reaches, it has heard only 134 cases filed over its entire history (Mitchell and Owsiak 2018), and even when the court has made decisions, those were sometimes not substantive rulings on the merits of the case. Usage rates may, however, be an inadequate means of measuring the effectiveness of a court, because they fail to capture out-of-court settlements achieved because of the court's presence or the general compliance with rules that stems from the court's existence (Shany 2015). The role of the ICJ in the settlement of disputes becomes muddied by the unwieldy and imprecise body of law it is charged with enforcing and the seeming lack of subject matter limitations (Gilligan, Johns, and Rosendorff 2010).

The ITLOS was implemented in 1996, fifty years after the ICJ, and represents a distinct amalgam of complex procedures outlined in the UN Convention on the Law of the Sea and its annexes. The court issues binding provisional rulings, but arbitration procedures serve as the basic mode for resolving disputes (Aust 2010). However, parties may also choose to litigate before the ICJ or to use a special arbitration mechanism. Jurisdiction of the court, unlike under the ICJ, is mandatory for nations that have signed the convention, but only under specific causes of action and notably excluding territorial claims. The caseload has been light—a total of fifteen cases as of mid-2009—and has primarily addressed seizures of vessels (MacKenzie, Romano et al. 2010; Alter 2014).

The WTO grew out of the General Agreement on Tariffs and Trade (GATT), which had served as the platform for multinational trade negotiations since 1948. The timing and impetus for its new configuration as the WTO in 1995 was the end of the Cold War and a recognition that the collapse of the Soviet Union would create new applications for membership and, consequently, greater difficulty in achieving structural reforms later (Alter 2014). By the end of 2017, 163 countries were members of the WTO. One essential new element of the WTO was the shift from diplomacy to legality, closer to hard law, with the creation of the Dispute Settlement Body (DSB) to resolve trade disputes. The DSB is explicitly prohibited from creating or altering any rights or obligations of the disputing parties under the terms of the WTO, but that attempt to preclude judicial creativity has not prevented panels of the DSB from relying on other treaties and customary international law in some decisions (Dunoff and Trachtman 2009).

The Law of the Sea Treaty relies on arbitration largely to settle disputes brought before it, whereas the WTO dispute settlement system has a more court-like structure, including a standing appellate body. At the base of the system are ad hoc panels, meaning that permanent judges do not hear the cases, and the contentious parties may propose other means of settlement, such as conciliation or mediation. Another unusual twist in the system is that decisions of the ad hoc panels are subject to review by the DSB, though in reality panel decisions are upheld unless a party chooses to appeal to the WTO Appellate Body, a "higher" court (MacKenzie, Romano et al. 2010). Unlike the ad hoc panels, the Appellate Body is staffed by seven judges serving four-year terms, all of whom hear every case (Aust 2010). The WTO dispute settlement system serves less to render binding decisions than to encourage nations in trade conflicts to find settlements, but through law-based negotiations (Steinberg 2002). Asymmetrical power relationships naturally play a role in bargaining (Conti 2008; Jackson and Volcansek 2009), and nations tend toward strategic behavior in pursuing litigation, often based largely on domestic politics (Davis and Shirato 2007).

The ICC is the newest of the international courts and began functioning in 2002; 123 countries were subject to the jurisdiction of the ICC in 2017. The ICC has jurisdiction over four types of crimes: (1) genocide, (2) crimes against humanity, (3) war crimes, and (4) aggression. The ICC will not hear cases unless the relevant domestic judicial system is unable or unwilling to prosecute. In other words, nations can prevent prosecutions from reaching the ICC if their own criminal justice systems hear the cases (Schabas 2004), a system known as "complementarity" (De Vos, Kendall, and Stahn 2015). Unlike the WTO, in which only nations are parties, individuals are the targets of the ICC, but only for actions that occurred after a nation signed the pact. Investigations may be triggered by state request or the prosecutors' own initiative, and states cannot accept or withhold jurisdiction on a case-by-case basis. Investigations also cannot be barred by immunities granted under national authority. The ICC's performance, as a relatively new international court, cannot be easily evaluated, but the mere existence of the court does not ensure that those committing atrocities will be punished (Simmons and Danner 2010). At the same time, the absence of prosecutions signals a positive accomplishment,

BOX 6.1 | **The International Criminal Court Investigates a Mali Police Chief**

Al Hassan Ag Abdoul Aziz Ag Mohamed Ag Mahmoud was brought before the International Criminal Court in 2018 on charges of crimes against humanity and war crimes for actions that occurred in 2012 and 2013 when he served as police chief under a jihadist occupation of Timbuktu in Mali. The specific charges included rape, torture, and sexual slavery, which encompassed brief forced marriages that often produced offspring. Al Hassan had about forty police officers under his command and allegedly took part in lashings and in the destruction of shrines of Muslim saints regarded as idolatrous. He had been arrested by French troops a year earlier and was handed over to Malian authorities, who in turn surrendered him to the ICC when a sealed arrest warrant was issued.

Source: Marlise Simons, "Rape Charges for Jihadist Police Chief," *New York Times,* April 5, 2018, A-8.

because it suggests that national criminal justice systems are functioning effectively (DeVos, Kendall, and Stahn 2015).

TRANSNATIONAL REGIONAL COURTS

At least twenty courts function over specific, geographically limited regions to adjudicate infractions of economic, political, or human rights agreements (PICT 2004). These tend to be found in Europe, the Americas, and more recently Africa. The trend to legalize and adjudicate regional agreements has not reached into Asia or the Middle East in the same way (Kahler 2000). The range is wide, as are the portfolios of the various judicial bodies. The two courts that have demonstrated both endurance and effectiveness reside in Europe: the EU's ECJ and the Council of Europe's ECtHR. These two serve well as examples of the functions and potential of other transnational judicial bodies. These two courts do not, however, bear much resemblance to others, such as the IACtHR, the dispute panels of NAFTA, the judicial bodies of Economic Community of West African States, the Southern Common Market (Mercosur), or the African Court on Human and People's Rights. Each court was created via multilateral negotiations to handle region- and mission-specific issues, and most have been created since 1990. The governance structures vary, but all are indicative of a push for regional solutions to economic and humanitarian problems (McCall Smith 2000). The ECJ and the ECtHR are the oldest and most active and therefore illustrate possible trajectories that others might follow. (For a brief comparison of twenty regional courts, see Alter 2014.)

The ECJ was created in 1952 as the enforcement arm of the European Coal and Steel Community, with only six member states, but it evolved in importance and authority along with its parent organization into the EU in 1993 and encompassed twenty-eight nations of Europe until the British signaled their exit in 2016. The original intent was to foster trade, but subsequently as new treaties were negotiated, social and political goals were added. The basic function of the ECJ has been to enforce the treaties and secondary legislation, and it hears cases alleging violations brought by the European Commission (the executive arm of the EU), member states, and private people or entities, as well as questions referred by national courts. Since 1989 the ECJ has been assisted by the Court of First Instance, which hears more routine and minor cases and whose decisions can usually be appealed to the ECJ.

The EU was designed to encourage private enforcement of European law through cases lodged with the ECJ, which has empowered the court and allowed it to make expansive interpretations and to enter the policy-making process (Kelemen 2011). Although most scholars conclude that the ECJ has developed into a powerful court, considerable disagreement persists about why that happened (Garrett, Kelemen, and Schultz 1998; Krehbiel, Gabel, and Carrubba 2018) and the consequences that flow from an empowered regional court (Blauberger 2014; Carrubba, Gabel, and Hankla 2012; Stone Sweet and Brunnell 2012). The ECJ stands as the oldest and most established regional tribunal and likely the most successful one (Blauberger and Schmidt 2017). As a result, some eleven "operational copies" of the ECJ have been created by regional agreements to replicate its design features. However, none of those has duplicated either the longevity or the effectiveness of the ECJ, largely because of factors specific to the regions in which they operate (Alter 2014).

The ECtHR claims its place as the second oldest regional transnational court, and its reach, constituencies, mandate, and

---

BOX 6.2 | Cuisine and the European Court of Justice

The original animating rationale for the European Union was to facilitate free trade, and therefore the European Court of Justice has often been called upon to adjudicate labels on foodstuffs. The court held that a German spirits maker might mislead or confuse consumers by its use of the term *glen* on its label for whiskey. Scotland is known for its production of Scotch whiskeys such as Glenmorangie, and the court reasoned that a German beverage called Glen Buchenbach might be assumed to be from Scotland.

Previously, the court had stated that products carrying labels such as "milk," "butter," or "cheese" must contain dairy products and dictated the specific properties required of items sold under the label "chocolate." It also prohibited calling a product "Champagne Sorbet" unless the distinctive flavor of champagne could be demonstrated.

Source: Amie Tsang, "Whiskey from a German Glen? The E.U. Demurs," *New York Times,* June 10, 2018, BU-6.

membership are distinct from but overlapping with the ECJ. The ECtHR was established in 1958 as the judicial organ of the Council of Europe to enforce national compliance with the European Convention on Human Rights. As of 2014, forty-seven nations were signatories of the convention. As under the ECJ, both individuals and governments, but overwhelmingly individuals, can bring cases; of those deemed admissible, individual petitioners have been successful in more than half of the cases decided. Not surprisingly, therefore, the caseload of the ECtHR has become staggering, with over 60,000 applications in 2017; 70,000 cases were deemed inadmissible that year, but 15,600 were decided. That is remarkable based on what is known about general levels of national compliance with other human rights treaties, particularly those without a transnational court to police national violations. Adherence to the Convention against Torture, for example, varies by nation. Those countries with effective domestic criminal justice and judicial

---

BOX 6.3 | **European Court of Human Rights and Political Expression**

In September 2007 Enric Stearn and Jaume Roura were charged by Spanish officials with the felony of insulting the monarch. At that time the movement for independence from Spain by the province of Catalonia was in its infancy. The two men burned an upside-down picture of the king and queen of Spain in a protest during a visit by King Juan Carlos I. Both men were convicted and given fifteen-month prison terms, later reduced to fines of €2,700 or about US$3,300 each. The Spanish Constitutional Court declined to hear Stearn and Roura's appeal. The two men then took their case to the European Court of Human Rights (ECtHR), which in 2018 overturned the convictions and ordered the Spanish government to reimburse the fines and to pay the men's legal costs for the case.

The ECtHR reasoned that burning the photograph was not a personal attack on the king, but rather a statement of opposition to the political system he represented. Therefore, it was not an incitement to hatred or violence, but merely an act of expression, justified political criticism.

Source: Raphael Minder, "Court Overturns Verdict Against Catalans," *New York Times*, March 14, 2018, A-5.

systems typically follow treaty dictates, and those lacking a robust judiciary do not (Powell and Staton 2009). The ECtHR presides over forty-seven signatory nations, and its effects have been uneven (Keller and Stone Sweet 2008). Within the orbit of the ECtHR, even Russia since 1998 accepts the court's compulsory jurisdiction and complies with dictates of the court, albeit reluctantly (Trochev 2009). The ECtHR has been deemed "the crown jewel of the world's most advanced systems for protecting civil and political liberties" (Helfer 2008, 125). Like the ECJ, the ECtHR has been imitated elsewhere, and one imitation, the IACtHR, has established a significant, though more limited, reputation (Pasqualucci 2003; Brewer-Carías 2009).

HYBRID COURTS

Hybrid or ad hoc courts, also known as international criminal tribunals (ICTs), have been created in much the same way as the Nuremburg and Tokyo Tribunals were at the end of World War II. Each was designed to address a specific conflict in which atrocities were alleged to have been committed and to punish culpable parties, but usually only if domestic courts did not or could not act or in conjunction with national institutions; hence the label "hybrid" (Cohen 2007). The seemingly repeated need to impanel such bodies led to the creation of the ICC, which should render future ICTs unnecessary. These courts were intended to facilitate transitional justice for fragmented societies by providing an accounting of past events and clarifying right and wrong. Whatever the UN mandate for a given ICT, little concrete law, beyond customary international law, guided proceedings, and they often amounted to ex post facto criminalization of acts (Carlson 2017).

The first ICT was that for the former Yugoslavia, established in 1993 to prosecute breaches of the Geneva Convention during the civil war in the Balkans. Interestingly, its jurisdiction was defined as concurrent with national courts, but with the authority to preempt domestic court proceedings (Aust 2010). This court, likely because it operated in The Hague in the Netherlands rather than in a more remote location, generated the greatest scholarly attention. The ICT for Rwanda demonstrated, however, that Western-inspired schemes were not capable of addressing human rights in the aftermath of mass violence (Uvin and Mironko 2003), and the ICTs in Cambodia, Sierra Leone, and East Timor, because of inadequate cooperation, excessive delays, and meager resources, also proved ineffective (Cohen 2007).

The ICT for the former Yugoslavia has been subject to more analyses and has been criticized for the number of acquittals, short sentences, and claims of partiality regarding which national groups were prosecuted (Hellman 2015). Even so, the ICT in Yugoslavia was found to be tough on sentencing when sexual assault was alleged, at least if assaults were in conjunction with other crimes and the level of command authority of the accused was high (King and Meernick 2005). Still, analysis of the sentences meted out by the ICTs for Yugoslavia, Rwanda, and Sierra Leone demonstrated a consistency with domestic and international tribunals' actions and focused on retribution and deterrence (Meernick 2011). Moreover, the ICTs served to form a "seabed" for the formation of the ICC by inserting individuals, not just nations, into international law and establishing their criminal liability (Sikkink 2011). Presumably, the ICC will now preclude resort to individual ICTs.

SPECIALIZED AND ADMINISTRATIVE TRIBUNALS

The Project on International Courts and Tribunals (PICT 2004) identified sixteen different administrative tribunals, each specializing in a single slice of commercial transactions, but that number has subsequently increased to twenty. The subject matter covered by the courts ranges from labor organization and migration to outer space and banking. Even appeals on NATO decisions can reach one of these, an arbitral tribunal. Many are only appellate courts to which administrative decisions can be appealed. Some would not qualify in normal or even technical parlance as courts. These multiple bodies allow for or facilitate transnational dispute resolution, but the political implications of their activities are minimal (PICT 2004).

ARBITRATION AND THE *LEX MERCATORIA*

All international and transnational courts were established because transactions of all kinds across national borders inevitably give rise to conflicts. Many, if not most, of the bodies created contain elements of compulsory jurisdiction for the nations that have ratified the relevant treaty, but some disputes require resolution across borders without either the involvement of a nation-state or acceptance of enforced jurisdiction. As a consequence, a number of bodies have been created with only arbitration or settlement as their goal. In addition, an informal system, disconnected from nation-states and any particular transnational body, has evolved, the so-called *lex mercatoria* or market law. Ten arbitral bodies exist, but arbitration also flourishes under other auspices, such as the International Chamber of Commerce, a relatively independent international commercial arbitrator (Grisel 2017).

The international arbitral boards function somewhat like mediators, in that they attempt to guide the disputing parties to an agreement, but if that does not occur, they can issue legally binding decisions. Commercial disputes subject to international arbitration tend to carry high stakes, though not ones necessarily directly tied to the political sphere. In 2013, 109 cases, each involving at least $500 million, were in the midst of international commercial arbitration under the International Chamber of Commerce; 58 of those cases carried claims of over $1 billion and 9 more than $9 billion (Grisel 2017). Though the disputes carried hefty price tags, national sovereignty and actual control were disconnected, and islands of private, transnational governance emerged (Stone Sweet 1999).

The need to resolve transnational commercial disputes beyond the purview of national legal systems and geographic boundaries has long been acknowledged, and the Permanent Court of Arbitration in the Hague was created by international convention in 1899 (MacKenzie, Romano, et al. 2010). In reality it cannot be considered either a court or permanent, because panels are appointed on an ad hoc basis as disputes are referred to it, and the body does not issue awards, though its panels do. The Permanent Court of Arbitration was designed to settle international disputes, whereas other bodies, informally created, address many other commercial disputes (MacKenzie, Romano, et al. 2010).

The myriad informal arbitration arrangements that comprise the *lex mercatoria* operate without national involvement, except where necessary to enforce decisions (Stone Sweet 2006). These are regimes based on private law. A company based in the United Kingdom, for example, conducts business with a firm in Japan. When writing the contract between the companies, how to resolve disputes can be specified—UK law, Japanese law, the Permanent Court of Arbitration, arbitration under the International Chamber of Commerce, or a privately agreed upon "court" that the parties to the contract design for their specific intentions. Often, however, the outcomes of these private agreements affect public goods, such as the Internet Corporation for Assigned Names and Numbers, which governs internet domain names (Wheatley 2010). Arbitration houses or private courts evolved as frequent substitutes for national courts, predicated on the basis of contracts, not bilateral or multilateral national agreements (Stone Sweet 2006).

COMPLIANCE AND ENFORCEMENT

Transnational and international courts are a relatively new phenomenon, and much remains unknown about the effects that they exert. Some obviously succeed in resolving disputes, and many have become highly empowered. The durability of some remains purely speculative, as a number have previously withered for lack of use or are extinct or abolished. The rise of so many courts also creates questions: which has jurisdiction, are the rulings of one respected by another, can nations or other entities forum shop (pick a particular court from which a favorable ruling can be anticipated), is the private *lex mercatoria* a more viable mechanism for resolving cross-border commercial disputes? Predicate to those questions, though, is an assessment of the effectiveness of courts that are not hinged to any national system of enforcement or tethered to a democratic mandate. The answers clearly vary by court, but the umbrella organization under which each court operates and the geographic region where its jurisdiction extends remain central to each court's viability. Perhaps most important, how do we know if a particular transnational or international court is effective?

Illustrations of the *in*effectiveness of courts in altering national behavior abound. In 2004 the ICJ ruled that some fifty Mexican nationals, who were convicted of crimes in the United States without being told of their right of access to the Mexican consulate, had been deprived of their rights under the Geneva Convention of 1963. That treaty had been ratified by the US Senate in 1969, but in 2008 the US Supreme Court upheld the conviction of one of the Mexican nationals on the grounds that the treaty was not self-executing (Jackson, Tolley, and Volcansek 2010). In 1995 a WTO dispute panel also decided against the United States in a dispute with Venezuela over restrictions on imported gasoline. The United States did not immediately change its restrictions, but rather reentered negotiations with Venezuela and ultimately lessened, but did not eliminate, them (Gilligan, Johns, and Rosendorff 2010). Were the ICJ and WTO decisions effective?

Yuval Shany (2015) argues that we have yet to identify and isolate metrics to measure the effectiveness of courts acting across national borders. Compliance with individual rulings, rates of usage, and changes in national behavior each capture a part of effectiveness, but not the overall picture. Even instances of "norm compliance," whereby one might infer that transnational and international court decisions deter certain national behaviors, may not be sufficient. Even so, social scientists and legal academics have attempted to gauge the impact of international and transnational courts.

A court's impact is difficult to attribute, as discussed in depth in the next chapter, largely because real-world events cannot be isolated from a host of other things occurring in a country's economic, political, and social environment. Actual world events cannot be placed in a test tube, nor can control groups be given a placebo instead of the "drug"—ruling—being tested. To complicate matters, as Alter (2014) notes, to argue that a nation has undergone "norm compliance," one would need to demonstrate usage, sensitivity to legality, a compliance constituency, and political support for a court. That's a tall order for social scientists to measure and for a transnational court to achieve. Regulation of transnational trade and monetary, environmental, or security policies might be gauged by some discrete, tangible indicators, but international human rights courts have responsibility for policing and often changing governmental activities that occur strictly within a nation's borders (Moravcsik 2000).

Concepts of national sovereignty stand as the major impediment to tightening ties and relinquishing authority to judicial bodies that lie beyond states. How is a nation compelled to address the mandates of such a court? The Westphalian view of national sovereignty—"the power to be left alone, to exclude, to counter any external meddling or interference" (Slaughter 2005, 267)—may never have existed other than as a legal, not a political, notion (Stone Sweet 1999). In reality, understandings of national sovereignty have modified and been reframed since the medieval era and cease to be monolithic when cross-national border transactions occur. Sovereignty now more aptly connotes something that is preceded by a modifier: shared, pooled, limited, relative, or competitive (Stack and Volcansek 2005). Figure 6.2 depicts the range of

Figure 6.2 Sovereignty costs of international courts

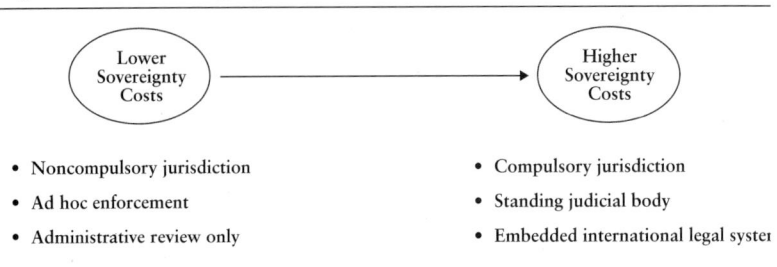

```
┌───────────┐                              ┌───────────┐
│  Lower    │                              │  Higher   │
│ Sovereignty├─────────────────────────────▶│Sovereignty│
│   Costs   │                              │   Costs   │
└───────────┘                              └───────────┘
```

- Noncompulsory jurisdiction
- Ad hoc enforcement
- Administrative review only

- Compulsory jurisdiction
- Standing judicial body
- Embedded international legal system

Source: Adapted from Karen J. Alter, "Delegating to International Courts: Self-Binding and Other-Binding Delegation," *Law and Contemporary Problems* 71 (2008):71.

features that impinge on national sovereignty, so-called sovereignty costs. The choice has ceased to be one between favoring a global rule of law or unilateralism that promotes foreign policy without concessions to global norms (Garth 2008). Not all national bending to international rules and enforcers of those rules results in compromised sovereignty, but some transnational courts—the ECJ and the ECtHR are excellent examples—exercise authority that does erode member nation's freedom to act outside the agreed upon norms (Alter 2008). Absent rules and nonlethal rule enforcers, such as courts, the international system might approach anarchy (Stack and Volcansek 2005).

The spread of multiple international and transnational courts has also created a potential for overlapping jurisdictions that can serve to mute the distinguishable effect of a given court. Positively, the availability of so many courts encourages nations to take disputes to court instead of resorting to force or unilateral actions (Linton and Tiba 2009). At the same time, potential litigants now often argue more fiercely for jurisdiction than on the merits of a case (Slaughter 2005). Countries and legal entities, including multiple possible non-state actors, forum shop based not only on which court may most likely render the preferred decision, but on which appeals more to domestic politics (Pekkanen, Solis, and Katada 2007) and what or where a precedent the party wants to achieve would best serve the litigator's interests (Busch 2007). Overlapping jurisdictions can also lead to conflicting jurisprudence (Linton and Tiba 2009) and require judges to consider provisions not included in that court's founding treaty, but rather other treaty documents (Pauwelyn and Salles 2009).

Possible complications arising from the proliferation of so many transnational courts can be discarded, however, if none or only some of the judicial bodies prove to be ineffective and incapable of altering or punishing behavior. At the same time, precisely what is meant by *effective*? At the very least, courts are not effective if their rulings are not followed by the litigants involved in the case, and transnational courts, more so than their domestic counterparts, "lack direct coercion mechanisms to compel either appearance or compliance" (Helfer and Slaughter 1997, 285). When a nation-state is a party to a case and loses, the interests of the national executive or legislature or both are directly affected, which can lead national governments to ignore, misapply, or block court rulings (Carrubba, Gabel, and Hankla 2008). Consensus seems to coalesce around the conclusion that some courts are more successful than others in having their decisions enforced, especially the EJC of the EU, which tends to achieve compliance generally with individual rulings and also affects domestic policy making more broadly (Blauberger and Schmidt 2017).

The effectiveness of a transnational or international court cannot be treated as a dichotomy: effective or not. Rather, a continuum between total ineffectiveness and total compliance proves a more fruitful approach (Helfer and Slaughter 1997). Attempts to assess the effectiveness of any transnational judicial organ across all cases can be fraught with pitfalls. Routine cross-border contract enforcement cannot be equated with politically charged conflicts such as war, terror, and human rights issues (Shany 2009). Moreover, individual empirical indicators of compliance necessarily fail to consider the time (immediate change in national policy versus a gradual, incremental adjustment over a period of years), the distance between the existing national policy and the change required by the court, and even how highly valued the national policy is by the relevant national stakeholders (Hillbrecht 2009). Enforcement of deep, well-developed treaties (hard law) varies from that of those characterized as shallow, aspirational ones (soft law) (Carrubba 2006).

The effectiveness of a court's decisions may best be measured indirectly by what happens outside of the courtroom. As is often the case in domestic courts, the threat of a court decision and knowledge of how that tribunal has acted previously can serve as the requisite incentive to settle a dispute without resorting to litigation (Mitchell and Owsiak 2018). Nation-states, particularly those in the EU, take into account the ECJ's jurisprudence when formulating policies so as to avoid potential future litigation (Martinsen 2015). Recognition of the option of taking cases to a transnational court can also foster legal mobilization that may actually result in more cases before domestic, not transnational, courts, where the jurisprudence of the transnational court can wield clout (Cichowski 2007).

International or transnational courts might be deemed ineffective measured by some indicators, in part because some nations simply lack the capacity to comply with decisions (Slaughter 2005), or the domestic audience costs for governmental authorities may appear too great for a state to comply (Tomz 2007). Even so, attempting even partial compliance can signal a credible commitment on the part of the nation (Simmons and Danner 2010). Unfortunately, in the area of human rights, that credible commitment is most likely observed in the nations that need it least (Helfer and Slaughter 1997).

Compliance with decisions of non-national courts is vexed with larger problems, as transnational judicial bodies lack the normal trappings of legitimacy and consent. The legitimacy of all courts can be problematic, as discussed in chapter 8, but those difficulties are heightened for courts operating beyond the nation-state and always absent any democratic mandate. Power dynamics inevitably play into implementation of transnational judicial rulings, and often no remedy results from litigation (Alter 2014).

CONCLUSION

Many decry the absence of a participatory-representative element in any aspect of international governance (de Burca 2008), but accountability mechanisms exist beyond democratic ones (Grant and Keohane 2004). That assertion, however, raises the question of to whom international courts (or other inter- and transnational bodies) are accountable (von Bogdandy and Venzke 2012). At the very least, abuses of authority should be recognized and those abusing should be accountable (Grant and Keohane 2004), but locating consent or pegging accountability in the international sphere can be tricky. Alter calls this "the democratic politics conundrum" (Alter 2014, 336), but that supposes rather idealistically that only democratic practices can legitimately undergird a political system. Ultimately, a nation that finds its interests damaged by international or transnational tribunals can withdraw, albeit with potential costs, from an international agreement.

Waves of renewed nationalism appearing in the first quarter of the twenty-first century may well slow the development of new transnational agreements and the process of globalization. They are unlikely, though, to roll back existing structures much because the interconnectivity of the world's economic and communications networks will not contract readily. The need for rules to govern cross-border transactions and norms and some means to enforce the rules stand as a powerful bulwark against withdrawal into Westphalian islands of strictly national governance.

7

The Impact of Courts

★ ★ ★

IN THE SPRING of 2018 Joshua Beard was convicted in Texas of killing his girlfriend's child two years earlier (Ramirez 2018). Beard was in police custody pending the outcome of any appeals, and no doubts arose that the court's judgment would be followed and that Beard would serve his prison time. On the same day, a continent away in Egypt, Hisham Geneina, a former high government official, was convicted in a military court of spreading false news about the nation's military that threatened national security. Mr. Geneina was already being held in jail, and the implementation of his five-year sentence was assured (Walsh 2018). Whether one who has been charged with a crime resides in a democratic or military system, the accused has most likely already been arrested, and the criminal system can be expected to smoothly implement the orders of a court.

Outside the criminal judicial system, however, an orderly and mechanistic enforcement of judicial officials' decisions cannot be routinely expected, because "courts cannot directly enforce their decisions" (Krehbiel 2016, 1). Securing execution of court orders typically falls on the party who won the case and can be both a time-consuming and expensive process. The Canadian province Alberta relies on a system typical of how many places enforce non-criminal settlements. The winning party in litigation must obtain a writ of enforcement once a court order has been issued. Multiple copies of that writ must be filed with an official judicial organ and may be rejected if any errors, even just in spelling, are detected.

The writ of enforcement must also be filed with the appropriate government agency, depending on how the winning litigant intends to obtain payments, such as the Personal Property Register and the Land Titles Office. These claims must be renewed every two years if the debt has not been fully repaid. After ten years, the judgment expires unless the victorious party has been fully compensated. Assuming that the amount owed is fully paid, the parties must complete and sign a discharge and obtain a "Satisfaction Piece" to file with the court (Central Alberta Community Legal Clinic 2017).

In other systems, enforcement may be simpler. The Russian security forces, acting under a 2016 antiterrorism law, sought to ban the Russian messaging service Telegram because it refused to allow access to encrypted messages. After an eighteen-minute court hearing, the security forces were granted a court order to shut down Telegram immediately, and the messaging service disappeared (MacFarquhar 2018). Similarly, in 2017 a US court of appeals ruled in a labor case on the use of punctuation involving a comma. One style places a comma after each item in a list (A, B, and C), whereas the other skips the comma after the penultimate item in that list (A, B and C). Readers may think that such a question belongs at a grammarians' conference rather than a court of law, but the court's decision favoring the comma after every item resulted in a $5 million settlement for overtime pay. Moreover, the legislature of the state of Maine promptly rewrote the law in question for clarification and used semicolons instead of commas in the replacement legislation (Victor 2018).

In other words, individual litigants in court cases may or may not have court decisions that affect them promptly and efficiently enforced. But does the same process follow decisions of nations' highest courts? Sometimes enforcement of high court orders proves even more vexing than of lower court decisions. The German Federal Constitutional Court and the US Supreme Court are generally regarded as among the most powerful national courts, but even their decisions are not always enforced, or at least are not implemented in full accordance with the court's mandate or intentions. The German Federal Constitutional Court, for example, ruled in 1995 on a state ordinance requiring display of a crucifix in public elementary schools. The German high court found that the requirement violated constitutional protections for religious and nonreligious beliefs. Even after the German state rewrote the offending law, crucifixes remained a legal requirement (Vanberg 2005).

The US Supreme Court has faced similar enforcement challenges. Anyone familiar with efforts to racially integrate public schools in the United States recognizes that the 1954 court decision ordering desegregation did not achieve its goal for decades and perhaps never did so as a national policy. Racial integration, however, poses a particular set of barriers because of the emotionally charged nature of the issue and the highly diffuse number of local and state actors under whose authority it rested to implement the decision. Even in a more or less technical separation of powers decision in 1983 that was directed at only one other institution, Congress, compliance was at best mixed. The court case involved a mechanism known as the legislative veto, whereby Congress would delegate authority to an executive agency, but Congress retained the power to veto any specific decision under that delegation by action of either chamber. The court ruled that any changes in delegation of authority must follow the same rules as required for passage of any law, that is, passage by both chambers and presentation to the president to sign or to veto. Congress dutifully removed legislative vetoes from some existing legislation, but subsequently, in just the ensuing ten years, passed more than two hundred new laws that contained the prohibited legislative veto (Vanberg 2005).

This chapter addresses the important question of what happens after a court decision is made. In other words, a court makes a decision and what, if anything, changes? Scholars refer to this as the impact of judicial rulings. The issue is even more acute for international and transnational courts in securing compliance with their decisions, as alluded to in chapter 6. At levels beyond the nation-state no executive usually exists to enforce laws, which compounds problems of enforcement. Importantly, national and multinational courts share the difficulty resulting from the absence of a judicially controlled enforcement mechanism. In other words, at whatever level they operate, do courts really matter?

Impact refers to how law affects behavior or, more closely tied to the emphasis of this book, how court decisions affect the behavior of institutions and individuals. The topic presents challenges because assessing the impact of a court decision requires attributing causation, not correlation. A happened and then B happened; did A cause B, or was the sequence of events merely coincidental? More specifically, did a court decision cause a change or did a court decision reflect or occur simultaneously with a change in behavior

(Friedman 2016)? Perhaps more important, did a court decision directly prompt a change, but not the one that was intended? These questions are important at the micro level; a court resolves a dispute through a legal decree, but does it resolve the conflict concretely? Addressing the other theme of this book, do empowered courts at the macro (societal or institutional) level achieve changes in the behavior of those who are not directly involved in the litigation before the court?

DEFINING IMPACT

Social scientists have a long history of trying to gauge the effects of judicial decisions, dating back at least six decades. Measuring the consequences of court pronouncements became necessary to answer a quite fundamental question: Can court actions make any major, long-term difference? Obviously court orders can directly affect the parties to litigation in criminal cases, divorce and child custody cases, contract suits, and commercial disputes. But what about broad policy pronouncements of the kind that courts exercising constitutional review sometimes make? Does school desegregation follow a decision of the US Supreme Court? Is air quality in New Delhi improved after a decision of the Indian Supreme Court? The whole efficacy of courts could potentially be undermined if no consequences accompany court decisions.

The term *impact* has been used variously, sometimes with greater precision than others. Theodore Becker (1969) equated impact with consequences, whereas Wasby (1970) used effects, and Becker and Feeley honed the term to mean "policy related consequences of a decision" (1973, 213). More recently *impact* has been imbued with greater specificity: "judicial path of causal influence" (Rosenberg 1992, 7) and "behavior that is causally related to some . . . decision" (Friedman 2016, 45). Causality has, in other words, become more key. Although imputing causation links court decisions more directly to changes (or not) in some political actors' or the public's behavior, it may also dilute recognition of what happens after judicial decisions, particularly those that might be called aspirational or symbolic. Using *impact* more broadly to capture what, if anything, happens in the aftermath of a court decision allows inclusion of indirect "ripple effects" (Friedman 2016) that might also be important politically or influence other potential litigants.

Achieving a desired result through a court decision, be it the resolution of a dispute or a broad policy pronouncement, can be best conceived of as a two-pronged process: the intent of the court and implementation or enforcement of the court's goal. Judges usually have a specific outcome in mind when they decide cases: to award custody to the person with whom a minor child can best thrive, to divide marital property equitably, to resolve a commercial dispute in fairness to all parties or in conformity with a contractor, or to force removal of religious symbols that might be seen as coercive from all public schools. Judges thus decide cases strategically, with a view to the reactions of others, including political actors and the public (Epstein and Knight 1998). Judges also expect their decisions to be enforced, "the Achilles heel" of judicial decision making (Gauri and Brinks 2008, 18).

Judges do, however, sometimes miscalculate, as we all do. The consequences of the 1973 *Roe v. Wade* decision by the Supreme Court that legalized abortion in the United States present an excellent example. Presumably the court intended that as a result of the decision, more women would gain access to safe, legal abortions during the first three months of a pregnancy and with certain limitations thereafter. Whether or not the number of legal abortions increased can be variously interpreted, but the kinds of facilities that provided abortions clearly changed after the decision. The reactions of other political actors were more pronounced. Fifty constitutional amendments, none successful, were introduced in Congress to overturn or limit the decision; more than three hundred laws were passed by states to limit access to abortion procedures (Canon and Johnson 1999). The chasm between the court's implicit goal and the achievement of that goal gaped wide.

Reactions to judicial pronouncements may result in compliance; for example, the disputed patent right is assumed by the party winning the litigation or states adjust their laws on access to abortion to conform with those outlined by the judges for second- and third-trimester abortions. Noncompliance with or outright defiance of the court ruling may also follow. More likely, as was the case with abortion in the United States, some form of evasion or avoidance follows (Benesh and Martinek 2012; Canon and Johnson 1999). The dilemma is multiplied exponentially for international and transnational courts, because compliance in that context depends on multilevel and diffuse actors. Potentially many

> **BOX 7.1** | **Potential Implementing Audiences for Court Decisions**
>
> - Immediate parties to litigation
> - National political actors
> - Other courts
> - Local and regional political actors
> - Bureaucratic agencies
> - Media
> - Special interest groups
> - The public

countries and a variety of political actors and publics must react to the decision (Carrubba and Gabel 2015).

There are several layers of possible implementing audiences, and multiples of those are necessarily involved for enforcement of international and transnational judicial rulings, depending on the number of countries implicated in a decision. Not all court decisions touch each of these audiences, but someone, other than the deciding court, must assume responsibility for enforcement of court decrees, and many of the audiences determine the rigor or absence thereof exerted to give effect to the judicial decision: comply, defy, evade, avoid, modify.

One factor that an implementing audience will include in its calculation of how to proceed will depend on the intrusiveness of the court decision, which can be substantial or merely cosmetic. A major policy shift demanded by a court order can constitute a major disruption, whereas other judicial decisions simply structure incentives for future litigation or generate publicity that can punish or reward (Epp 2008) or merely resolve the single dispute being litigated.

Scholars pose different theories about how much court decisions can affect policy. The dynamic court model holds that courts can serve as the catalysts for major social change when legislative bodies fail to act. Publics tend to trust courts, because courts rely on a process that is accepted as yielding proper decisions. The constrained court model, however, holds that courts are limited in what they can accomplish because of the legal framework in which they must work, their dependence on other political actors, and their lack of independent enforcement capability (Hume 2018). The dialogue model argues that, unlike under the dynamic court theory, courts act in a dialogue with other political actors whereby a court decision opens a conversation with, say, the legislative body to craft new laws to comport with the court ruling (Macfarlane 2012). Finally, the backlash model proposes that courts, as occurred in the aftermath of the 1973 US Supreme Court decision on abortion, provoke a reaction against the ruling and can thereby block the intended effects (Keck 2009).

Theories can only speculate on and attempt to explain events; consequently, none of these models purports to explain the results of all court decisions or even reactions to all decisions of any given court. Many, if not most, court decisions affect only the immediate parties to a dispute. Others present routine legal questions that understandably result in routine decisions. Still others ask only that a court interpret an ambiguous law or contract and produce, at most, tiny ripples. Only the most intrusive decisions, those that potentially alter policy or present a different way of perceiving an issue, can illustrate a dynamic or constrained court or produce a dialogue or a backlash.

The dynamic court model, the one that most judicial champions espouse, can often be linked with judicially created or protected rights that had previously been unrecognized. The proponent most often tied to this theory is Charles Epp (1998), who demonstrated how judicial actions lent muscle to previously skeletal rights in the United States, India, Great Britain, and Canada. Even his account, however, focused on how court decisions signaled to implementing audiences and created incentives for subsequent legal mobilization. He did not assert that the judicial pronouncements alone achieved substantial social or political change.

Many other researchers have argued that courts are more likely constrained in their ability to foster change and consequently often resort to strategic decision making. In those cases, courts often support government policies that might not be legally defensible, prioritizing politics over legality or illegality. In institutionally insecure environments, such as Argentina, Venezuela, and Mexico in the mid-1990s, courts were likely constrained because of the tenuous nature of judges' tenure in office (Helmke 2005). The same critique was offered regarding the European Court of Justice, because that court presumably often acted strategically to avoid being overridden by governments of member states (Carrubba, Gabel, and Hankla 2008), although that argument has been challenged (Stone Sweet and Brunnell 2012). Even the US Supreme Court has been depicted as constrained and therefore as adopting obfuscating language to avoid conflicts with a politically hostile Congress (Owens, Wedeking, and Wohlfarth 2013). Courts can also be constrained in conflicts between military and civilian authorities, as was the case in Colombia, Peru, and Mexico in the latter part of the twentieth century. The constrained courts in those situations chose to position themselves as mediators between the competing authorities by avoiding creation of winners and losers in their decisions (Ríos-Figueroa 2016).

The backlash theory of judicial impact most commonly relies on the consequences of the 1954 decision of the US Supreme Court to force racial desegregation of public schools (Rosenberg 1991), but was more recently applied in the United States to reactions to judicial treatment of homosexuality (Keck 2009). Efforts to avoid backlash reactions were demonstrated in the case of the Mexican Supreme Court, which attempted to publicize its decisions to garner public support and preempt negative reactions (Staton 2006). The dialogue theory of impact has been most closely associated with the South African Supreme Court (Klug 2013), but has been disproved in the Canadian context. Interestingly, the absence of a dialogue between judicial and legislative authorities in Canada has been attributed to the inclination of legislators to dutifully acquiesce to court rulings (Macfarlane 2012).

What prompts individual litigants or political actors to comply, as Canadian legislators apparently do, or to choose another response? Much can be explained as self-regulation, when people believe they are obliged to comply and the laws imposed are consistent with their values (Tyler 2008). The clarity of the decision, the effectiveness of its communication, and the political environment of the implementing audiences also drive choices about compliance versus other courses of action (Canon and Johnson 1999). The degree of fragmentation or the porousness of institutional structures impedes the implementation of any public policy, including ones made by judges (Epp 2008). Fragmentation that interferes with implementation may not be only institutional, but also ideological or partisan.

DISPUTE RESOLUTION (MICRO LEVEL)

The overwhelming majority of the work that courts do involves resolving disputes between litigants seeking distribution of some good, service, or right and not issuing policy pronouncements. Decisions in individual cases, particularly at the trial level, can nonetheless have an impact beyond the direct parties to a case. Yet individual, private law cases are also very fact specific and, even more complicating, usually involve only orders, not explanatory opinions. Therefore, generalizing about outcomes can be risky at best. However, large damage awards in one case may offer an incentive to negotiate settlements in subsequent ones. Likewise, severe penalties in criminal cases or a penchant to favor one gender over another in child custody disputes may signal to other potential litigants what to expect if their cases are pursued. Ripple effects result from some individual private law litigation, as well as criminal cases, at least within localized jurisdictions. Even authoritarian regimes employ courts through private litigation to monitor low-level bureaucratic malfeasance as well as to impose social control (Magaloni 2008).

Thus, when the Chinese government became concerned in the early twenty-first century about the growth of excessive private debt following a binge of commercial and individual borrowing and about the murky, unregulated, shadow banking system that lent considerable sums to fuel lavish purchases and acquisitions, it turned to its courts. Wu Xiaohui had risen from working as a car salesman to owning the extensive Anbang Insurance Group. The company under Wu's leadership had borrowed heavily to make purchases such as the Waldorf Astoria Hotel in New York City and other famous properties. Wu was arrested in 2017 and in the next year was convicted of fraudulently taking more than $10 billion from investors. Wu was sentenced to eighteen years in prison, and the government mounted a month-long campaign in advance of the sentencing to publicize the criminality behind Anbang's financial rise. Though the specific case involved only a single corporation and a single businessman, a motive driving the conviction and lengthy sentence was to send a message—ripple effects—to other large, overleveraged Chinese conglomerates (Stevenson 2018).

The activity of courts in handling legal disputes depends on both supply and demand. Accessibility, public perceptions of judicial

> **BOX 7.2** | **Ripple Effects of Trial Court Decisions**
>
> In January 2016 Salam Aldeen, the Danish founder of the non-profit Team Humanity, and four others were arrested by Greek authorities during the Syrian refugee crisis for illegally bringing migrants into Greece. The five were volunteers who rescued people whose boats were in peril as they made their way from Turkey to the Greek Island of Lesbos in the Aegean Sea. The charges were viewed by many as criminalizing humanitarian acts, but reactions to the almost historic migration into Europe provoked by the Syrian Civil War made the case a politically charged one.
>
> More than two years later, a Greek court on Lesbos cleared the five of all charges. The five men, from Denmark and Spain, were freed and allowed to return to their native countries, but the case had much larger implications. It signaled to national authorities, particularly those bordering the Mediterranean Sea where most immigrants attempted marine crossings, that courts were not likely to uphold similar arrests. Thus, future arrests and prosecutions might be considered differently.
>
> *Source:* Niki Kitsantonis, "Migrant Rescuers Cleared in Greece," *New York Times*, May 8, 2018, A-11.

impartiality, and the legal rules available drive the supply side. The legal rules in even the most mundane disputes reflect politics; "laws are how politics communicates with judges and how judges know what is expected of them" (Gauri and Brinks 2008, 17). The demand side of the calculus to resort to courts to resolve conflicts assumes its shape from the availability of competent legal assistance, and legal talent usually requires considerable financial resources. Thus, although exceptions can be found, financial realities generally mean that private legal claims are more likely to be brought by the more affluent than by underprivileged segments of society (Gauri and Brinks 2008). Courts cannot initiate actions, but must wait for controversies to be brought to them, and a number of countries, notably Japan, have devised alternative avenues for individuals to assert legal claims (Haley 2018). Nevertheless, the financial wherewithal needed to pursue legal claims has largely excluded the poor. In Brazil, for example, health litigation has been used to force the government to provide expensive medical treatments, but only for those who can afford to assert their claims in court (Ferraz 2011). A right to housing, while recognized by the South African Constitutional Court, has not been translated into individual relief for anyone lacking shelter (Khosla 2018).

The impact of court decisions in private litigation before judges tends to be limited. Ripple effects may occur, but they are most likely contained within the purview of a given legal community and probably pursued only by those possessed of more than meager means. That does not minimize the consequences of judicial resolution of controversies, but often what occurs at the micro-individual level has few, if any, consequences beyond the parties to the case.

POLICY AND INSTITUTIONAL CHANGE (MACRO LEVEL)

Conventional wisdom holds, and is supported by dramatic examples from around the world, that courts cause major shifts in policies. The dynamic court model suggests that such is the normal result of court activities, and thus macro-level effects constitute the primary focus of those studying impact. Did a judicial decision actually change something for people beyond the immediate litigants in a case? As noted previously, one school of thought, represented by Gerald Rosenberg (1991), argues that courts do not cause or even nudge social change. The opposing view, that typically associated with the writings of Charles Epp (1998), claims that courts can and do serve as catalysts for social change if a decision can spark legal mobilization. Most likely, reality lies somewhere between those two poles and varies according to specific judicial pronouncements, the political and economic climate, and the proclivities of other political actors and public opinion. To attribute impact to a judicial decision, one must look also at the concentric circles that radiate out from a decision, the immediate and more distant ripple effects.

Macro effects of court decisions tend to be linked primarily to the use of constitutional review, though corruption cases involving political elites or decisions regarding elections can also trigger social or political shifts. The very act of a court's intervening in public policy choices raises the question of what role judges should play in politics, both in democracies and in authoritarian regimes. When high courts inject themselves into making policy choices, are they invading the political space allotted to legislatures and executives or rather acting, at least in the context of democratic governments, to protect rights from overbearing governments and the rights of those minorities who, by definition, cannot be protected at the ballot box (Bricker 2016)? The implications or impact of court decisions rest, though, on assumptions that are potentially more important.

Judicial decisions, be they from trial or from constitutional courts, cannot self-execute, but rather "hinge on responses from a wide array of actors" (Rodríguez-Garavito, 2010, 1674), ranging from other government actors and other courts to legal activists, the media, and potential litigants. In each instance, those implementing or interpreting a judicial decree weigh the "correctness" of the decision against their own values and the appropriateness of a court's rather than the legislature's making that determination. Usually, executives and legislatures are the most proximate institutions affected by a high court decision and hold the options of complying with, defying, ignoring, or evading the intended outcomes of the ruling. Legislatures may choose to override the decision, and executives may (or may not) implement them as they see fit (Carrubba, Gabel, and Hankla 2008). In the United States, congressional overrides of court interpretations of laws—excluding declarations of unconstitutionality—occur frequently and often with little or no publicity (Eskridge 2014). American state legislatures are more likely, on the other hand, to react more immediately to rulings on constitutionality by their own courts than to ones by the US Supreme Court (Bosworth 2017). Implementation beyond the immediate parties to a case typically relies on lower courts to follow faithfully the policy dictates of a constitutional court. Lower courts often provide the essential link in enforcement. Ideological differences have been theorized as playing a role in how lower courts apply decisions of the US Supreme Court, but even so, hierarchical control appears to be powerful and effective (Westerland et al. 2010).

Courts presumably want their decisions to be enforced and may therefore act strategically to fashion rulings that may prove more palatable to those on whom the court must rely to obtain implementation. That means that the rights or goods that should, at least theoretically, drive judicial decisions may be tempered in light of potential reactions (Bricker 2016). Thus, for example, when the Italian Constitutional Court was called upon in 2015 to consider the validity of the so-called Robin Hood Tax, which had been passed to achieve a balanced national budget, it considered the significant financial implications of a "normal" ruling of unconstitutionality. The court adopted the language of "reasonableness" in its decision to maintain the constitutional mandate of a balanced budget and to uphold a discriminatory tax imposed to reach that goal (Bergonzini 2016). On the other hand, the Colombian Constitutional Court did not seek to make social policy, but rather was drawn into decisions on campaign financing scandals, extradition policies, and demilitarized zones. It failed to act strategically and was met by significant attempts in the legislature to limit its authority (Cepeda-Espinoza 2004).

One avenue available to courts for both self-protection and enhancement of the potential for compliance with their decisions lies in public opinion. Public opinion has been demonstrated to affect the US Congress's inclination to act against the highest court (Clark 2009). Similarly, in Poland before the national populist wave, the Constitutional Court acted more boldly when its position was bolstered by public support (Bricker 2016). Courts therefore often attempt to woo public support by, for example in Germany, holding public oral hearings to enhance the visibility of possible controversial cases. In Mexico, likewise, the Supreme Court mounts public relations campaigns, complete with detailed press releases, to publicize what could be divisive decisions (Staton 2006).

Courts attempt, in other words, to secure compliance with their judgments, but are those efforts successful? The intersection of the micro with the macro can be helpful in assessing how successful implementation of court decisions is. One study of social and economic rights in five countries estimated how many people actually benefited from social policy decisions issued by their nations' highest courts that involved (1) a demand on the government for a service or good at the state's expense; (2) regulation of a good or service such as health care; and (3) rights in public service, such as rights in education as opposed to an education. Brinks and Gauri (2012) estimated that almost eight million people in Brazil directly benefited from health litigation, whereas fewer than 350,000 gained from similar court rulings in South Africa. Many conclusions might be inferred about the variation in magnitude between those two countries, but the more important finding is that judicial decisions by the highest court in each country positively impacted many multiples beyond those who were parties to the cases. The

> **BOX 7.3** | **Public Reaction to Sentences**
>
> During the famous running of the bulls in Pamplona, Spain, in 2016, five men sexually assaulted a woman, but according to the three-judge panel that tried the case, did not rape her. The prosecutor had sought twenty-three-year terms for gang rape, but the men were instead each given nine years in prison for the lesser offense of sexual abuse. The judicial decision that the men's actions constituted sexual abuse instead of rape was based on Spain's criminal code, which stipulated that rape must involve violence or intimidation.
>
> More than thirty-five thousand people protested in Pamplona after the sentencing decision. The association of Spanish judges called for the resignation of the Spanish minister for justice for having questioned the handling of the case, and the Spanish government promised to review how rape is defined in the 1995 criminal code.
>
> *Source:* From Raphael Minder, "Spanish Officials Defend Justiciary as Protesters Fume over Sexual Assault Case," *New York Times*, April 30, 2018, A-4.

impact of those decisions was government compliance that affected thousands of people.

The micro/macro impact of four student free speech decisions made by the US Supreme Court, however, presents a different twist. That court had broadly upheld free speech rights for students attending public schools and then, over the following decades, slowly reined in the expressive freedoms that students possess. The macro-level impact could be measured, though with great difficulty, by ascertaining what limitations schools continue to place on students and also the success of litigants challenging those restrictions in lower courts. However, at the micro level, the students directly involved in those four cases present a counterintuitive lesson. In three of the cases, the student litigants won before the highest US court, but the impact was not what might have been anticipated. In the first broad case, few ripple effects followed because lawyers were disinclined to take cases that offer limited monetary rewards. One student litigant felt vindicated by the court's decision and was permitted to serve as a commencement speaker. Another case, however, initially resulted in a victory but was followed by considerable subsequent litigation in retaliation against the student's father. The financial costs of the litigation and the loss of the father's job led both father and son to move (Moss 2011).

The problems of macro-level impact arise—or not—when speaking of international and transnational court decisions. Although total compliance could not be demonstrated, full compliance with the IACtHR was found in almost one-third of the cases and partial compliance in 40 percent (Reid 2018). Studies of the United Nations Charter of Human Rights show that nations signing the treaty were at least "nudged" toward compliance with the standards articulated (Simmons 2009, 355). In the case of hybrid courts, particularly those in the former Yugoslavia, civil society actors, both domestic and international, were central to achieving compliance (Lamont 2010).

If international agreements that are enforced in courts achieve compliance, that impact can reach across several countries. Achieving even one-third compliance, as was attributed to rulings of the IACtHR, exerts significant positive changes in the lives of thousands. Yet discerning impact across several countries presents measurement and methodological challenges. Those problems are compounded where conflicts were averted because of the existence of an enforcing court or when the threat of litigation forced a resolution.

DO COURTS MATTER?

Federalist 78 offers a time-honored depiction of judiciaries as the least dangerous branch of government, having "neither force nor will, but only judgement . . . [dependent on] the aid of the executive arm for the efficacy of its judgements" ([1787] 1970, 504). Those words, penned to persuade during the ratification of the US Constitution in 1789, aimed to mollify fears of a judicial power "altogether unprecedented in a free country" (Storing 1985, 163). Indeed, more than two-thirds of the Anti-Federalists opposing the constitution found problems with the proposed US federal judiciary (Main 1961), and the eighteenth-century experiment with a wholly independent judiciary with the power of constitutional review was the ancestor to most contemporary constitutional and international/transnational courts and even many trial courts. Though judges have been empowered in many parts of the world, some basic limitations on their authority remain constant.

Courts everywhere serve as passive actors that cannot seek the conflicts or controversies that come before them. Some event must trigger a dispute, and someone must approach a court seeking resolution. Thus, will is absent. So likewise is force, since courts do not control, at least directly, a police or military contingent to impose their decisions on recalcitrant actors. Compliance with court decisions depends on both litigants and enforcers. The impact of court rulings must always be seen as filtered by factors beyond the control of judges.

The difficulty in assessing direct impact of court decisions resides in the attribution of causality. Did a court decision prompt a change in policy, or was public and political sentiment coincidentally shifting at the proximate time of a decision? Did a lag occur between a judicial ruling and a policy change that muddies ascertainment of a court's role in the final outcome? Did a court decision merely ratify an existing, but perhaps not legally sanctioned, activity, such as homosexual conduct or extramarital sexual relations? Were ripple effects from a court decision visible, though not directly related? Does a ruling directly affect the legal system, such as lower court actions, but have no further ramifications?

The questions surrounding the impact of judicial decisions are numerous. Some potentially unconstitutional policies may not be enacted because lawmakers anticipate judicial reactions (Stone Sweet and Brunnell 1998b), and earlier decisions often shape future legislative deliberations quietly to avoid legal difficulties later (Blauberger and Schmidt 2017). Legislators may likewise be emboldened to retaliate against a court if public opinion—the voters—also oppose a decision or direction in which a court appears to be moving (Clark 2009). Conversely, even for international tribunals, courts are protected if others appear inclined to punish those attacking a court or defying a ruling (Carrubba and Gabel 2015).

All of these considerations call into question the dynamic court model, in which a court makes a decision and implementation regularly follows on the part of both political actors and other affected audiences. Indeed, one of the major limitations cited in support of the constrained court model is the inability of courts to enforce their rulings, along with judges' ties to political elites that compromise independence and the necessity of public support (Rosenberg 1991). The dialogue model of high courts links most closely to places with weak form constitutional review (Tushnet 2008) and where competing political elites vie for power (Ríos-Figueroa 2016).

> **BOX 7.4** | **Public Preferences in Bermuda Override Supreme Court Decision**
>
> In May 2017, when the Bermuda Supreme Court overruled the country's law banning same-sex marriages, Winston and Greg Godwin-DeRoche won their suit to enable them to marry. Bermuda had rejected same-sex marriage in a referendum in 2016, but that apparently did not influence the decision of the British overseas territory's highest court a year later. The backlash, however, was sufficient that nine months after the court decision, the national parliament reinstated the ban. However, Parliament, in the Domestic Partnership Act of 2017, did recognize same-sex domestic partnerships, while still denying them the right to marry. The original litigants, even though they had won their case in Bermuda, were married in Canada. Eight other same-sex couples who were married in the nine-month interim between the court decision and the signing of the new law were allowed to retain their married status.
>
> *Source:* Megan Specia, "Bermuda Revokes Same-Sex Marriage," *New York Times*, February 9, 2018, A-8.

The suggested conclusion, then, is that courts must act strategically if they expect to see their decisions implemented. Judges may act or presume to act strategically or even as they perceive the law to dictate yet nonetheless miscalculate. Judges, after all, do not possess the powers of oracles or prescience in all cases. Sometimes decisions are implemented as intended, but judges have been unable to foresee the side effects that are too often, like those of some pharmaceuticals, negative (Friedman 2016).

Abortion in the United States presents one example of unintended consequences. Prior to the 1973 decision to legalize abortion, in many cases public support for liberalization was growing and opposition was disorganized. Rather than seeking a dialogue with legislative bodies, the US Supreme Court chose a legal path—privacy, which is not explicitly protected in the constitution—to forge a strictly judicial road to liberalization and excluded legislative dialogue. Thus, almost five decades later the abortion issue in the United States remains pivotal, driving many electoral choices from the presidency to legislatures and emerging as the litmus test for Supreme Court nominees on both sides of the debate (Silverstein

2009). The Supreme Court succeeded, in other words, in politicizing an issue, and the ripple effects persist some fifty years later.

More recently, the Kenyan Supreme Court became embroiled in the 2017 presidential election. An election was held August 8, 2017, but it was invalidated by the Supreme Court the next month, which declared it "invalid, null, and void" despite the fact that the court itself acknowledged no proof of systematic rigging, but rather "irregularities and illegalities" (Economist 2017f). A new election was then scheduled for late October, but the main opposition candidate withdrew. On the eve of the second election, the Kenyan Supreme Court accepted a petition to determine the credibility of the second election. However, the hearing was attended by only two of the seven judges; the hearing was canceled for lack of a quorum (Moore 2017a). The incumbent president, Uhuru Kenyatta, who had been declared the victor in the first election, won handily in the second as well, but at great expense to the national treasury ($500 million for just the first election) (Economist 2017f), a dent in the reputation of the nation's highest court, and a possible blow to democracy in East Africa.

Courts are most effective when they retain public respect and act in a guardian, not political, capacity. Are policy choices better made by judges or by those in the elected branches of government (Geyh 2016)? Potent arguments have been made on both sides of that question; clearly independent judiciaries have been demonstrated to extend the longevity of democracies (Lane and Ersson 2000), but not all court decisions achieve the desired impact. The law expressed through judicial pronouncements can serve as an instrument of social and political reforms, but they necessarily rely on a variety of audiences and allies to realize change (Epp 2008). They remain, however, a single instrument, one cog, in the machinery of government, not the only or even primary one.

8

The Legitimacy of Courts

★ ★ ★

HUMAN RIGHTS LAWYER Jiang Tianyong, who was known for his vigorous defense of dissidents, had his license to practice law in China revoked by the government in 2009, but he nonetheless continued to counsel dissidents. Consequently, in July 2015, while he was meeting with clients, he was arrested and held in secret detention until his trial a year later in the capital of Hunan Province. His trial was streamed live on the internet and shown on television news, as Mr. Jiang calmly confessed to attempting to overthrow the Communist Party. His family and supporters claimed that the confession was the result of torture during his long incarceration (Buckley 2017).

Later that year, the government of Cambodia filed a lawsuit against the opposition Cambodian National Rescue Party alleging that the CNRP was engaged in a US-backed plan to overthrow the authoritarian prime minister, Hun Sen. Within a month, the Cambodian Supreme Court, whose chief judge also holds a high-ranking post in the governing party and is a close associate of the prime minister, announced that the opposition party was officially dissolved. That ruling immediately barred all sitting parliamentarians in the opposition from continuing in their positions and prevented the party from contesting elections in the future. Members of the CNRP denied that they had any intentions beyond competing in the national elections in 2018 and hoping to gain power legally through the electoral process. No appeal is possible from decisions of the Cambodian Supreme Court; therefore the decision essentially rendered Cambodia a one-party nation for the first time since the end of the Khmer Rouge era in 1999 (Wallace 2017).

In 2018 a court in Jodhpur, India, sentenced a seventy-seven-year-old Hindu religious leader, Asaram Bapu, to life imprisonment for the rape of a sixteen-year-old peasant girl. The trial took five years, but many advocates for women's rights were heartened that a venerated Hindu leader, adored by millions and with close connections to politicians, could be convicted and harshly sentenced (Economist 2018a).

Reading about these three separate judicial decisions evokes distaste for the first two and perhaps a smile of justice served in the last. Why? What strikes us as repugnant about a rights lawyer, who may have been tortured, publicly confessing to sedition, or a judge, crony of the sitting prime minister, eliminating any meaningful opposition in the next election? What, on the other hand, seems satisfying about hearing that even a powerful man will be punished for sexually assaulting a poor young woman? One explanation can be found in how the decisions resonate in our own value systems. Another might be that our sense of "justice" or how judicial authorities wield their power evoked a response. More basic, though, is that our sense of the legitimacy of those decisions causes us to respond negatively or positively.

Legitimacy may be among the slipperiest terms in the political lexicon and, as discussed in this chapter, can be bandied about often and defined rarely. The most agreed upon definition of legitimacy—if any—is the generic one offered by Seymour Martin Lipset: "The capacity of the system to engender and maintain the belief that the existing political institutions are the most appropriate ones for society" (1963, 64). Legitimacy should not necessarily be equated with actual performance of a regime, but rather carries an evaluative connotation. As amorphous as the term may be, all topics covered in this book coalesce around it. Legal traditions, the health of the legal profession, judicial authority and independence, constitutional review, and transnational law and courts carry no significance if courts are believed to act illegitimately, and all contribute to or detract from the ability of courts to be seen as appropriate for society.

Applying the concept of legitimacy to courts poses particular difficulties. A natural tension resides between the empowerment of courts and the role of courts in dispute resolution. Triadic dispute settlement succeeds only when all parties to the litigation believe that the judge acts impartially and is wholly dispassionate about who wins and loses and what is won or lost. Judicial empowerment, however, adds a feature that potentially impinges on impartiality. What if the judge also considers the preservation or aggrandizement of power by the court or the larger judiciary when deciding a dispute? This possible dilemma emerges regardless of the legal tradition—common, civil, Islamic, or customary—and at all levels of courts in judicial hierarchies and reaches those operating outside the realm of the nation-state.

The legal profession in each national jurisdiction provides the pool from which judges are drawn, except, of course, usually in the customary legal tradition. Therefore, the availability of trained lawyers and the quality of their education affects both sides of the empowerment-impartiality equation. So too, the perceived mores, whether taught or simply absorbed, of both the legal profession and the corps of judges are important. Is a certain level of corruption, be it political or financial or personal, generally tolerated? Are allegiances to a political persuasion, ethnic or gender identity, or a religious belief accepted or even tolerated in either the legal profession or the judiciary? Is a socioeconomic hierarchy regularly considered in the outcome of cases? Any such calculation beyond the parameters set by law that enter into judicial decision making can taint the balance, particularly by compromising judicial impartiality.

The judicial role as prescribed by law—de jure—and the de facto realities of how judges decide likewise affect institutional legitimacy and that of individual judges. The latitude for action by judges largely depends on the mechanisms used for selection and the parameters set for tenure, removal, and compensation. Those limitations, as prescribed by law and described in chapter 4, are frequently warped or distorted by political realities. Nonetheless, the combination of de facto and de jure rules limiting or liberating judges, along with the political climate in which they work, determines whether judges are executors, delegates, guardians, or political. That, in turn, can be reflected in the perceptions of the proper or valid—legitimate, if you will—role for judges.

Delegate and executor judges, as discussed in chapter 4, rarely confront temptations toward judicial empowerment. Guardian and political judges may, however, consider the ramifications of some decisions for institutional or personal empowerment. Guardian and political judges typically are armed with constitutional review authority. They may therefore intrude into the political space of executives and legislatures, thereby empowering or diminishing the courts. The exercise of constitutional review provides a lure for judges to act in an empowering manner. Notably, judicial empowerment is intrinsically neither positive nor negative, but minimizing or expanding the possible authority of the courts affects public and elite perceptions of the propriety of judicial decisions.

The inability of judges to enforce their decisions directly may be the most constraining factor for judicial empowerment. Total dependence on a variety of audiences to interpret and apply judicial decisions can render courts impotent, however impartial and faithful to the law they may be. Why then do political actors implement court decisions that they find distasteful, and why does the public accept rulings of the courts? The evaluative belief or perception that the courts and their decisions are legitimate nurtures or even forces compliance. In democratic regimes, public—electoral—perceptions are important, but even in authoritarian regimes some segment of political actors must likewise embrace that view. The legitimacy of lawmakers, laws, and courts undergirds the rule of law. The law itself, however, is not neutral; "it favors some values or policies, it favors certain groups within society" (Hendley 1996, 115). Law is produced by a political process, but rational-legal authority constitutes "the pillar of legitimacy in our contemporary world" (Friedman 2016, 197). Without it, judicial pronouncements, even impartial ones, lack sway. Legitimacy stands as especially important for courts, which lack any independent coercive power. Courts, unlike other political actors, lack an electoral mandate and are usually only indirectly accountable or answerable to the public. Courts need institutional legitimacy for acquiescence to their decisions, particularly controversial or politically charged ones (Vibert 2007). The ante is upped even higher for international and transnational courts (Helfer and Alter 2013; Grant and Keohane 2004). The conflicting and at times contradictory treatment of institutional legitimacy has not, however, diminished the consensus that institutional legitimacy remains "the most important political capital courts possess" (Gibson 2008, 59).

DEFINING AND RECOGNIZING LEGITIMACY

The legitimacy of a country, government, leaders, laws, and institutions shares many properties with the element of mercury. One cannot quite pin it down, but it can be useful when carefully confined and calibrated in a thermometer. Though we seek to define the term with some precision, doing so may be akin to US Supreme Court justice Potter Stewart's famous 1961 comment about obscenity in Jacobellis v. Ohio: "I know it when I see it." At the same time, however, no more salient quality exists for courts than that they be seen as legitimate. Democracies presumptively gain legitimacy through elections, if elections are believed to be free and fair. Many nations, of course, are not democracies, though they may be quasi-democracies. And violation or evasion of law occurs in those regimes if people see them as illegitimate (Friedman 2016). In failed democracies or even failed states, like Sudan, if law replaces violence, the government may be illegitimate, but its authority is accepted (Massoud 2013). Citizens and subjects, not nation-states, comply with or consent to governments and implicitly confer legitimacy; consequently, a given regime may be viewed as legitimate by some but not by others (Hardin 2007).

Relying on Lipset's (1963) definition, how do we know what institutions are appropriate for society? Courts in particular must be cast as legitimate for the rule of law to flourish, but the phrase "rule of law" proves almost as elusive as the term legitimacy. Most scholars accept the notion that the rule of law constitutes a condition in which the government is not the product of a single will (Sánchez-Cuenca 2003). The absence of the rule of law can perhaps best be captured in the likely apocryphal proclamation of French king Louis XIV, "L'Etat, c'est moi" ("The State is me"). Thus, dictatorships cannot by definition produce the rule of law. Rather, the common statement that no one is above the law, that a "set of stable political rules and rights appl[y] impartially to all citizens" (Weingast 1997, 245) may best approximate the essence of the rule of law. That condition exists where people trust their government and "perceive that government is producing outcomes consistent with their expectations" (Hetherington 2007, 9).

The rule of law and government legitimacy are not synonymous, but the twin concepts tend to be mutually reinforcing. The rule of law can be ascertained a bit more readily than can legitimacy. When political, economic, and other elites follow the same rules as everyone else and are punished equivalently when they do not, the active presence of the rule of law exists. Legitimacy, on the other hand, relies on individual beliefs or perceptions, which makes getting a handle on the absence or presence of it difficult. Therefore, scholars use indicators or manifestations of legitimacy or illegitimacy to attempt to discern when it exists. Diffuse support

(Gibson, Caldeira, and Baird 1998), institutional loyalty (Bülmann and Kunz 2011), reservoir of goodwill (Gibson and Nelson 2016), and confidence (Bülmann and Kunz 2011) can each reflect legitimacy. Every one of these indicators captures how the public can disapprove of any specific law, policy, or decision but still support the institution responsible for it.

How then can courts achieve and sustain confidence, trust, diffuse support, or a reservoir of goodwill in the public's eyes? Many courts, though hardly all, are perceived as being outside of politics and carry a reputation for rectitude and expertise (Tate 1995). A degree of symbolism, often cultivated by courts, tends to underscore a sense of moral authority in judiciaries. Courts rely on a different style of decision making, once couched in the language of law and jurisprudential doctrine (Callander and Clark 2017; Bartels 2009). Procedural fairness is typically believed to drive judicial decisions, rather than the rough and tumble of negotiation and bargaining that characterizes political decisions. At the root of each of these assumed traits of courts and judges is the belief that courts act independently of political elites and impartially with respect to who wins and who loses. Thus, we are skeptical when a Chinese human rights lawyer who has been secretly detained confesses to sedition or when a Cambodian court effectively eliminates all opposition to the ruling regime.

Courts perceived as exhibiting the traits of independence and impartiality seemingly can sustain goodwill even in the face of unpopular decisions. The US Supreme Court, for example, ventured into the heart of partisan politics in 2000 when it decided the case of *Bush v. Gore*, which determined the outcome of a presidential election. Though the framing of the case influenced perceptions—"stealing the election" versus "purely legal concerns"—diffuse support for or the legitimacy of the US highest court remained high (Nicholson and Howard 2003). Moreover, even when US citizens fully recognize the ideological and partisan motives behind some Supreme Court decisions, they grant the court legitimacy and believe that the justices exercise their discretion in a principled manner (Gibson and Caldeira 2011). The newer South African Constitutional Court does not, on the other hand, benefit from perceptions of legitimacy sufficient to garner compliance or acquiescence with its decisions (Gibson and Caldeira 2003).

Public perceptions of a court's performance vary by issue areas. Some people pay greater attention to labor-management disputes, whereas others care about the processing of criminal cases, and yet others are interested in freedom of expression. Sadly, most people have only a vague notion of what judiciaries or high courts do, much less about the decisions that result, but most nonetheless have a sense of the legitimacy or illegitimacy of a court's rightful ability to make a decision. A court's reservoir of goodwill or legitimacy also changes with issues.

CREATING, SUSTAINING, AND FORFEITING LEGITIMACY

Courts and governments can exercise authority through systems of reward and punishment, but those constitute expensive and not always effective mechanisms. Institutions that possess the quality of legitimacy, alternatively, are able to foster compliance with their orders through a sense of obligation to obey (Tyler 2008). How, then, are courts able to create an aura of legitimacy around their actions that can compel compliance? A court's or the courts' reputation for impartiality is paramount. As discussed in chapter 1, the entire premise behind seeking a neutral third party to resolve a dispute rests on the belief that the intervening mediator does not favor either party; the situation is not two against one. Potentially politically divisive issues, such as deciding claims to disputed land in the aftermath of South Africa's system of apartheid, were successfully handled by the Lands Claim Court in large part because of its reputation for impartiality (Farmbry and Harper 2005). Maintenance of perceptions of impartiality and, indeed, the essence of it is best assured when the judiciary as an institution is independent. Preservation of institutional independence generally depends on the actions of other institutional players. Courts have proven to be the most institutionally protected when governmental power is fragmented and party competition is robust (Ríos-Figueroa 2007). That typically holds true for advanced democracies, but a study of a broader group of ninety-seven democracies demonstrated that in developing democracies, intense political competition diminishes the institutional independence of judiciaries (Aydin 2013).

Institutional independence is valued because it presumably fosters impartiality in decisions in individual cases. In the context of determining winners and losers, detachment stands as paramount, but who should legally win or lose in any given case is not always readily apparent. Individual people form their opinions about courts from their own experiences (Bülmann and Kunz 2011), and consequences of judicial decisions frequently reach beyond the immediate parties and involve other institutions of the regime. When the action of another political institution or actor is in question, the practice of deference may be the more viable avenue for creating and sustaining the legitimacy of the courts. That is, of course, if the other political actor did not clearly act wrongly. Legal criteria for making that call are often vague and imprecise. What constitutes "reasonable?" What does "clearly" mean? In such situations, what makes the court's "reasonable" solution preferable to that of another political institution (Vermeule 2007)? A show of deference, not to be confused with subservience, allows courts to lay the foundation for mutual respect of their decisions by other political authorities.

Many courts, particularly high courts, choose to create a particular image by maintaining a relatively low profile, as befits an institution exercising moral authority, and by surrounding themselves with symbolic trappings, such as the robes worn by many judges, to enhance that appearance. Courts, like any other institution, must still be visible to gain public legitimacy. To form attitudes, whether negative or positive, people need information. For example, almost a quarter of a century ago, Gibson and Caldeira (1995) surveyed Europeans about the legitimacy of or diffuse support for the European Court of Justice, the highest court of the EU. Most people were relatively unaware of the court. Hence, without knowledge, diffuse support was minimal. Attitudes toward the court, not surprisingly, ran parallel to public perceptions of the court's parent organization. People who were skeptical or nonsupportive of the EU similarly withheld support for its highest court. The European Court of Justice was a relatively new and consequently unknown entity, which also suggests that the longevity of a court influences the extent of the reservoir of goodwill that the public grants to it. That may explain part of the vulnerability of courts in new democracies.

Should courts look to public opinion, the source of their legitimacy, when making decisions? The logic of judicial impartiality and the expected role of courts in protecting minority rights in liberal democracies would argue against that. However, the US Supreme Court has been shown to follow public opinion on at least some issues (McGuire and Stimson 2004). Moreover, as noted previously, constitutional courts tend to act more boldly and less deferentially when bolstered by high levels of public support. Do the judges choose that course consciously?

The institutional independence of courts and consequently their ability to act impartially are most likely to be in peril where courts are most empowered, when they may exercise constitutional review. Likewise, institutional legitimacy may also be at greatest risk. Courts in democracies in particular have become progressively more empowered. The dicey aspect of the use of constitutional review lies in its potential to reflect or to be interpreted as an assertion of institutional rivalry (Vanberg 2000), rather than as an explication of the law.

Constitutional review has both its advocates and its critics. It provides an avenue for minorities and the poor to seek protection, but conversely, it may also allow an unelected, socioeconomic elite to substitute its will for those with democratic accountability gained at the ballot box (Tate 1995). It can monitor the boundaries of legal actions by political institutions and, through the interpretative process, give life to the law. For others, it stifles deliberative democracy (Stone Sweet 2000).

Whatever virtues or vices may be attributed to constitutional review, the power has been granted to courts or a court, at least on paper, in more than half of the nations in the world. The issue therefore becomes, how do courts empowered with constitutional review use that authority in a manner that does not compromise their legitimacy? Too often, the judicialization of politics can lead to politicization of the judiciary (Domingo 2004), which in turn has the potential to strip courts of their claim to moral authority, procedural fairness, and formal reasoning based on rectitude and expertise. Indeed, constitutional review can aggravate "the pathologies of representative democracy" (Fox and Stephenson 2011) more than facilitate democratic goals.

A number of factors come into play, whether the judges are conscious of them or not, in responding to petitions for constitutional review. Many scholars discount the role that the actual written law, particularly constitutions, assumes in judicial decisions, because "legal rules are often indeterminate and do not always yield a single right answer to the questions raised" (Dyevre 2010, 311). If the "law" does not offer at least some constraint on judges' decisions, what guides them? Consistency can be a major factor, even in non-common-law countries, if only to signal to potential litigants what the probabilities of winning might be if litigation is pursued. That leaves the policy preferences of judges, internal bargaining on collegial courts, and strategic calculations of possible response of legislators and the executive as the determining factors (Dyevre 2010).

The debate over the meaning of the Second Amendment to the US Constitution and the US Supreme Court's 2008 decision may prove illustrative. Naturally, one may merely speculate about what influenced that decision beyond the written law and judicial precedents, but the Second Amendment states succinctly: "A well-regulated militia being necessary to the security of a free state, the right of the people to keep and bear arms shall not be infringed." In the case of *District of Columbia v. Heller* (2008), the majority of the highest court interpreted that provision as protecting one's right to possess firearms in the home for self-defense. In the preceding year, respected Harvard law professor Mark Tushnet (2007) published a scholarly analysis of the arguments, law, and precedents that were relevant to the meaning of the Second Amendment and concluded that whether gun control or gun rights advocates had a stronger case depended on the interpretive tools followed. However, in his own words, "gun control advocates have a significantly stronger case than their adversaries if . . . [the issue] is treat[ed] as an ordinary constitutional question" (2007, 71). A majority of the Supreme Court reached the opposite conclusion.

If judges employ constitutional review to reach a conclusion that would not be reached using the ordinary judicial tools, how does that decision achieve legitimacy? Remember that legitimacy attaches to institutions, not through understanding or agreeing with any single decision. Rather, legitimacy can best be understood as a reservoir of goodwill that may be deep or shallow and diffuse support. Most US citizens, even those who are advocates for both sides of the firearms debate, are unaware of and likely uninterested in the reasoning used by the country's highest court, and probably even fewer read the Tushnet analysis. Even though most people comprehend that judges on the highest US court decide cases based on their ideological and political biases, they still accord legitimacy to judicial decisions because of the perception that the decisions are principled and sincere (Gibson and Caldeira 2011).

The legitimacy of judicial institutions hinges on their interpretations of law, and "law, then, cannot be detached from political systems and behaviors" (Massoud 2013, 5). Courts, even in more vexed political systems, such as the military tribunals in the

Israeli-occupied territories of Palestine, derive their legitimacy through respect for the institution, its compatibility with the larger national criminal system, and recognition that the occupied territories were not part of Israel. Thus, the legitimacy of the court system hangs on the perceived legitimacy of the state (Hajjar 2005).

The accepted linkage that courts' legitimacy depends to a large measure on the perceived legitimacy of the political regime appears to be contradicted by empirical realities or perhaps by who assigns a label to a regime as legitimate or not. The World Values Survey, a global network of social scientists, conducts survey waves across the world to ascertain beliefs and values. The 2010–2014 survey included sixty countries and eighty-five thousand respondents. One question asked:

> I am going to name a number of organizations. For each one, could you please tell me how much confidence you have in them? Is it a great deal of confidence, quite a lot of confidence, not much confidence, or none at all? The courts.

Rather than listing all sixty countries' responses, table 8.1 presents the Leaders (highest confidence ratings) and Laggards (lowest confidence ratings) (World Values Survey 2017). Of the top nine countries where courts have achieved the highest levels of confidence, Germany and Sweden are the only Western nations included. Qatar, number 1, and Jordan, number 7, are both Middle Eastern monarchies. Hong Kong is now governed from Beijing, and Singapore is autocratic. Many readers may have to consult a map to locate the Central Asian nation of Uzbekistan or the South Pacific country of Malaysia. Even China ranked ahead of Germany. The Laggards are not quite as surprising, as all except Russia have suffered from civil wars, abrupt regime changes, or political instability in recent years. In the United States, only 8.9 percent of the respondents had a great deal of confidence in the courts, and 44.9 percent had quite of lot of confidence. Australia, New Zealand, and Spain were in the same range (World Values Survey 2017).

How does one interpret these counterintuitive results? The most obvious inference that can be made relates to the expectation that only democracies can nurture judiciaries with high levels of legitimacy. Not so. The other apparently fallacious assumption defied by these findings is that Western values are most conducive to institutional legitimacy. Yet, if one returns to Lipset's classic

Table 8.1 Confidence in Courts

	Great Deal of Confidence (%)	Quite a Lot of Confidence (%)	Total Confidence (%)
Leaders			
Qatar	66.9	23.9	90.8
Hong Kong	38.0	47.5	85.5
Singapore	25.1	58.2	83.3
Uzbekistan	53.8	28.4	82.2
Malaysia	25.7	54.5	80.2
Sweden	18.6	56.9	75.0
Jordan	42.6	30.9	73.5
China	21.1	50.0	71.1
Germany	17.0	54.3	64.3
Laggards			
Peru	3.7	13.7	17.4
Argentina	2.9	15.6	18.5
Yemen	5.0	15.3	20.3
Slovenia	2.4	22.3	24.7
Ukraine	3.0	22.2	25.2
Chile	2.8	23.4	26.2
Armenia	3.4	26.4	29.8
Trinidad & Tobago	6.9	24.3	31.2
Russia	4.9	27.6	32.5

Source: World Values Survey, 2010–2014. http://www.worldvaluessurvey.org/WVSOnline.jsp.

definition, legitimacy involves "the belief that the existing political institutions are the most appropriate ones for the society" (1963, 64). Obviously, those residing in Qatar, Hong Kong, Singapore, China, and other highly ranked nations perceive that the judicial systems of their countries are indeed the most appropriate ones for their societies. Naturally, people "make inferences and draw conclusions about particular institutions based on their general values and preferences" (Caldeira and Gibson 1995).

CONCLUSION

How should we view and assess courts: our own national ones, those in other places, and those acting outside of the nation-state? Presumably the World Values Survey findings challenge us to discard some of our preconceived notions and ethnocentric biases. Therein lies one of the virtues of studying political phenomena comparatively. The study of comparative politics also teaches that generalizing across nations and societies is a fraught exercise.

A basic question that must guide comparative inquiry, particularly when the focus is law, courts, and politics, must be: What are we trying to explain? In social science parlance, what is the dependent variable? Is the focus on dispute resolution or on judicial intrusion into public policy? Is it the ability of transnational or international courts to alter national behavior? Is it what guides judges in reaching their conclusions? Often the answers to any of these questions cross-nationally will vary. What comparative analysis cannot do is determine that any given system serves in all contexts as better than others.

Most scholars concede that institutional legitimacy undergirds whatever authority courts possess. In authoritarian regimes, the significant coercive power of the state may serve to bolster the authority of judicial decisions, but does that make the authority of the courts more or less legitimate? The answer depends largely on what indicator is appropriate to ascertain and measure legitimacy, a term that is inherently evaluative. In an authoritarian regime, legitimacy may depend less on the attitudes of the populace than on those holding the levers of power. Yet even in China and Singapore people have greater confidence in their courts than do those in much of Europe and North America. More important, is confidence in the judicial apparatus equivalent to legitimacy?

More questions than answers arise. Some of those questions remain, nonetheless, basic to our understanding of how courts and judges resolve disputes and conserve or expand judicial power. Neither dispute resolution nor empowerment counts unless courts have the legitimacy to achieve compliance with their decisions and attitudinal changes that align with their rulings (Gibson and Caldeira 2003). These goals remain as important for resolution of individual disputes as for decisions addressing highly charged political controversies.

Most of the attention and contention about courts and their proper role in the political sphere focus on constitutional review. Though constitutional review had been largely a peculiarity of the US political system until after World War II, it was adopted widely as a standard feature of constitutions written or rewritten after the end of that war and again in the aftermath of the Cold War near the conclusion of the twentieth century. The inclusion of provisions for constitutional review was driven by a recognition that some institution was needed to definitively interpret constitutions, which are otherwise no more than "words, texts, pieces of paper" (Friedman 2016, 198). Whether short and vague like the US document or detailed and long as has become the vogue, considerable latitude resides in constitutions for interpretation and discretion (Friedman 2016).

The second motivation for adoption of constitutional review in more recent constitutions was the new push to protect human rights. A rights culture emerged following World War II, heralded by the adoption of the United Nations Universal Declaration of Human Rights in 1948. Those rights were proclaimed as universal, "truly transnational" (Piana, 2010, 55). The precise enumeration of rights in national constitutions, however, varies (Friedman 2016), and the legal tradition of a country emerges most strongly when those rights are compared. Most customary legal traditions rely on human hierarchies, and some strands of the Islamic legal tradition tend to parcel out rights by gender. But whatever rights can be found in the texts and words of constitutions are reduced to mere rhetoric if they cannot be enforced (Friedman 2016). The protection of human rights has proven to be more closely tied to de facto judicial independence than to the presence of constitutional review authority (Volcansek and Lockhart 2012).

Both catalysts for incorporating constitutional review—definitive interpretation and human rights protection—are laudable and rational. How, though, are judges to establish and preserve legitimacy when deciding the constitutional validity of actions of other institutional and political actors, especially those that infringe rights? Do they follow John Hart Ely's (1980) admonition to restrict themselves to a purely referee role, do they test potential solutions against the political posturing a decision might provoke (Fox and Stephenson 2011), or do they substitute their policy preferences for those of other political actors? The judicial dilemma, then, is that best stated by James Gibson: "Judges' decisions are a function of what they prefer to do, tempered by what they think they ought to do, but constrained by what they perceive is feasible to do" (1983, 9). The legitimacy of courts and judges may be jeopardized if they are perceived as following their personal preferences, not understanding the feasible limits of their activity, or ignoring what they ought to do.

Four ideal categories of judges are discussed in chapter 4, and those ideal types can serve to illustrate how judges exercising constitutional review can potentially shore up or forfeit legitimacy. Executor judges are limited by both low autonomy and low authority. As such, they are unlikely to possess constitutional review authority. The Chinese judiciary might be characterized as executors (Cabestan 2005); being held outside the political sphere, they garner little visibility but, according to the World Values Survey, have achieved a goodly measure of confidence or legitimacy. Delegate judges, with little autonomy but significant discretion, might also attain a high level of goodwill unless the absence of secure tenure in office leads them to be subservient to the government in power and skews their interpretation and application of the law.

Guardian judges have limited discretion but strong insulation for their positions. Such judges are well-positioned to accumulate a reservoir of goodwill because their independence allows them to act with neither fear nor favor. Their constricted purview for judicial creativity makes their intrusion into the most hotly contested controversies unlikely. Guardian judges, because of their secure autonomy, may be more likely to protect fundamental rights against the state, despite their presumably limited field of action (Guarnieri and Pederzoli 2002). Political judges are most likely to wade into public view and political controversy because they are well-protected in office and have been granted a high level of discretion. How those twin attributes are employed likely determines the measure of legitimacy they enjoy. Political judges are best equipped to be perceived as both empowered and activist. Notably, activist almost always carries a pejorative connotation, because of the implication that the judiciary encroaches on the rightful prerogatives of other political actors. Consequently, whether judges are empowered or activist depends largely on the policy domain in question and the perceptions of those assessing court decisions.

Political judges or courts risk jeopardizing legitimacy most when they too boldly challenge either other political actors or deeply held societal values. The risks are more precarious in new or consolidating democracies, in which courts do not benefit from a lengthy history that allows them to build both familiarity and respect. Courts in Bulgaria, Hungary, and Poland, for example, acted quite decisively in the first decade after the establishment of democracy at the end of the Communist era. Where uncertainty affected the political realm, as in Bulgaria, judicial-political conflicts resulted (Magalhães 1999). Later, with populist parties in control of government, the courts in Poland and Hungary emerged quickly as targets of the populist regimes. A study of eight post-Communist nations—Czech Republic, Estonia, Georgia, Latvia, Lithuania, Moldova, Russia, and Slovakia—concluded that the new constitutional courts acted as political ones when the party systems were fragmented and when the courts held a good measure of popular trust and confidence (Smithey and Ishiyama 2002).

Courts do not function in a vacuum but are embedded in larger political frameworks and environments. Thus, the workings of other mechanisms in political systems inevitably affect how courts are perceived and treated. The desirable balance between courts and other institutional and political actors can be located differently for democracies, quasi-democratic regimes, and authoritarian ones. In authoritarian systems and probably some quasi-democratic regimes, courts venture into the political arena at their peril. Even so, courts can act as executors or delegates and decide disputes in ways that are perceived to be fair. Fulfilling that function seemingly satisfies the public and facilitates the flourishing of judicial legitimacy, as the World Values Survey results demonstrate. Constitutional review, where it might be conferred, is best exercised sparingly and prudently.

Courts in many democracies, primarily where constitutional review authority has been placed in a judicial body, may enter willingly or be thrust or pulled into the more bare-knuckle world of politics and be called upon to referee boundaries among political institutions and assert individuals' rights against government agencies or other possibly powerful interests. Self-restraint on the part of judges in the political fray presents a safe and viable strategy, but that course of action can also erode the rule of law and deprive people of human rights. A single judicial decision may be unpopular, but because of broader public support for the courts, not damaging to legitimacy (Gibson and Nelson 2016). Power configurations within government and society prove crucial, then, to conservation of both judicial authority and legitimacy. Political pluralism is essential to the preservation of courts' viability, independence, and legitimacy (Dargent 2011), because one-party states deny courts potential support from the opposition. Competitive elections emerge as crucial to the efficacy of courts, particularly when deciding political controversies or against the regime (Ríos-Figueroa 2007). Even in democracies that practice political pluralism and hold fair, competitive elections, courts are more efficacious when intervening in the political sphere if a self-enforcing equilibrium imposes self-restraint upon all institutions and protects the weakest, the judiciary.

Many courts and court systems have survived bruising battles with other political institutions and emerged with their legitimacy, that wellspring of political goodwill, intact. The US Supreme Court stands as an exemplar of that conclusion. That court benefits from longevity and visibility. The Supreme Court has similarly survived the rise of political realism, which has revealed that political rule makers, including judges, behave according to a different set of evaluative standards (Erman and Möller 2018). Citizens of the United States, in other words, recognize that judges' decisions are influenced by a wide array of factors, including partisan and ideological ones. Nevertheless, "they continue to express confidence in the courts; but that does not mean that they necessarily approve of extralegal stimuli driving judicial decisions" (Geyh 2016, 77). Gibson and Caldeira (2011) explain this paradox by asserting that the public views the partisan or ideological predilections of judges as being applied in a "principled" way.

Courts that engender high levels of public confidence employ the symbols of fairness and legality (Gibson and Caldeira 2011). They also follow prescribed procedures that are designed to give the appearance of "judicial competence, integrity, impartiality, and independence" (Geyh 2016, 106). Both civil and common law traditions design procedures, at least theoretically, to attain applications of the law that are "known to all, equally applicable to all, and offering equal protection to all" (Vibert 2007, 119). Presumably, customary and Islamic legal traditions also seek consistency in rulings, albeit within the hierarchies of those traditions. No system can guarantee that all decisions treat the litigants fairly in all instances, in part because the law too often is obscure and parties to cases are hardly alike (Vibert 2007). Perceptions that the machinery of justice strives to accomplish fairness creates the aura that courts and their judgments are legitimate. Legitimacy, after all, bears an emotive rather than a moral or an empirical quality (Hardin 2007). Even when judges render decisions that make public policy, people seem to understand that "policy is not the same as politics" (Friedman 2016, 199).

The credibility of political institutions—including courts—began to be assertively challenged in a number of democracies as the twenty-first century entered its second decade. Populist parties of both the Left and the Right challenged and often defeated established political parties across Europe, and a populist movement drove Great Britain's exit from the EU and placed outsider Donald Trump as president of the United States. Even the Philippines and Brazil were not immune to the populist wave. A coherent definition of "populism" is elusive, but most varieties of it share two common traits: an anti-elite bias and a distrust of globalism and global governance systems. Courts and judges became targets of both strands, because judges share the label of elites and courts reside staunchly in the so-called establishment. If global governance systems are assailed, then the courts that enforce their rules are likewise under attack.

Scholars bemoan the possible "end to the democratic century" (Mounk and Foa 2018), attempt to diagnose the malady that is affecting democracies (Inglehart 2018), and prescribe means for saving democracy (Mead 2018). Perhaps liberal democracy is not a panacea. A corollary to that implicates courts, particularly those exercising constitutional review. If liberal democracy relies on courts exercising constitutional review to protect those who are unprotected via the ballot box, what rationale remains for their authority? What fate awaits courts in democratic systems when confidence in them—their legitimacy—is lower in democratic nations than in authoritarian or quasi-democratic countries, as the World Values Survey has demonstrated?

The value of analyzing courts around the world and attempting to learn from how other places seek to locate fairness and integrity in their judicial apparatus has rarely seemed more timely. Have courts in liberal democracies been empowered excessively or insufficiently? What characteristics of courts in Qatar, Hong Kong, and Singapore inspire such high levels of public support and legitimacy? Do courts have a role to play in improving living standards, policing boundaries on immigration, and setting limitations to religious expression?

Courts help to define the rules of the game, both at the political and individual levels. They interpret constitutions, laws, and contracts, all of which are not imposed externally but rather develop within a political context (Marsh and Olsen 1984). Courts serve as the linchpin for the rule of law and, as Alexis de Tocqueville marveled after his visit to the United States in 1831, judges' decisions are followed even when they run counter to the wishes of public officials. What de Tocqueville observed in the United States is, of course, the basic element of the rule of law. The rule of law took root first in Europe and North America and then spread. Guillermo O'Donnell wondered if the rule of law could flourish when "the tradition of individual autonomy is weak or disputed and where deep inequality persists" (2000, 28). An apt question. The rule of law requires courts and judges to exist, and understanding the varied routes to establishing courts that are perceived as legitimate in the public's eye can lead to the creation and preservation of all important elements of the rule of law and human rights.

References

★ ★ ★

Abel, Richard L. 1973. A Comparative Theory of Dispute Institutions in Society. *Law & Society Review*, 8: 249–347.
Abbott, Frederick M. 2000. NAFTA and the Legalization of World Politics: A Case Study. *International Organization*, 54: 519–47.
Abbott, Kenneth W., Robert O. Keohane, Andrew Moravcsik, Anne-Marie Slaughter, and Duncan Snidal. 2000. The Concept of Legalization. *International Organization*, 54: 401–19.
Abbott, Kenneth W., and Duncan Snidal. 2000. Hard and Soft Law in International Governance. *International Organization*, 54: 421–56.
Agabin, Pacifico. 2012. The Philippines. In Vernon Valentine Palmer (ed.), *Mixed Jurisdictions Worldwide: The Third Legal Family*. Cambridge, UK: Cambridge University Press, 452–80.
Alberts, Susan. 2009. How Constitutions Constrain. *Comparative Politics*, 41: 127–43.
Albertyn, Catherine. 2005. Defending and Securing Rights through Law: Feminism, Law and the Courts in South Africa. *Politikon*, 32: 217–37.
Allee, Todd L., and Paul K. Huth. 2006. Legitimizing Dispute Settlement: International Legal Rulings as Domestic Political Cover. *American Political Science Review*, 100: 219–34.
Almond, Gabriel A., and G. Bingham Powell Jr. 1996. *Comparative Politics: A Theoretical Framework*. New York: HarperCollins College Publishers.
Alter, Karen J. 2006. Private Litigants and the New International Courts. *Comparative Political Studies*, 39: 22–49.
———. 2008. Delegating to International Courts: Self-Binding vs. Other-Binding Delegation. *Law and Contemporary Problems*, 71: 37–76.

———. 2011. The Global Spread of European Style International Courts. *West European Politics*, 35: 135–54.

———. 2014. *The New Terrain of International Law*. Princeton, NJ: Princeton University Press.

Alter, Karen J., and Laurence R. Helfer. 2010. Nature or Nurture? Judicial Lawmaking in the European Court of Justice and the Andean Tribunal of Justice. *International Organization*, 64: 563–92.

Alter, Karen J., and Jeanette Vargas. 2003. Explaining Variation in the Uses of European Litigation Strategies. *Comparative Political Studies*, 33: 452–482.

Amar, Vikram David, and Mark V. Tushnet. 2009. *Global Perspectives on Constitutional Law*. New York: Oxford University Press.

Amaral-Garcia, Sofia, Nuno Garoup, and Veronica Grembi. 2009. Judicial Independence and Party Politics in the Kelsenian Constitutional Courts: The Case of Portugal. *Journal of Empirical Legal Studies*, 6: 381–404.

American Lawyer. 2015. 2015 Global 100: Top-Grossing Law Firms in the World. https://www.law.com/americanlawyer/almID/1202471809600/2015-Global-100-TopGrossing-Law-Firms-in-the-World-/ (accessed 10/2/18).

Anderson, J. N. D. 1959. *Islamic Law in the Modern World*. New York: New York University Press.

Aust, Anthony. 2010. *Handbook of International Law*. Cambridge, UK: Cambridge University Press.

Aydin, Aylin. 2013. Judicial Independence across Democratic Regimes: Understanding the Varying Impact of Political Competition. *Law and Society Review*, 47: 105–34.

Badrinarayana, Deepa. 2014. India's State of Legal Education: The Road from NLSIU to Jindal. *Journal of Legal Education*, 63: 521–23.

Barsotti, Vittoria, Paolo G. Carozza, Marta Cartabia, and Andrea Simoncini. 2016. *Italian Constitutional Justice in Global Context*. Oxford: Oxford University Press.

Bartels, Brandon L. 2009. The Constraining Capacity of Legal Doctrine on the U.S. Supreme Court. *American Political Science Review*, 103: 474–95.

Bartlett, Nicola. 2015. Adultery: Which Countries Are the Most Unfaithful? *Mirror*, February 29. https://www.mirror.co.uk/news/world-news/adultery-countries-most-unfaithful-5188791 (accessed 9/9/2018).

Basabe-Serrano, Santiago. 2014. Determinants of Judicial Dissent in Contexts of Extreme Institutional Instability. *Journal of Politics in Latin America*, 6: 83–107.

Baum, Lawrence. 1997. *The Puzzle of Judicial Behavior*. Ann Arbor: University of Michigan Press.

———. 2006. *Judges and Their Audiences*. Princeton, NJ: Princeton University Press.

BBC. 2015. Burundi: Court Backs President Nkurunziza on Third Term. *BBC News*, May 5. http://www.bbc.com/news/world-africa-32588658 (accessed 6/30/2016).
Becker, Theodore L. 1969. *The Impact of Supreme Court Decisions*. New York: Oxford University Press.
Becker, Theodore L., and Malcolm M. Feeley. 1973. *The Impact of Supreme Court Decisions*. 2nd ed. New York: Oxford University Press.
Beer, Caroline C. 2006. Judicial Performance and the Rule of Law in Mexican States. *Latin American Politics and Society*, 40: 33–62.
Belge, Ceren. 2006. Friends of the Court. *Law and Society Review*, 40: 653–92.
Benesh, Sara C., and Wendy L. Martinek. 2012. Lower Court Compliance with Precedent. In Kevin T. McGuire (ed.), *New Directions in Judicial Politics*. New York: Routledge, 259–76.
Bergonzini, Chiara. 2016. The Italian Constitutional Court and Balancing the Budget. *European Constitutional Law Review*, 12: 177–91.
Berman, Harold J. 1983. *Law and Revolution: The Formation of the Western Legal Tradition*. Cambridge, MA: Harvard University Press.
Beširević, Violeta. 2015. Governing Without Judges: The Politics of the Constitutional Court in Serbia. *I-Con*, 12: 954–79.
Biddulph, Sarah. 2010. Legal Education in the People's Republic of China. In Stacey Steel and Katheryn Taylor (eds.), *Legal Education in Asia*. London: Routledge, 260–77.
Bizimana, Syldie, Jean-Claude Burakarafitiva, and Javier Ncanatwi. 2012. Update: The Burundi Legal System and Research. http://nyulawglobal.org/globalex/burundi.html (accessed 6/29/2016).
Blauberger, Michael. 2014. National Responses to European Court Jurisprudence. *West European Politics*, 37: 457–74.
Blauberger, Michael, and Susanne K. Schmidt. 2017. The European Court of Justice and Its Political Impact. *West European Politics*, 40: 907–18.
Bliss, Lisa. 2014. Lessons Learned from Teaching Clinical Legal Education in Thailand. *Journal of Legal Education*, 63: 524–31.
Blondel, Jean. 1995. *Comparative Government: An Introduction*. London: Prentice-Hall.
Bonneau, Chris W., and Melinda Gann Hall. 2009. *In Defense of Judicial Elections*. London: Routledge.
Bosworth, Matthew H. 2017. Legislative Responses to Unconstitutionality. *Journal of Law and Courts*, 5: 243–66.
Bowen, John R. 2000. Consensus and Suspicion: Judicial Reasoning and Social Change in an Indonesian Society, 1960–1994. *Law and Society Review*, 34: 97–127.
———. 2007. Fairness and Law in an Indonesian Court. In R. Mark Feener and Mark E. Cammack (eds.), *Islamic Law in Contemporary Indonesia*. Cambridge, MA: Harvard University Press, 170–92.

Brace, Paul, Jeff Yates, and Brent D. Boyea. 2012. Judges, Litigants, and the Design of Courts. *Law and Society Review*, 46: 497–522.

Brenner, Saul, and Harold J. Spaeth. 1995. *Stare Indecisis: The Alteration of Precedent on the Supreme Court, 1946–1992*. Cambridge, UK: Cambridge University Press.

Brewer-Carías, Alla R. 2009. *Constitutional Protection of Human Rights in Latin America: A Comparative Study of Amparo Proceedings*. Cambridge, UK: Cambridge University Press.

Bricker, Benjamin. 2016. *Visions of Judicial Review*. Colchester, UK: ECPR Press.

Brinks, Daniel M. 2003. Informal Institutions and the Rule of Law. *Comparative Politics*, 36: 1–19.

———. 2005. Judicial Reform and Independence in Brazil and Argentina. *Texas International Law Journal*, 40: 595–622.

Brinks, Daniel M., and Varun Gauri. 2008. A New Policy Landscape: Legalizing Social and Economic Rights in the Developing World. In Daniel M. Brinks and Varun Gauri (eds.), *Courting Social Justice: Judicial Enforcement of Social and Economic Rights in the Developing World*. Cambridge, UK: Cambridge University Press, 303–52.

———. 2012. The Law's Majestic Equality? The Distributive Impact of Litigating Social and Economic Rights. http://openknowledge.worldbank.org/bitstream/handle/10986/3287/W155199.pdf?sequence=1 (accessed 4/13/2018).

Brodie, Ian. 2002. *Friends of the Court: The Privileging of Interest Group Litigants in Canada*. Albany: State University of New York Press.

Brouard, Sylvain. 2009a. The Constitutional Council: The Rising Regulator of French Politics. In Sylvain Brouard, Andrew M. Appleton, and Amy G. Mazur (eds.), *The French Fifth Republic at Fifty*. Houndsmills, UK: Palgrave Macmillan, 99–117.

———. 2009b. The Politics of Constitutional Veto in France. *West European Politics*, 32: 384–403.

Brouard, Sylvain, and Christoph Hönnige. 2017. Constitutional Courts as Veto Players. *European Journal of Political Science*, 56: 529–52.

Brown, Nathan J. 1997. *The Rule of Law in the Arab World: Courts in Egypt and the Gulf*. Cambridge, UK: Cambridge University Press.

Buckley, Chris. 2017. Chinese Rights Lawyer Confesses to Subversion. *New York Times*, August 23, A-5.

Bühlmann, Marc, and Ruth Kunz. 2011. Confidence in the Judiciary: Comparing the Independence and Legitimacy of Judicial Systems. *West European Politics*, 34: 317–45.

Busch, Marc L. 2007. Overlapping Institutions, Forum Shopping and Dispute Settlement in International Trade. *International Organization*, 61: 735–61.

Cabestan, Jean-Pierre. 2005. The Political and Practical Obstacles to the Reform of the Judiciary and the Establishment of a Rule of Law in China. *Journal of Chinese Political Science*, 10: 43–64.

Caldeira, Gregory A., and James L. Gibson. 1995. The Legitimacy of the Court of Justice in the European Union: Models of Institutional Support. *American Political Science Review*, 89: 356–76.

Callander, Steven, and Tom S. Clark. 2017. Precedent and Doctrine in a Complicated World, *American Political Science Review*, 111: 184–203.

Calvert, Randall L., Matthew D. McCubbins, and Barry R. Weinghast. 1989. A Theory of Political Control and Agency Discretion. *American Journal of Political Science*, 33: 588–611.

Cameron, Charles M., and Jonathan P. Kastellec. 2016. Are Supreme Court Nominations a Move-the-Median Game? *American Political Science Review*, 110: 778–97.

Cammack, Mark E., Helen Donovan, and Tim V. Heaton. 2007. Islamic Divorce Law and Practice in Indonesia. In R. Mark Feener and Mark E. Cammack (eds.), *Islamic Law in Contemporary Indonesia*. Cambridge, MA: Harvard University Press, 99–127.

Cann, Damon M., Chris W. Bonneau, and Brent D. Boyea. 2012. Campaign Contributions and Judicial Decisions in Partisan and Nonpartisan Elections. In Kevin T. McGuire (ed.), *New Directions in Judicial Politics*. New York: Routledge, 38–52.

Cann, Damon M., and Jeff Yates. 2008. Homegrown Institutional Legitimacy. *American Politics Research*, 36: 297–329.

Canon, Bradley C., and Charles A. Johnson. 1999. *Judicial Policies: Implementation and Impact*. Washington, DC: CQ Press.

Carlson, Kerstin Bree. 2017. International Criminal Law and Its Paradoxes. *Journal of Law and Courts*, 5: 33–53.

Carp, Robert A., Ronald Stidham, and Kenneth L. Manning. 2014. *Judicial Process in America*. Los Angeles, CA: Sage.

Carnwath, Robert. 2004. Do We Need a Supreme Court? *Political Quarterly*. https://doi.org/10.1111/j.1467-923X.2004.00609.x.

Carroll, Wayne. 2004. Liberalization of National Legal Admissions Requirements in the European Union. *Pennsylvania State International Law Review*, 22: 563–87.

Carrubba, Clifford J. 2006. Courts and Compliance in International Regulatory Regimes. *Journal of Politics*, 67: 669–89.

Carrubba, Clifford J., Matthew Gabel, and Charles Hankla. 2008. Judicial Behavior under Political Constraints: Evidence from the European Court of Justice. *American Political Science Review*, 102: 435–52.

———. 2012. Understanding the Role of the European Court of Justice in European Integration. *American Political Science Review*, 106: 214–22.

Carrubba, Clifford J., and Matthew J. Gabel. 2015. *International Courts and the Performance of International Agreements*. Cambridge, UK: Cambridge University Press.

Carter, Connie. 2010. Specialized Intellectual Property Courts in the People's Republic of China. In Andrew W. Harding and Penelope (Pip) Nicholson (eds.), *New Courts in Asia*. London: Routledge, 101–18.

Carter, Sarah. 2015. Update: A Guide to the UK Legal System. http://www.nyulawglobal.org/globalex/United_Kingdom1.html (accessed 5/18/17).

Casey, Nicholas. 2018. Bolivia Tells President His Term Is Up. *New York Times*, January 28, A-6.

Central Alberta Community Legal Clinic. 2017. Enforcing a Court Judgement by a Writ of Enforcement. http://www.communitylegalclimic.net/programs-services/dial-a-law/enforcing-a-court-judgement (accessed 4/25/2018).

Cepeda-Espinosa, Manuel José. 2004. Judicial Activism in a Violent Context: The Origin, Role, and Impact of the Colombian Constitutional Court. *Washington University Global Studies Law Review*, 3: 629–700.

Chavez, Rebecca Bill. 2003. The Construction of the Rule of Law in Argentina: A Tale of Two Provinces. *Comparative Politics*, 35: 417–37.

———. 2004. *The Rule of Law in Nascent Democracies: Judicial Politics in Argentina*. Stanford, CA: Stanford University Press.

———. 2007. The Appointment and Removal Process for Judges in Argentina: The Role of Judicial Councils and Impeachment Juries in Promoting Judicial Independence. *Latin American Politics and Society*, 49: 33–55.

Cheeseman, Nick. 2011. How an Authoritarian Regime in Burma Used Special Courts to Defeat Judicial Independence. *Law and Society Review*, 45: 801–30.

Chen, Thomas Chih-Hsuiung. 2012. Legal Education Reform in Taiwan. *Journal of Legal Education*, 62: 32–65.

Chua, Lynette J. 2014. *Mobilizing Gay Singapore: Rights and Resistance in an Authoritarian State*. Philadelphia: Temple University Press.

CIA World Factbook. 2016. Africa: Burundi. http://www.cia.gov/library/publications/resources/the-world-factbook/.

———. 2017. U.S. Department of State: Diplomacy in Action. http://www.cia.gov/library/publications/the-world-factbook (accessed 8/2/2017).

Cichowski, Rachel A. 2007. *The European Court and Civil Society: Litigation, Mobilization, and Governance*. Cambridge, UK: Cambridge University Press.

Clark, Tom S. 2006. Judicial Decision Making during Wartime. *Journal of Empirical Legal Studies*, 3: 397–419.

———. 2008. A Principal-Agent Theory of En Banc Review. *Journal of Law, Economics, and Organization*, 25: 55–79.

———. 2009. The Separation of Powers, Court Curbing, and Judicial Legitimacy. *American Journal of Political Science*, 53: 971–89.

———. 2011. *The Limits of Judicial Independence*. Cambridge, UK: Cambridge University Press.

Cochrane, Joe. 2017. Christian Governor in Indonesia Found Guilty of Blasphemy Against Islam. *New York Times*, May 9. https://www.nytimes.com/2017/05/09/world/asia/indonesia-governor-ahok-basuki-tjahaja-purnama-blasphemy-islam.html (accessed 9/9/2018).

Cohen, Davis. 2007. "Hybrid" Justice in East Timor, Sierra Leone, and Cambodia: "Lessons Learned" and Prospects for the Future. *Stanford Journal of International Law*, 43. https://heinonline.org/HOL/LandingPage?handle=hein.journals/stanit43&div=5&id=&page= (accessed 9/29/2007).

Collins, Paul M., and Lauren A. McCarthy. 2017. Friends and Interveners: Interest Group Litigation in a Comparative Context. *Journal of Law and Courts*, 5: 55–80. https://www.journals.uchicago.edu/doi/abs/10.1086/690275 (accessed 9/10/18).

Comella, Victor Ferreres. 2011. The Rise of Specialized Constitutional Courts. In Tom Ginsburg and Rosalind Dixon (eds.), *Comparative Constitutional Law*. Cheltenham, UK: Edward Elgar, 265–77.

Constituteproject.org. 2015. Burundi Constitution, 2005. https://aceproject.org/ero-en/regions/africa/BI/burundi-constitution-2005-english (accessed 7/16/2016).

Conti, Joseph A. 2008. The Good Case: Decisions to Litigate at the World Trade Organization, *Law and Society Review*, 42: 145–81.

Couso, Javier A. 2003. The Politics of Judicial Review in Chile in the Era of Democratic Transition, 1990–2002. *Democratization*, 10: 70–91.

———. 2005. The Judicialization of Chilean Politics: The Rights Revolution That Never Was. In Rachel Siedler, Line Schjolden, and Alan Angell (eds.), *The Judicialization of Politics in Latin America*. New York: Palgrave, 105–30.

Crisis Group. 2016. Burundi: A Dangerous Third Term. https://www.crisisgroup.org/africa/central-africa/burundi/burundi-dangerous-third-term (accessed 9/10/2018).

Dahl, Robert A. 1957. Decision-Making in a Democracy. *Journal of Public Law*, 6: 279–98.

Dam, Kenneth W. 2006. Legal Institutions, Legal Origins, and Governance. John M. Olin Program in Law and Economics Working Paper No. 303.

Damaška, Mirjan R. 1986. *The Faces of Justice and State Authority: A Comparative Approach to the Legal Process*. New Haven, CT: Yale University Press.

Dargent, Eduardo. 2011. Determinants of Judicial Independence: Lessons from Three "Cases" of Constitutional Courts in Peru (1982–2007). *Journal of Latin American Studies*, 41: 251–78.

Davis, Christina L., and Yuki Shirato. 2007. Firms, Governments, and WTO Adjudication: Japan's Selection of WTO Disputes. *World Politics*, 59: 274–313.
De Burca, Gráinne. 2008. Developing Democracy Beyond the State. *Columbia Journal of Transnational Law*, 46:101–58.
De Franciscis, Maria Elisabetta. 1996. Italy. In Mary L. Volcansek (ed.), *Judicial Misconduct: A Cross-National Comparison*. Gainesville: University Press of Florida, 49–66.
De Groot-Van Leeuwen, Leny E. 2006. Merit Selection and Diversity in the Dutch Judiciary. In Kate Malleson and Peter H. Russell (eds.), *Appointing Judges in an Age of Judicial Power: Critical Perspectives from around the World*. Toronto: University of Toronto Press, 145–58.
De Poorter, Jurgen C. A. 2013. Constitutional Review in the Netherlands. *Utrecht Law Review*, 9: 89–105.
De Sousa Santos, Boaventura. 2006. The Heterogeneous State and Legal Pluralism in Mozambique. *Law and Society Review*, 40: 39–75.
De Vos, Christian M., Sara Kendall, and Carsten Stahn. 2015. Introduction. In Christian M. De Vos, Sara Kendall, and Carsten Stahn (eds.), *Contested Justice: The Politics and Practice of International Criminal Court Interventions*. Cambridge, UK: Cambridge University Press, 1–20.
Della Porta, Donatella. 2001. A Judge's Revolution? Political Corruption and the Judiciary in Italy. *European Journal of Political Research*, 39: 1–21.
Dickens, Charles. (1853) 1996. *Bleak House*. London: Penguin Books.
Domingo, Pilar. 2002. Judicial Independence: The Politics of the Supreme Court in Mexico. *Journal of Latin American Studies*, 32: 705–35.
———. 2004. Judicialization of Politics or Politicization of the Judiciary? Recent Trends in Latin America. *Democratization*, 11: 104–126.
Dotan, Yoav. 1999. Public Lawyers and Private Clients: An Empirical Observation on the Relative Success Rates of Cause Lawyers. *Law & Policy*, 21: 401–25.
Driscoll, Amanda, and Michael J. Nelson. 2015. Judicial Selection and the Democratization of Justice. *Journal of Law and Courts*, 3: 1–35.
Dunoff, Jeffrey L., and Joel P. Trachtman (eds.). 2009. *Ruling the World? Constitutionalism, International Law, and Global Governance*. Cambridge, UK: Cambridge University Press.
Dyevre, Arthus. 2010. Unifying the Field of Comparative Judicial Politics: Towards a General Theory of Judicial Behavior. *European Political Science Review*, 2: 297–327.
———. 2015. Technocracy and Distrust: Revisiting the Rationale for Constitutional Review. *International Journal of Constitutional Review*, 13: 30–60.
Economist. 2017a. Bleak House. July 1, 39.

———. 2017b. Brazil's Painful Political Purge. July 15, 32.
———. 2017c. Gay Across the Straits. June 3, 36.
———. 2017d. More Blinkered than Blind. October 14, 34.
———. 2017e. The Punishments of Sisi Fus. June 10, 48.
———. 2017f. The Rematch: Kenyan Politics. September 9, 43.
———. 2018a. Almost Getting Away with It. April 28, 36.
———. 2018b. Back to the Old Days. May 19, 39.
Edelman, Martin. 1994. *Courts, Politics, and Culture in Israel*. Charlottesville: University of Virginia Press.
eDiplomat. 2005. Burundi. http://www.ediplomat.com/np/post_reports/pr_bi.htm (accessed 6/30/2016).
EHEA. 2016. An Overview of the Bologna Process 2016. https://www.eacea.ec.europa.eu/national-policies/eurydice/files/bologna_internetz_0.pdf (accessed 5/25/17).
Ely, John Hart. 1980. *Democracy and Distrust: A Theory of Judicial Review*. Cambridge, MA: Harvard University Press.
Emont, Jon. 2017. A Shariah Experiment Becomes a Model in Indonesia. *New York Times*, January 13, A-9.
Engel, David M. 2009. Landscapes of the Law: Injury, Remedy, and Social Change in Thailand. *Law and Society Review*, 43: 61–94.
Epp, Charles R. 1998. *The Rights Revolution: Lawyers, Activists and Supreme Courts in Comparative Perspective*. Chicago: University of Chicago Press.
———. 2008. Law as an Instrument of Social Reform. In Keith E. Whittington, R. Daniel Kelemen, and Gregory A. Caldiera (eds.), *Oxford Handbook of Law and Politics*. Oxford: Oxford University Press, 595–613.
Epperly, Brad, and Monica Lineberger. 2018. Strategic Behavior of Comparative Courts. In Robert M. Howard and Kirk A. Randazzo (eds.), *The Routledge Handbook of Judicial Behavior*. New York: Routledge, 239–94.
Epstein, Lee, and Jack Knight. 1998. *The Choices Justices Make*. Washington, DC: CQ Press.
Epstein, Lee, Jack Knight, and Olga Shvetsova. 2001. Comparing Judicial Selection Systems. *William and Mary Bill of Rights Law Journal*, 10: 7–36.
Erie, Matthew S. 2009. Legal Education Reform in China through U.S.-Inspired Transplants. *Journal of Legal Education*, 59: 60–96.
Erman, Eva, and Niklas Möller. 2018. Political Legitimacy for Our World: Where Is Political Realism Going? *Journal of Politics*, 80: 525–38.
Ernst, Jeff, and Elisabeth Malkin. 2018. Honduran Leader Begins 2nd Term Amid Protests. *New York Times*, January 29, A-14.
Eskridge, William N. 2014. Congressional Overrides of Supreme Court Statutory Interpretation Decisions, 1967–2011. Yale Law School Faculty Scholarship Series, Paper-4888.

Farmbry, Kyle, and Raina Harper. 2005. Institutional Legitimacy Building in a Context of Transition: The South African Land Claims Court. *Public Administration Review*, 65: 678–86.

Faure, Michael G., and A.V. Raja. 2010. Effectiveness of Environmental Public Interest litigation in India. *Fordham Environmental Law Review*, 21: 239–94.

Federalist Papers. (1787) 1970. New York: Modern Library.

Feld, Lars P., and Stefan Voigt. 2003. Economic Growth and Judicial Independence: Cross-Country Evidence Using a New Set of Indicators. *European Journal of Political Economy*, 19: 497–527.

Feldman, Noah. 2008. Why Shariah? *New York Times Magazine*, March 16. http://www.nytimes.com/2008/03/16/magazine/16Shariah-t.html (accessed 1/8/2017).

Ferejohn, John. 2002. Judicializing Politics, Politicizing Law. *Law and Contemporary Problems*, 65: 41–69.

Ferejohn, John, and Pasquale Pasquino. 2003. Rule of Democracy and Rule of Law. In José María Maravall and Adam Przeworski (eds.), *Democracy and the Rule of Law*. Cambridge, UK: Cambridge University Press, 242–60.

Ferejohn, John, Frances Rosenbluth, and Charles Shipan. 2007. Comparative Judicial Politics. In Carles Boix and Susan C. Stokes (eds.), *The Oxford Handbook of Comparative Politics*. Oxford: Oxford University Press, 727–51.

Ferraz, Octavio Luiz Motta. 2011. Harming the Poor Through Social Rights Litigation: Lessons from Brazil. *Texas Law Review*, 89: 1643–68.

Finkel, Jodi. 2005. Judicial Reform as Insurance Policy: Mexico in the 1990's. *Latin American Politics and Society*, 47: 87–113.

———. 2008. *Judicial Reform as Political Insurance: Argentina, Peru, and Mexico in the 1990s*. Notre Dame, IN: Notre Dame Press.

Fiss, Owen M. 1993. The Right Degree of Independence. In Irwin P. Stotzsky (ed.), *Transition to Democracy in Latin America*. Boulder, CO: Westview Press, 55–72.

Flemming, Roy B., and Glen S. Krutz. 2002. Repeat Litigators and Agenda Setting on the Supreme Court of Canada. *Canadian Journal of Political Science*, 35: 811–33.

Fox, Justin, and Matthew C. Stephenson. 2011. Judicial Review as a Response to Political Posturing. *American Political Science Review*, 105: 397–414.

Friedman, Lawrence M. 2016. *Impact: How Law Affects Behavior*. Cambridge, MA: Harvard University Press.

Friedman, Tom. 2017. *Thank You for Being Late*. New York: Farrar, Straus, and Giroux.

Frison-Roche, François, and Spas-Dimitrov Sodev. 2005. The Issues Involved in the Reform of the Bulgarian Judicial System. *International Review of Administrative Sciences*, 71: 593–606.

Fu, Yulin. 2017. The Chinese Supreme People's Court in Transition. In C. H. (Remco) van Rhee and Yulin Fu (eds.), *Supreme Courts in Transition in China and the West*. Cham: Springer, 13–36.
Galanter, Marc. 1974. Why the "Haves" Come out Ahead: Speculation on the Limits of Legal Change. *Law & Society Review*, 9: 95–160.
Gallagher, Mary E. 2006. Mobilizing Law in China. *Law and Society Review*, 40: 783–816.
Gargarella, Roberto. 2004. In Search of Democratic Justice—What Courts Should Not Do: Argentina, 1983–2002. In Siri Gloppen, Roberto Gargarella, and Elin Skaar (eds.), *Democratization and the Judiciary*. London: Frank Cass, 181–97.
Garoupa, Nino, and Tom Ginsburg. 2008a. Guarding the Guardians: Judicial Councils and Judicial Independence. University of Chicago Public Law and Legal Theory Working Paper No. 250.
———. 2008b. Judicial Audiences and Reputation: Perspectives from Comparative Law. *Columbia Journal of Transnational Law*, 47: 451–90.
Garrett, Geoffrey, R. Daniel Kelemen, and Heiner Schultz. 1998. The European Court of Justice, National Governments, and Legal Integration in the European Union. *International Organization*, 52: 149–76.
Garth, Bryant G. 2008. The Globalization of the Law. In Keith E. Whittington, R. Daniel Kelemen, and Gregory A. Caldeira (eds.), *Oxford Handbook of Law and Politics*. Oxford: Oxford University Press, 245–66.
Gauri, Varum, and Daniel M. Brinks. 2008. A New Policy Landscape. In Varum Gauri and Daniel M. Brinks (eds.), *Courting Social Justice*, Cambridge, UK: Cambridge University Press, 303–52.
Gee, Graham, Robert Hazell, Kate Malleson, and Patrick O'Brien. 2015. *The Politics of Judicial Independence in the UK's Changing Constitution*. Cambridge, UK: Cambridge University Press.
Geeroms, Sofie M. F. 2014. Comparative Law and Legal Translation. In Mary Ann Glendon, Paolo G. Carozza, and Colin B. Picker (eds.), *Comparative Legal Traditions: Text, Materials and Cases on Western Law*. St. Paul, MN: West Academic, 271–78.
Geissel, Brigitte, Marianne Kneuer, and Hans-Joachim Lauth. 2016. Measuring the Quality of Democracy. *International Political Science Review*, 37: 571–79.
Gelber, Katharine. 2004. High Court Review 2003: The Centenary Year. *Australian Journal of Political Science*, 39: 331–47.
George, Alexander L., and Andrew Bennett. 2005. *Case Studies and Theory Development in the Social Sciences*. Cambridge, MA: MIT Press.
Gerring, John. 2007. The Case Study: What It Is and What It Does. In Carles Boix and Susan C. Stokes (eds.). *The Oxford Handbook of Comparative Politics*. Oxford: Oxford University Press, 90–122.

Gettleman, Jeffrey. 2015. With Burundi's President Sticking to Power, Violence Is on the Rise. *New York Times*, December 2, A-12.

———. 2016. Burundi Moves to Quit International Criminal Court, Raising Fears of Exodus. *New York Times*, October 13, A-10.

Geyh, Charles Gardner. 2008. The Endless Judicial Selection Debate and Why It Matters for Judicial Independence. http://www.repository.law.indiana.edu/facpub/55 (accessed 10/18/17).

———. 2016. *Courting Peril: The Political Transformation of the American Judiciary*. Oxford: Oxford University Press.

Gibler, Douglas M., and Kirk A. Randazzo. 2011. Testing the Effects of Independent Judiciaries on the Likelihood of Democratic Backsliding. *American Journal of Political Science*, 55: 696–709.

Gibson, James L. 1983. From Simplicity to Complexity. *Political Behavior*, 5: 7–49.

———. 2008. Challenges to the Impartiality of State Supreme Courts: Legitimacy Theory and "New-Style" Judicial Campaigns. *American Political Science Review*, 102: 59–75.

———. 2012. *Electing Judges: The Surprising Effects of Campaigning on Judicial Legitimacy*. Chicago: University of Chicago Press.

Gibson, James L., and Gregory A. Caldeira. 1995. The Legitimacy of Transnational Legal Institutions: Compliance, Support, and the European Court of Justice. *American Journal of Political Science* 39: 459–89.

———. 2003. Defenders of Democracy? Legitimacy, Popular Acceptance, and the South African Constitutional Court. *Journal of Politics*, 65: 1–30.

———. 2011. Has Legal Realism Damaged the Legitimacy of the U.S. Supreme Court? *Law and Society Review*, 45: 195–219.

Gibson, James L., Gregory Caldeira, and Vanessa Baird. 1998. On the Legitimacy of National High Courts. *American Political Science Review*, 92: 343–58.

Gibson, James L., and Michael J. Nelson. 2016. Change in Institutional Support for the U.S. Supreme Court: Is the Court's Legitimacy Imperiled by the Decisions It Makes? *Public Opinion Quarterly*, 80: 622–41.

Gillespie, John. 2011. Exploring the Limits of the Judicialization of Urban Land Disputes in Vietnam. *Law and Society Review*, 45: 241–75.

Gilligan, Michael, Leslie Johns, and B. Peter Rosendorff. 2010. Strengthening International Courts and the Early Settlement of Disputes. *Journal of Conflict Resolution*, 54: 5–38.

Ginsburg, Tom. 2001. Economic Analysis and the Design of Constitutional Courts. *Theoretical Inquiries in Law*. http://find.galegroup.com.ezproxy.tcu.edu/itx/start.do?prodId+AONE (accessed 9/29/07).

———. 2003. *Judicial Review in New Democracies: Constitutional Courts in Asian Cases*. Cambridge, UK: Cambridge University Press.

———. 2004. Transforming Legal Education in Japan and Korea. *Penn State International Law Review*, 22: 433–39.
———. 2008a. The Global Spread of Constitutional Review. In Keith E. Whittington, R. Daniel Kelemen, and Gregory A. Caldeira (eds.), *Oxford Handbook of Law and Politics*. Oxford: Oxford University Press, 81–98.
———. 2008b. The Judicialization of Politics. In Keith E. Whittington, R. Daniel Kelemen, and Gregory A. Caldeira (eds.), *Oxford Handbook of Law and Politics*. Oxford: Oxford University Press, 119–41.
Glendon, Mary Ann, Paolo G. Carozza, and Colin B. Picker. 2014. *Comparative Legal Traditions: Text, Materials and Cases on Western Law*. St. Paul, MN: West Publishing Company.
Glenn, H. Patrick. 2014. *Legal Traditions of the World*. Oxford: Oxford University Press.
Gloppen, Siri. 2004. The Accountability Function of the Courts in Tanzania and Zambia. In Siri Gloppen, Roberto Gargarella, and Elin Skaar (eds.), *Democratization and the Judiciary: The Accountability Function of Courts in New Democracies*. London: Frank Cass, 112–36.
Gloppen, Siri, Bruce M. Wilson, Roberto Gargarella, Elin Skaar, and Morten Kinander. 2010. *Courts and Power in Latin America and Africa*. New York: Palgrave Macmillan.
Graber, Mark A. 2005. Constructing Judicial Review. *Annual Review of Political Science*, 8: 425–51.
Grant, Ruth W., and Robert O. Keohane. 2004. Accountability and Abuses of Power in World Politics. International Law and Justice Working Paper 2004/7. http://www.iilj.org/wp-content/uploads/2016/11/Grant-et-al-Accountability-and-Abuses-of-Power-in-World-Politics-2004.pdf (accessed 9/10/2018).
Grendstad, Gunner, William R. Shaffer, and Eric Waltenburg. 2015. *Policy Making in an Independent Judiciary: The Norwegian Supreme Court*. Colchester, UK: ECPR Monographs.
Grisel, Florian. 2017. Competition and Cooperation in International Commercial Arbitration: The Birth of a Transnational Legal Profession. *Law and Society Review*, 51: 790–824.
Guarnieri, Carlo. 2015. The Courts. In Erik Jones and Gianfranco Pasquino (eds.), *Oxford Handbook of Italian Politics*, Oxford: Oxford University Press, 120–31.
Guarnieri, Carlo, and Patrizia Pederzoli. 2002. *The Power of Judges: A Comparative Study of Courts and Democracy*. Oxford: Oxford University Press.
Haimerl, Maria. 2017. Turkish Constitutional Court under Amended Turkish Constitution. https://verfassungsblog.de/the-turkish-constitutional-court-under-the-amended-turkish-constitution/ (accessed 12/24/2017).

Hajjar, Lisa. 2005. *Courting Conflict: The Israeli Military Court System in the West Bank and Gaza*. Berkeley: University of California Press.

Haley, John Owen. 2018. The Myth of the Reluctant Litigant. In Carroll Seron (ed.), *The Law and Society Canon*. London: Routledge, 123–54.

Hallaq, Wael B. 2002. Muslim Rage and Islamic Law. *Hastings Law Journal*. http://repository.uchastings.edu/tobriner/3 (accessed 7/13/2017).

———. 2009. *An Introduction to Islamic Law*. Cambridge, UK: Cambridge University Press.

———. 2016. Early Ijtihād and the Later Construction of Authority. In Wael B. Hallaq (ed.), *The Formation of Islamic Law*. London: Routledge, 351–66.

Hamoudi, Haider Ala. 2014. *Negotiating in Civil Conflict*. Chicago: University of Chicago Press.

Hardin, Russell. 2007. Compliance, Consent, and Legitimacy. In Carles Boix and Susan C. Stokes (eds.), *Oxford Handbook of Comparative Politics*. Oxford: Oxford University Press, 236–55.

Haveman, Roelef H. 2011. Gacaca in Rwanda: Customary Law in Case of Genocide. In Jeanmarie Fenrich, Paolo Galizzi, and Tracy Higgins (eds.), *The Future of African Customary Law*. Cambridge, UK: Cambridge University Press, 387–420.

Hawes, Colin. 2006. Improving the Quality of the Judiciary in China: Recent Reforms to the Procedures for Appointing, Promoting and Discharging Judges. In Kate Malleson and Peter H. Russell (eds.), *Appointing Judges in an Age of Judicial Power: Critical Perspectives from around the World*. Toronto: University of Toronto Press, 395–419.

Haynie, Stacia L. 1994. Resource Inequalities and Litigation Outcomes in the Philippine Supreme Court. *Journal of Politics*, 56: 752–72.

———. 1995. Resource Inequalities and Regional Variation in Litigation Outcomes in the Philippine Supreme Court, 1961–1986. *Political Research Quarterly*, 48: 371–80.

———. 1997. Courts and Revolution: Independence and Legitimacy in the New Republic of South Africa. *Justice System Journal*, 19: 167–79.

———. 2007. Experienced Advocates and Litigation Outcomes: Repeat Players in the South African Supreme Court of Appeal. *Political Research Quarterly*, 60: 443–53.

Helfer, Laurence R. 2008. Redesigning the European Court of Human Rights: Embeddedness as a Deep Structural Principle of the European Court of Human Rights. *European Journal of International Law*, 19: 125–59.

Helfer, Laurence R., and Karen J. Alter. 2013. Legitimacy and Lawmaking: A Tale of Three International Courts. *Theoretical Inquiries in Law*, 14: 479–503.

Helfer, Laurence R., and Anne-Marie Slaughter. 1997. Toward a Theory of Effective Supranational Adjudication. *Yale Law Journal*, 107: 273–391.

Hellman, Matias. 2015. Challenges and Limitations of Outreach from the ICTY to the ICC. In Christian De Vos, Sara Kendall, and Carsten Stahn (eds.), *Contested Justice: The Politics and Practice of International Criminal Court Interventions*. Cambridge, UK: Cambridge University Press, 251–71.

Helmke, Gretchen. 2005. *Courts under Constraints: Judges, Generals and Presidents in Argentina*. Cambridge, UK: Cambridge University Press.

Helmke, Gretchen, and Steven Levitsky. 2004. Informal Institutions and Comparative Politics: A Research Agenda. *Perspectives on Politics*, 2: 725–40.

Helmke, Gretchen, and Frances Rosenbluth. 2009. Regimes and the Rule of Law. *Annual Review of Political Science*, 12: 345–66.

Hendley, Kathryn. 1996. *Trying to Make Law Matter: Legal Reform and Labor Law in the Soviet Union*. Ann Arbor: University of Michigan Press.

Henisz, Witold. 2000. The Institutional Environment for Economic Growth. *Economics and Politics*, 12: 1–31.

Henrysson, Elin, and Sandra F. Joireman. 2009. On the Edge of the Law: Women's Property Rights and Dispute Resolution in Kisii, Kenya. *Law and Society Review*, 43: 39–59.

Herron, Erik S., and Kirk A. Randazzo. 2003. The Relationship Between Independence and Judicial Review in Post-Communist Courts. *Journal of Politics*, 65: 422–38.

Hetherington, Marc J. 2007. *Why Trust Matters: Declining Political Trust and the Demise of American Liberalism*. Princeton, NJ: Princeton University Press.

Hilbink, Lisa. 2007. *Judges beyond Politics in Democracy and Dictatorship: Lessons from Chile*. Cambridge, UK: Cambridge University Press.

———. 2008. Agents of Anti-Politics: Courts in Pinochet's Chile. In Tom Ginsburg and Tamir Moustafa (eds.), *Rule by Law: The Politics of Courts in Authoritarian Regimes*. Cambridge, UK: Cambridge University Press, 102–31.

Hillbrecht, Courtney. 2009. Rethinking Compliance: The Challenges and Prospects of Measuring Compliance with International Human Rights Tribunals. *Journal of Human Rights Practice*, 1: 362–79.

Himonga, Chuma. 2011. The Future of Living Customary Law in African Legal Systems in the Twenty-First Century and Beyond, with Special Reference to South Africa. In Jeanmarie Fenrich, Paolo Galizzi, and Tracy E. Higgins (eds.), *The Future of African Customary Law*. Cambridge, UK: Cambridge University Press, 31–57.

Hirschl, Ran. 2000. "Negative" Rights vs. "Positive" Entitlements: A Comparative Study of Judicial Interpretations of Rights in an Emerging Neo-Liberal Economic Order. *Human Rights Quarterly*, 22: 1060–98.

———. 2001. The Political Origins of Judicial Empowerment through Constitutionalization: Lessons from Israel's Constitutional Revolution. *Comparative Politics*, 33: 315–35.

———. 2004a. "Juristocracy"—Political, Not Juridical. *The Good Society*, 13: 6–11.

———. 2004b. *Towards Juristocracy: The Origins and Consequences of the New Constitutionalism*. Cambridge, MA: Harvard University Press.

———. 2008. The Judicialization of Politics. In Keith E. Whittington, R. Daniel Kelemen, and Gregory A. Caldeira (eds.), *Oxford Handbook of Law and Politics*. Oxford: Oxford University Press, 119–41.

———. 2010. *Constitutional Theocracy*. Cambridge, MA: Harvard University Press.

Holyoke, Thomas T. 2003. Choosing Battlegrounds: Interest Group Lobbying Across Multiple Venues. *Political Research Quarterly*, 56: 325–36.

Hofnung, Menachem, and Keren Weinshall-Margel. 2011. Judicial Rejection as Substantive Relief: The Israeli Supreme Court and the "War on Terror." In Mary L. Volcansek and John F. Stack Jr. (eds.), *Courts and Terrorism: Nine Nations Balance Rights and Security*. Cambridge, UK: Cambridge University Press, 150–68.

Hönnige, Christoph. 2009. The Electoral Connection. *West European Politics*, 32: 963–84.

Hoover, Dennis R., and Kevin R. den Dulk. 2004. Christian Conservatives Go to Court: Religion and Legal Mobilization in the United States and Canada. *International Political Science Review*, 25: 9–34.

Horobin, William. 2015. Christine Lagarde Shouldn't Face Negligence Charges, French Prosecutors Say. http://www.wsj.com/articles/christine-lagarde-shouldnt-face-negligence-charges-say-french-prosecutors-1443020724 (accessed 9/10/18).

Horowitz, Donald L. 2006. Constitutional Courts: A Primer for Decision Makers. *Journal of Democracy*, 17: 125–37.

———. 2013. *Constitutional Change and Democracy in Indonesia*. Cambridge, UK: Cambridge University Press.

Howard, A. E. 2001. Judicial Independence in Post-Communist Central and Eastern Europe. In David M. O'Brien and Peter H. Russell (eds.), *Judicial Independence in the Age of Democracy: Critical Perspectives from around the World*. Charlottesville: University Press of Virginia, 89–110.

Howard, Robert M., and Henry F. Carey. 2004. Is an Independent Judiciary Necessary for Democracy? *Judicature*, 87: 284–90.

Huang, Kuo-Chang, Chang-Ching Lin, and Kong-Pin Chen. 2014. Do Rich and Poor Behave Similarly in Seeking Legal Advice? *Law and Society Review*, 48: 193–223.

Hulls, Rob. 2017. Indigenous Courts Help to Balance the Scales. *The Australian*, June 9, 13.

Hume, Robert J. 2018. *Judicial Behavior and Policymaking*. Lanham, MD: Rowman & Littlefield.

Hurd, Ian. 2017. *How to Do Things with International Law*. Princeton, NJ: Princeton University Press.

Iaryczower, Matías, Pablo R. Spiller, and Marian Tommasi. 2002. Judicial Independence in Unstable Environments: Argentina 1935–1998. *American Journal of Political Science*, 46: 699–716.

Ietswaart, Heleen F. P. 1990. The International Comparison of Court Caseloads: The Experience of the European Working Group. *Law and Society Review*, 24: 571–93.

Inglehart, Ronald. 2018. The Age of Insecurity: Can Democracy Save Itself? *Foreign Affairs*, 97: 20–28.

Irish, Charles R. 2008. Reflections on the Evolution of Law and Legal Education in China and Vietnam. *Wisconsin International Law Journal*, 25: 243–54.

Jackson, Donald W., Michael C. Tolley, and Mary L. Volcansek. 2010. Conclusion. In Donald W. Jackson, Michael C. Tolley, and Mary L. Volcansek (eds.), *Globalizing Justice: Critical Perspectives on Transnational Law and the Cross-Border Migration of Legal Norms*. Albany: State University of New York Press, 267–78.

Jackson, Donald W., and Mary L. Volcansek. 2009. Human Rights or Trade Protection? US Politics and the World Trade Organization. *Australian Journal of Political Science*, 44: 155–72.

Jacobsohn, Gary Jefferey. 2003. *The Wheel of Law: India's Secularism in Comparative Constitutional Context*. Princeton, NJ: Princeton University Press.

Jain, M. P. 2000. The Supreme Court and Fundamental Rights. In S. K. Verman Kusum (ed.), *Fifty Years of the Supreme Court of India: Its Grasp and Reach*. Oxford: Oxford University Press, 1–101.

Jambholkar, Lakismi. 2007. Conflict of Laws. In S. K. Verman Kusum (ed.), *Fifty Years of the Supreme Court of India: Its Grasp and Reach*. Oxford: Oxford University Press, 650–81.

Janin, Hunt, and André Kahlmeyer. 2007. *Islamic Law: The Sharia from Muhammad's Time to the Present*. Jefferson, NC: McFarland and Co., Inc.

Johns, Leslie. 2009. Judicial Bias and Heterogeneity in International Courts. Paper presented at the Workshop on Law, Politics, and Human Rights at Emory University, March.

Joireman, Sandra F. 2004. Colonization and the Rule of Law: Comparing the Effectiveness of Common and Civil Law Countries. *Constitutional Political Economy*, 15: 3–20.

Jung, Jai Kwan, and Christopher Deering. 2013. Constitutional Choices: Uncertainty and Institutional Design in Democratising Nations. *International Political Science Review*, 36: 60–77.

Ka'bah, Rifyal. 2007. Islamic Law in Court Decisions and Fatwa Institutions in Indonesia. In R. Michael Feener and Mark E. Cammack (eds.), *Islamic Law in Contemporary Indonesia*. Cambridge, MA: Harvard University Press, 83–98.

Kahler, Miles. 2000. Legalization as a Strategy: The Asia-Pacific Case. *International Organization*, 54: 549–71.

Kahn-Fogel, Nicholas A. 2012. The Troubling Shortage of African Lawyers. *University of Pennsylvania Journal of International Law*, 33: 719–89.

Kanter, James. 2017. An Olio of EU Rules, Leading to Food Fights. *New York Times*, June 22, B-2.

Kapiszewski, Diana. 2011. Tactical Balancing. *Law and Society Review*, 45: 471–506.

Kapiszewski, Diana, and Matthew M. Taylor. 2008. Doing Courts Justice? Studying Judicial Politics in Latin American. *Perspectives on Politics*, 6: 741–67.

Katzenstein, Suzanne. 2014. In the Shadow of Crisis: The Creation of International Courts in the Twentieth Century. *Harvard International Law Journal*, 55: 151–209.

Kavanagh, Aileen. 2015. What's So Weak about "Weak Form Review"? The Case of the UK Human Rights Act 1998. *International Journal of Constitutional Law*, 13: 1008–39. https://academic.oup.com/icon/article/13/4/1008/2450828 (accessed 9/9/2018).

Keck, Thomas M. 2009. Beyond Backlash: Assessing the Impact of Judicial Decisions on LBGT Rights. *Law and Society Review*, 43: 151–85.

Keith, Linda Camp. 2002. Constitutional Provisions for Individual Human Rights (1977–1996): Are They More Than Mere "Window Dressing?" *Political Research Quarterly*, 55: 111–43.

Kelemen, R. Daniel. 2001. The Limits of Judicial Power: Trade-Environment Disputes in the GATT/WTO and the EU. *Comparative Political Studies*, 34: 622–50.

———. 2011. *Eurolegalism: The Transformation of Law and Regulation in the European Union*. Cambridge, MA: Harvard University Press.

Kelemen, R. Daniel, and Mitchell A. Orenstein. 2016. Europe's Autocracy Problem. *Foreign Affairs*, January 7. https://www.foreignaffairs.com/articles/poland/2016-01-07/europes-autocracy-problem (accessed 9/9/2018).

Keller, Helen, and Alec Stone Sweet. 2008. *A Europe of Rights: The Impact of the ECHR on National Legal Systems*. Oxford: Oxford University Press.

Kennedy, David. 2009. The Mystery of Global Governance. In Jeffrey L. Dunoff and Joel P. Trachtman (eds.), *Ruling the World? Constitutionalism, International Law, and Global Governance*. Cambridge, UK: Cambridge University Press, 37–68.

Khosla, Madhav. 2018. Making Social Rights Conditional: Lessons from India. *International Journal of Constitutional Law*, 8: 739–65.

King, Kimi, and James Meernick. 2005. Bringing Her Out of the Shadows: An Empirical Analysis of Sentences in Rape Cases before the International Criminal Tribunal for the Former Yugoslavia. In Mary L. Volcansek and John F. Stack Jr. (eds.), *Courts Crossing Borders: Blurring the Lines of Sovereignty*. Durham, NC: Carolina Academic Press, 183–212.

Kjeldgaard-Pedersen, Astric. 2010. The Evolution of the Right of Individuals to Seize the European Court of Human Rights. *Journal of the History of International Law*, 12: 267–306.

Klerman, Daniel M., Paul G. Mahoney, Holger Spamann, and Mark I. Weinstein. 2011. Legal Origin or Colonial History? *Journal of Legal Analysis*, 3: 379–409.

Klug, Heinz. 2013. Constitutional Authority and Judicial Pragmatism: Politics and Law in the Evolution of South Africa's Constitutional Court. In Diana Kapiszewski, Gordon Silverstein, and Robert A. Kagan (eds.), *Consequential Courts: Judicial Roles in Global Perspective*. Cambridge, UK: Cambridge University Press, 93–113.

Kommers, Donald P., and Russell A. Miller. 2012. *The Constitutional Jurisprudence of the Federal Republic of Germany*. Durham, NC: Duke University Press.

Kono, Daniel Y. 2007. Making Anarchy Work: International Legal Institutions and Trade Cooperation. *Journal of Politics*, 69: 746–59.

Koopmans, Tim. 2003. *Courts and Political Institutions: A Comparative View*. Cambridge, UK: Cambridge University Press.

Kornhauser, Lewis A. 1992. Modeling Collegial Courts II: Legal Doctrine. *Journal of Law, Economics, and Organization*, 8: 441–70.

Kornhauser, Lewis A., and Lawrence G. Sager. 1986. Unpacking the Court. *Yale Law Journal*, 96: 82–117.

Krehbiel, Jay N. 2016. The Politics of Judicial Procedures: The Role of Public Oral Hearings in the German Constitutional Court. *American Journal of Political Science*, 60: 1–16.

Krehbiel, Jay N., Matthew J. Gabel, and Clifford J. Carrubba. 2018. The European Court of Justice. In Robert M. Howard and Kirk A. Randazzo (eds.), *The Routledge Handbook of Judicial Behavior*. New York: Routledge, 467–90.

Kretzmer, David. 2002. *The Occupation of Justice: The Supreme Court of Israel and the Occupied Territories*. Albany: State University of New York Press.

Kumar, C. Raj. 2013. Legal Education, Globalization, and Institutional Excellence. *Indiana Journal of Global Legal Studies*, 20: 221–52.
Kuong, Teilee. 2011. Legal Education in Cambodia. In Stacy Steele and Kathryn Taylor (eds.), *Legal Education in Asia*. London: Routledge, 278–97.
Kushkush, Isma'il. 2015. Burundi Court Backs President's Bid for Third Term. *New York Times*, May 5 (accessed 9/9/2018).
La Porta, Rafael, Florencia López-de-Silanes, Cristian Pop-Eleches, and Andrei Shleifer. 2004. Judicial Checks and Balances, *Journal of Political Economy*, 112: 445–81.
Lamont, Christopher K. 2010. *International Criminal Justice and the Politics of Compliance*. Farnham, Surrey, UK: Ashgate.
Landa, Dimitri, and Jeffrey R. Lax. 2009. Legal Doctrine on Collegial Courts. *Journal of Politics*, 71: 946–63.
Lane, Jan-Erik, and Svante Ersson. 2000. *The New Institutional Politics: Performance and Outcomes*. London: Routledge.
Larkins, Christopher. 1996. Judicial Independence and Democratization: A Theoretical and Conceptual Analysis. *American Journal of Comparative Law*, 44: 605–26.
———. 1998. The Judiciary and Delegative Democracy in Argentina. *Comparative Politics*, 30: 423–42.
Lax, Jeffrey. 2011. The New Judicial Politics of Legal Doctrine. *Annual Review of Political Science*, 14: 131–57.
Leme de Barros, Marco Antonio Loschiavo. 2017. Constitutional Design and Brazilian Judicial Review. *Revista Opinoca Juridica*, 15: 180–206.
Lemieux, Scott E. 2017. Judicial Supremacy, Judicial Power, and Finality of Constitutional Rulings. *Perspectives on Politics*, 15: 1067–81.
Lerner, Renée Lettow. 2001. The Intersections of Two Systems: An American Trial for an American Murder in the French Cour d'Assises. In Mary Ann Glendon, Paolo G. Carozza, and Colin B. Picker (eds.), *Comparative Legal Traditions: Text, Materials and Cases on Western Law*. St. Paul: West Academic Publishing, 248–68.
Levi-Faur, David. 2005. The Political Economy of Legal Globalization. *International Organization*, 59: 451–62.
Leyland, Peter. 2007. *The Constitution of the United Kingdom: A Contextual Analysis*. Oxford: Hart Publishing.
Lijphart, Arend. 2012. *Patterns of Democracy: Government Forms and Performance in Thirty-Six Countries*. 2nd ed. New Haven, CT: Yale University Press.
Linnan, David K. 2010. "Reading the Tea Leaves" in the Indonesian Commercial Court. In Andrew Harding and Penelope (Pip) Nicholson (eds.), *New Courts in Asia*. London: Routledge, 56–80.
Linton, S., and F. K. Tiba. 2009. The International Judges in an Age of Multiple International Courts and Tribunals. *Chicago Journal of International Law*, 9: 407–70.

Linzer, Drew A., and Jeffrey K. Staton. 2015. A Global Measure of Judicial Independence, 1948–2012. *Journal of Law and Courts*, 3: 223–56.

Lipset, Seymour Martin. 1963. *Political Man: The Social Bases of Politics*. Garden City, NY: Anchor Books.

Lyman, Rick. 2017a. Plan by Poland to Control Its Courts Draws a Rebuke. *New York Times*, February 27, A-8.

———. 2017b. Poland's Siege on Democracy Targets Courts. *New York Times*, July 20, A-1.

MacCormaic, Ruadhán. 2016. *The Supreme Court*. London: Penguin Books.

Macfarlane, Emmett. 2012. Dialogue or Compliance? Measuring Legislatures' Policy Responses to Court Rulings on Rights. *International Political Science Review*, 34: 39–56.

———. 2013. *Governing from the Bench: The Supreme Court of Canada and the Judicial Role*. Vancouver: University of British Columbia Press.

MacFarquhar, Neil. 2018. Russian Court Bans Telegram App After an 18-Minute Hearing, *New York Times*, April 14, A-4.

MacKenzie, Ruth, Kate Malleson, Penny Martin, and Phillipe Sands. 2010. *Selecting International Judges: Principles, Process, and Politics*. Oxford: Oxford University Press.

MacKenzie, Ruth, Cesare Romano, Yuval Shany, and Phillipe Sands. 2010. *The Manual on International Courts and Tribunals*. Oxford: Oxford University Press.

Magalhães, Pedro C. 1999. The Politics of Judicial Reform in Eastern Europe. *Comparative Politics*, 32: 43–62.

Magaloni, Beatriz. 2008. Authoritarianism, Democracy and the Supreme Court: Horizontal Exchange and the Rule of Law in Mexico. In Scott Mainwaring and Christopher Welna (eds.), *Democratic Accountability in Latin America*. Oxford: Oxford University Press, 266–306.

Mahoney, James. 2007. Qualitative Methodology and Comparative Politics. *Comparative Political Studies*, 40: 122–44.

Main, Jackson Turner. 1961. *The Anti-Federalists: Critics of the Constitution 1781–1788*. Chicago: Quadrangle Paperbacks.

Mair, Peter. 1996. Comparative Politics: An Overview. In Robert E. Goodin and Hans-Kieter Klingmann (eds.), *A New Handbook of Political Science*. Oxford: Oxford University Press, 309–35.

Maisel, Peggy. 2006. Expanding and Sustaining Clinical Legal Education in Developing Countries. *Fordham International Law Journal*, 30: 374–420.

Malleson, Kate. 2006. Introduction. In Kate Malleson and Peter H. Russell (eds.), *Appointing Judges in an Age of Judicial Power: Critical Perspectives from around the World*. Toronto: University of Toronto Press, 3–12.

Maravall, José María. 2003. The Rule of Law as a Political Weapon. In José María Maravall and Adam Przeworski (eds.), *Democracy and the Rule of Law*. Cambridge, UK: Cambridge University Press, 261–301.

Marsh, James G., and Johan P. Olsen. 1984. The New Institutionalism: Organizational Factors in Political Life. *American Political Science Review*, 78: 734–49.

Massoud, Mark Fathi. 2013. *Law's Fragile State: Colonial, Authoritarian, and Humanitarian Legacies in Sudan*. Cambridge, UK: Cambridge University Press.

Martinsen, Dorte Sindbjerg. 2015. *An Ever More Powerful Court? The Political Constraints of Legal Integration in the European Union*. Oxford: Oxford University Press.

Matsui, Shigenori. 2006. The Protection of "Fundamental Human Rights" in Japan. In Randall Peerenboom, Carole J. Petersen, and Albert H. Y. Chen (eds.), *Human Rights in Asia: A Comparative Legal Study of Twelve Asian Jurisdictions, France and the USA*. London: Routledge, 121–57.

———. 2010. The Intellectual Property Court of Japan. In Andrew Harding and Pip Nicholson (eds.), *New Courts in Asia*. London: Routledge, 63–100.

———. 2012. The Future of Law Schools in Japan. *Journal of Legal Education*, 62: 3–31.

Mattei, Ugo. 1997. Three Patterns of Law: Taxonomy and Change in the World's Legal Systems. *American Journal of Comparative Law*, 45: 5–44.

Mayer, Lawrence C. 1989. *Redefining Comparative Politics: Promise Versus Performance*. Newbury Park, CA: Sage Publications.

McCall Smith, James. 2000. The Politics of Dispute Settlement Design: Explaining Legalism in Regional Trade Pacts. *International Organization*, 54: 137–80.

McGuire, Kevin T., and James A. Stimson. 2004. The Least Dangerous Branch Revisited: New Evidence on Supreme Court Responsiveness to Public Opinion. *Journal of Politics*, 66: 1018–35.

McQuoid, Mason D. 2013. Access to Justice in South Africa. *Oñati Socio-Legal Series*, 561–79.

Mead, Walter Russell. 2018. The Big Shift: How American Democracy Fails Its Way to Success. *Foreign Affairs*, 97: 10–19.

Meernick, James. 2011. Sentencing Rationales and Judicial Decisional Making at the International Criminal Tribunals. *Social Science Quarterly*, 92: 588–608.

Melone, Albert P. 1996. The Struggle for Judicial Independence and the Transition Toward Democracy in Bulgaria. *Communist and Post-Communist Studies*, 29: 231–43.

Melton, James, and Tom Ginsburg. 2014. Does De Jure Judicial Independence Really Matter? *Journal of Law and Courts*, 2: 188–217.

Mendelski, Martin. 2012. EU-Driven Reforms in Romania: A Success Story? *East European Studies*, 28: 23–42.

Merryman, John Henry, and Rogelio Pérez-Perdomo. 2007. *The Civil Law Tradition: An Introduction to the Legal Systems of Europe and Latin America*. Stanford, CA: Stanford University Press.

Meydani, Assaf. 2011. *The Israeli Supreme Court and the Human Rights Revolution: Courts as Agenda Setters*. Cambridge, UK: Cambridge University Press.

Michelson, Ethan. 2006. The Practice of Law as an Obstacle to Justice. *Law and Society Review*, 40: 1–38.

———. 2013. Women in the Legal Profession, 1970–2010. *Indiana Journal of Global Legal Studies*, 20: 1071–1137.

Minder, Raphael. 2018. Court Overturns Verdict Against Catalans, *New York Times*, March 4, A-5.

Minzer, Carl F. 2009. Judicial Disciplinary Systems for Incorrectly Decided Cases. *New Mexico Law Review*, 39: 63–87.

Mitchell, Sara McLaughlin, and Andrew P. Owsiak. 2018. The International Court of Justice. In Robert M. Howard and Kirk A. Randazzo (eds.), *The Routledge Handbook of Judicial Behavior*. New York: Routledge, 445–66.

Montesquieu, Baron Charles-Louis de Secondat. (1748) 1949. *The Spirit of the Laws*. Translated by Thomas Nugent. New York: Hafner Publishing Co.

Montoya, Juny. 2010. The Current State of Legal Education Reform in Latin America. *Journal of Legal Education*, 59: 545–66.

Moore, Jina. 2017a. Revote in Kenya Raises Challenges for a Young Democracy. *New York Times*, October 26, A-4.

———. 2017b. Trying to Sidestep a Potential Scandal, Burundi Quits International Criminal Court. *New York Times*, October 28, A-4.

Moral, Mert, and Efe Tokdemir. 2017. Judges "En Garde." *International Political Science Review*, 38: 264–80.

Moravcsik, Andrew. 2000. The Origins of Human Rights Regimes: Democratic Delegation in Postwar Europe. *International Organization*, 54: 217–52.

Morton, F. L. 2006. Judicial Appointments in Post-Charter Canada: A System in Transition. In Kate Malleson and Peter H. Russell (eds.), *Appointing Judges in an Age of Judicial Power: Critical Perspectives from around the World*. Toronto: University of Toronto Press, 56–79.

Moss, Scott A. 2011. The Overhyped Path from Tinker to Morse: How the Student Speech Cases Show the Limits of Supreme Court

Decisions—for the Law and for the Litigants. *Florida Law Review*, 63: 1407–57.

Mounk, Yascha, and Roberto Stefan Foa. 2018. The End of the Democratic Century: Autocracy's Global Ascendance. *Foreign Affairs*, 97: 29–38.

Moustafa, Tamir. 2003a. Law and Resistance in Authoritarian States: The Judicialization of Politics in Egypt. *Law and Social Inquiry*, 28: 883–930.

———. 2003b. Law versus the State: The Judicialization of Politics in Egypt. *American Bar Foundation*, 2003: 883–930.

———. 2007a. Mobilising the Law in an Authoritarian State: The Legal Complex in Contemporary Egypt. In Terence C. Halliday, Lucien Karpik, and Malcolm M. Feeley (eds.), *Fighting for Political Freedom: Comparative Studies of the Legal Complex and Political Liberalism*. Oxford: Hart Publishing.

———. 2007b. *The Struggle for Constitutional Power: Law, Politics, and Economic Development in Egypt*. Cambridge, UK: Cambridge University Press.

Moustafa, Tamir, and Tom Ginsburg. 2008. Introduction: The Functions of Courts in Authoritarian Politics. In Tom Ginsburg and Tamir Moustafa (eds.), *Rule by Law: The Politics of Courts in Authoritarian Regimes*. Cambridge, UK: Cambridge University Press, 1–22.

Murphy, Tim. 2011. Map: Is Adultery Illegal? http://www.motherjones.com/mojo/2011/11/is-Adultery-illegal-map (accessed 12/22/2016).

Mutua, Makau. 1999. The African Human Rights Court: A Two-Legged Stool. *Human Rights Quarterly*, 21: 342–63.

———. 2001. Justice Under Siege: The Rule of Law and Judicial Subservience in Kenya. *Human Rights Quarterly*, 23: 96–118.

Ng'wanakilala, Fumbuka. 2015. African Leaders Urge Burundi to Postpone Polls. *Reuters*, May 31. https://www.reuters.com/article/us-burundi-politics/african-leaders-urge-burundi-to-postpone-polls-idUSKBN0OG0K020150531 (accessed 8/4/2016).

Nicholson, Stephen P., and Robert M. Howard. 2003. Framing Support for the Supreme Court in the Aftermath of *Bush v. Gore*. *Journal of Politics*, 65: 676–95.

North, Douglass C., and Barry R. Weingast. 1989. Constitutions and Commitment: The Evolution of Institutions Governing Public Choice in Seventeenth-Century England. *Journal of Economic History*, 49: 803–32.

Oba, Abdulmumini A. 2011. The Future of Customary Law in Africa. In Jeanmarie Fenrich, Paolo Galizzi, and Tracy E. Higgins (eds.), *The Future of African Customary Law*. Cambridge, UK: Cambridge University Press, 58–81.

O'Brien, David M. 1996. *To Dream of Dreams: Religious Freedom and Constitutional Politics in Postwar Japan*. Honolulu: University of Hawaii Press.

———. 2006. The Politics of Judicial Selection and Appointments in Japan and Ten Southeast Asian Countries. In Kate Malleson and Peter H. Russell (eds.), *Appointing Judges in an Age of Judicial Power: Critical Perspectives from around the World*. Toronto: University of Toronto Press, 355–74.

———. 2011. Detentions and Security versus Liberty in Times of National Emergency. In Mary L. Volcansek and John F. Stack Jr. (eds.), *Courts and Terrorism: Nine Nations Balance Rights and Security*. Cambridge, UK: Cambridge University Press, 9–32.

O'Donnell, Guillermo. 1999. Horizontal Accountability in New Democracies. In Andreas Schedler, Larry Diamond, and Marc F. Plattner (eds.), *The Self-Restraining State: Power and Accountability in New Democracies*. Boulder, CO: Lynne Rienner Publishers.

———. 2000. The Judiciary and the Rule of Law. *Journal of Democracy*, 11: 25–31.

———. 2001. Democracy, Law, and Comparative Politics. *Studies in Comparative International Development*, 36: 7–36.

Olowofoyeku, A. A. 1989. The Beleaguered Fortress: Reflections on the Independence of Nigeria's Judiciary. *Journal of African Law*, 33: 55–71.

Örücü, Esin. 2008. What Is a Mixed Legal System: Exclusion or Expansion? *Electronic Journal of Comparative Law*, 12: 1–18.

Oseguera, Silvia Inclán. 2009. Judicial Reform in Mexico. *Political Research Quarterly*, 62: 753–66.

Ostberg, C. L., and Matthew E. Wetstein. 2007. *Attitudinal Decision Making in the Supreme Court of Canada*. Vancouver: University of British Columbia Press.

Owens, Ryan J., Justin Wedeking, and Patrick C. Wohlfarth. 2013. How the Supreme Court Alters Opinion Language to Evade Congressional Review. *Journal of Law and Courts*, 1: 35–59.

Padovano, Fabio, Grazia Sgarra, and Nadia Fiorino. 2003. Judicial Branch, Checks and Balances and Political Accountability. *Constitutional Political Economy*, 14: 47–70.

Palmer, Alex W. 2017. The Last Line of Defense. *New York Times Magazine*, July 30, 25–48.

Palmer, Vernon Valentine. 2012. *Mixed Jurisdictions Worldwide: The Third Legal Family*. Cambridge, UK: Cambridge University Press.

Parsons, Jemme, and Jamhari Makruf. 2010. Islamic Legal Education in Indonesia. In Stacy Steel and Kathryn Taylor (eds.), *Legal Education in Asia*. London: Routledge, 298–324.

Pasqualucci, Jo M. 2003. *The Practice and Procedure of the Inter-American Court of Human Rights*. Cambridge, UK: Cambridge University Press.

Pauwelyn, Joost, and Manfred Elsig. 2011. The Politics of Treaty Interpretation: Variations and Explanations across International Tribunals. October 6. https://papers.ssrn.com/sol3/papers.cfm?abstract_id=1938618 (accessed 9/9/2018).

Pauwelyn, Joost, and Luiz Eduardo Salles. 2009. Forum Shopping before International Tribunals: (Real) Concerns, (Im)Possible Solutions. *Cornell International Law Journal*, 42: 77–118.

Peerenboom, Randall. 2006. An Empirical Overview of Rights Performance in Asia, France and the USA: The Dominance of Wealth in the Interplay of Economics, Culture, Law and Governance. In Randall Peerenboom, Carole J. Petersen, and Albert H. Y. Chen (eds.), *Human Rights in Asia: A Comparative Legal Study of Twelve Asian Jurisdictions, France and the USA*. London: Routledge, 1–64.

———. 2008. Judicial Independence in China. La Trobe Law School Legal Studies Research Paper No. 2008/11. https://papers.ssrn.com/sol3/papers.cfm?abstract_id=1283179 (accessed 9/9/2018).

Pekkanen, Saadia, Mireya Solís, and Saori N. Katada. 2007. Trading Gains for Control: International Trade Forums and Japanese Economic Diplomacy. *International Studies Quarterly*, 51: 945–70.

Pereira, Anthony W. 2005. *Political (In)Justice: Authoritarianism and the Rule of Law in Brazil, Chile, and Argentina*. Pittsburgh: Pittsburgh University Press.

———. 2008. Of Judges and Generals: Security Courts Under Authoritarian Regimes in Argentina, Brazil, and Chile. In Tom Ginsburg and Tamir Moustafa (eds.), *Rule by Law: The Politics of Courts in Authoritarian Regimes*. Cambridge, UK: Cambridge University Press, 23–57.

Perez-Liñan, Anibal, Barry Ames, and Mitchell A. Seligson. 2006. Strategy, Careers, and Judicial Decisions: Lessons from the Bolivian Courts. *Journal of Politics*, 68: 284–95.

Phan, Pamela N. 2005. Clinical Legal Education in China. *Yale Human Rights and Development Law Journal*, 8: 117–52.

Piana, Daniela. 2010. *Judicial Accountabilities in New Europe: From Rule of Law to Quality of Justice*. Farnham, Surrey, UK: Ashgate.

PICT. 2004. Project on International Courts and Tribunals. http://www.pict-pcti.org. (accessed 6/3/09).

Pierce, Jason. 2008. Institutional Cohesion in the High Court of Australia. *Commonwealth and Comparative Politics*, 46: 318–40.

Popova, Maria. 2010. Political Competition as an Obstacle to Judicial Independence. *Comparative Political Studies*, 43: 1202–24.

Powell, Emilia Justyna, and Sara McLaughlin Mitchell. 2007. International Court of Justice and the World's Three Legal Systems. *Journal of Politics*, 69: 397–415.

Powell, Emilia Justyna, and Jeffrey K. Staton. 2009. Domestic Judicial Institutions and Human Rights Treaty Violation. *International Studies Quarterly*, 53: 149–74.
Rahimi, Babak. 2012. Democratic Authority, Public Islam, and Shi'ia Jurisprudence in Iran and Iraq: Hussain Ali Montazeri and Ali Sistani. *International Political Science Review*, 33: 193–208.
Ramirez, Domingo. 2018. Arlington Man Sentenced to Life in Prison for 2014 Murder of Toddler. *Star-Telegram*, April 25, 5A.
Ramseyer, J. Mark. 1994. The Puzzling (In)dependence of Courts: A Comparative Approach. *Journal of Legal Studies*, 23: 721–48.
Ramseyer, J. Mark, and Eric B. Rasmusen. 2001. Why Are Japanese Judges So Conservative in Politically Charged Cases? *American Political Science Review*, 95: 331–49.
———. 2003. *Measuring Judicial Independence: The Political Economy of Judging in Japan*. Chicago: University of Chicago Press.
Reichman, Amnon. 2013. Judicial Constitution Making in a Divided Society: The Case of Israel. In Diana Kapiszewski, Gordon Silverstein, and Robert A. Kagan (eds.), *Consequential Courts*. Cambridge, UK: Cambridge University Press, 233–61.
Reid, Rebecca. 2018. Turning to Regional Courts: The Inter-American Court of Human Rights. In Robert M. Howard and Kirk A. Randazzo (eds.), *The Routledge Handbook of Judicial Behavior*. New York: Routledge, 491–508.
Riddell, Troy Q. 2004. The Impact of Legal Mobilization and Judicial Decisions. *Law and Society Review*, 33: 583–609.
Rincker, Meg, Ghazia Aslam, and Mujtaba Isani. 2017. Crossed My Mind, but Ruled It Out. *International Political Science Review*, 38: 246–63.
Ríos-Figueroa, Julio. 2007. Fragmentation of Power and the Emergence of an Effective Judiciary in Mexico, 1994–2002. *Latin American Politics and Society*, 49: 31–57.
———. 2016. *Constitutional Courts as Mediators: Armed Conflict, Civil-Military Relations, and the Rule of Law in Latin America*. Cambridge, UK: Cambridge University Press.
Ríos-Figueroa, Julio, and Jeffrey K. Staton. 2009. Unpacking the Rule of Law: A Review of Judicial Independence Measures. Paper presented at the Workshop on Law, Politics and Human Rights, Emory University, March.
Rodríguez-Garavito, César. 2010. Beyond the Courtroom: The Impact of Judicial Activism on Socioeconomic Rights in Latin America. *Texas Law Review*, 89: 1668–98.
Rosen, Lawrence. 2006. *Law as Culture: An Invitation*. Princeton, NJ: Princeton University Press.
Rosenberg, Gerald N. 1991. *The Hollow Hope: Can Courts Bring About Social Change?* Chicago: University of Chicago Press.

———. 1992. Judicial Independence and the Reality of Political Power. *Review of Politics*, 54: 369–98.

Rothmayr, Christine. 2001. Towards the Judicialisation of Swiss Politics? *West European Politics*, 24: 77–94.

Russell, Peter H. 2001. Toward a General Theory of Judicial Independence. In David M. O'Brien and Peter H. Russell (eds.), *Judicial Independence in the Age of Democracy: Critical Perspectives from around the World*. Charlottesville: University Press of Virginia, 1–24.

———. 2006. Conclusion. In Kate Malleson and Peter H. Russell (eds.), *Appointing Judges in an Age of Judicial Power: Critical Perspectives from around the World*. Toronto: University of Toronto Press, 420–36.

Sánchez-Cuenca, Ignacio. 2003. Power, Rules, and Compliance. In José María Maravall and Adam Przeworski (eds.), *Democracy and the Rule of Law*. Cambridge, UK: Cambridge University Press, 62–93.

Santiso, Carlos. 2003. Economic Reform and Judicial Governance in Brazil: Balancing Independence with Accountability. *Democratization*, 10: 161–80.

Santora, Marc. 2015. As Burundians Vote, Many Are Afraid to Pick a Side. *New York Times*, July 22, A-5.

Santora, Marc, and Joanna Berendt. 2017. Poland Overhauls Courts, and Critics See Retreat from Democracy. *New York Times*, December 20. https://nytimes.com/2017/12/20/world/europe/eu-poland-law.html (accessed 12/24/2017).

Sarbah, John Mensah. (1904) 2015. *Fanti Customary Laws, 1904*. London: Forgotten Books.

Sartori, Giovanni. 1987. *The Theory of Democracy Revisited*. Chatham, NJ: Chatham House Publishers, Inc.

Sathe, S. P. 2002. *Judicial Activism in India: Transgressing Borders and Enforcing Limits*. Oxford: Oxford University Press.

Schabas, William A. 2004. *An Introduction to the International Criminal Court*. Cambridge, UK: Cambridge University Press.

Schedler, Andreas. 2004. Arguing and Observing: Internal and External Critiques of Judicial Impartiality. *Journal of Political Philosophy*, 12: 245–65.

Scheppele, Kim Lane. 2003. Constitutional Negotiations: Political Contexts of Judicial Activism in Post-Soviet Europe. *International Sociology*, 18: 219–38.

Schönfelder, Bruno. 2005. Judicial Independence in Bulgaria: A Tale of Splendour and Misery. *Europe-Asia Studies*, 57: 61–92.

Schubert, Frank August. 2015. *Introduction to Law and the Legal System*. Stamford, CT: Cengage Learning.

Schultz, Kai. 2018. Activists Cheer as India's Supreme Courts Orders a Review of Ban on Gay Sex. *New York Times*, January 9, A-4.

Schwartz, Alex, and Melanie Janelle Murchison. 2016. Judicial Impartiality and Independence in Divided Societies. *Law and Society Review*, 50: 821–55.

Schwartz, Herman. 2000. *The Struggle for Constitutional Justice in Post-Communist Europe*. Chicago: University of Chicago Press.

Sezgin, Yüksel. 2017. How a Constitutional Amendment Could End Turkey's Republic. *Washington Post*, January 24. https://www.washingtonpost.com/news/monkey-cage/wp/2017/01/24/how-a-constitutional-amendment-could-end-turkeys-republic/?utm_term=.886fbb5ebf79 (accessed 10/2/18).

Shambayati, Hootan, and Essen Kirdiş. 2009. In Pursuit of "Contemporary Civilization": Judicial Empowerment in Turkey. *Political Research Quarterly*, 62: 767–80.

Shany, Yuval. 2009. No Longer a Weak Department of Power? Reflections on the Emergence of a New International Judiciary. *European Journal of International Law*, 20: 73–91.

———. 2015. Assessing the Effectiveness of International Courts. *European Yearbook of International Law*, 6: 423–26.

Shapiro, Martin. 1981. *Courts: A Comparative and Political Analysis*. Chicago: University of Chicago Press.

———. 2003. Judicial Review in Developed Democracies. *Democratization*, 10: 7–26.

Shapiro, Martin, and Alec Stone. 1994. The New Constitutional Politics of Europe. *Comparative Political Studies*, 26: 397–420.

Sherman, Edward. 2002. Group Litigation under Foreign Legal Systems. *De Paul Law Review*, 52: 401–32.

Shipan, Charles R. 2000. The Legislative Design of Judicial Review: A Formal Analysis. *Journal of Theoretical Politics*, 12: 269–304.

Siddique, Osama. 2014. Legal Education in Pakistan. *Journal of Legal Education*, 63: 499–511.

Sieder, Rachel. 2005. Introduction. In Rachel Sieder, Line Schjolden, and Alan Angell (eds.), *The Judicialization of Politics in Latin America*. New York: Palgrave Macmillan, 1–20.

Sieder, Rachel, Line Schjolden, and Alan Angell. 2003. Renegotiating Law and Order. *Democratization*, 10: 137–60.

Sikkink, Kathryn. 2011. *The Justice Cascade: How Human Rights Prosecutions Are Changing World Politics*. New York: W. W. Norton & Co.

Silverstein, Gordon. 2008. Singapore: The Exception That Proves Rules Matter. In Tom Ginsburg and Tamir Moustafa (eds.), *Rule by Law: The Politics of Courts in Authoritarian Regimes*. Cambridge, UK: Cambridge University Press, 73–101.

———. 2009. *Law's Allure: How Law Shapes, Constrains, Saves, and Kills Politics*. Cambridge, UK: Cambridge University Press.

Simmons, Beth A. 2008. International Law and International Relations. In Keith E. Whittington, R. Daniel Kelemen, and Gregory A. Caldeira (eds.), *Oxford Handbook of Law and Politics*. Oxford: Oxford University Press, 187–208.

———. 2009. *Mobilizing for Human Rights: International Law in Domestic Politics*. Cambridge, UK: Cambridge University Press.

Simmons, Beth A., and Allison Danner. 2010. Credible Commitments and the International Criminal Court. *International Organization*, 64: 225–56.

Slaughter, Anne-Marie. 2005. *A New World Order*. Princeton, NJ: Princeton University Press.

Smithey, Shannon Ishiyama. 2000. Judicious Choices: Designing Courts in Post-Communist Politics. *Communist and Post-Communist Studies*, 33: 163–82.

Smithey, Shannon Ishiyama, and John Ishiyama. 2002. Judicial Activism in Post-Communist Politics. *Law and Society Review*, 36: 719–42.

Smyth, Russell. 2000. The "Haves" and the "Have Nots": An Empirical Study of the Rational Actor and Party Capability Hypotheses in the High Court 1948–99. *Australian Journal of Political Science*, 35: 255–74.

Spamann, Holger. 2009. Contemporary Legal Transplants: Legal Families and the Diffusion of (Corporate) Law. *Brigham Young University Law Review*, 2009: 1813–77.

Staats, Joseph, and Glen Biglaiser. 2011. Effects of Judicial Strength and Rule of Law on Portfolio Investment in the Developing World. *Social Science Quarterly*, 92: 609–35.

Stack, John F., Jr., and Mary L. Volcansek. 2005. Courts Crossing Borders. In Mary L. Volcansek and John F. Stack Jr. (eds.), *Courts Crossing Borders: Blurring the Lines of Sovereignty*. Durham, NC: Carolina Academic Press, 3–10.

Starr, June. 1992. *Law as Metaphor: From Islamic Courts to the Palace of Justice*. Albany: State University of New York Press.

Staton, Jeffrey K. 2006. Constitutional Review and the Selective Promotion of Case Results. *American Journal of Political Science*, 50: 98–112.

Steinberg, Richard H. 2002. In the Shadow of Law or Power? Consensus-Based Bargaining and Outcomes in the GATT/WTO. *International Organization*, 56: 339–74.

Stevenson, Alexandra. 2018. With Resolve, China Tackles Growing Debt. *New York Times*, May 11, B-1.

Stone, Alec. 1989. In the Shadow of the Constitutional Council: The "Juridicisation" of the Legislative Process in France. *West European Politics*, 12: 12–34.

Stone Sweet, Alec. 1992. *The Birth of Judicial Politics in France: The Constitutional Council in Comparative Perspective.* New York: Oxford University Press.
———. 1999. Islands of Transnational Governance. Paper presented at the workshop "Boundaries, Territory, and the State," University of California, Berkeley.
———. 2000. *Governing with Judges: Constitutional Politics in Europe.* Oxford: Oxford University Press.
———. 2002. Constitutional Courts and Parliamentary Democracy. *West European Politics,* 25: 77–100.
———. 2003. Why Europe Rejected American Judicial Review: And Why It May Not Matter. *Michigan Law Review,* 101: 2744–80.
———. 2006. The New *Lex Mercatoria* and Transnational Governance. *Journal of European Public Policy,* 13: 627–46.
Stone Sweet, Alec, and Thomas Brunnell. 1998a. Constructing a Supranational Constitution: Dispute Resolution and Governance in the European Community. *American Political Science Review,* 92: 63–80.
———. 1998b. The European Court and the National Courts: A Statistical Analysis of Preliminary References, 1961–95. *Journal of European Public Policy,* 5: 66–97.
———. 2012. The European Court of Justice, State Noncompliance, and the Politics of Override. *American Political Science Review,* 106: 204–12.
Stone Sweet, Alec, and Wayne Sandholtz. 1998. Integration, Supranational Governance, and the Institutionalization of the European Polity. In Wayne Sandholtz and Alec Stone Sweet (eds.), *European Integration and Supranational Governance.* Oxford: Oxford University Press, 1–26.
Storing, Herbert J. 1985. *The Anti-Federalist: Writings by the Opponents of the Constitution.* Chicago: University of Chicago Press.
Strohmeyer, Hansjörg. 2001. Collapse and Reconstruction of a Judicial System. *American Journal of International Law,* 45: 46–63.
Swanson, Ana. 2018. U.S. Is Poised to Impose Metal Tariffs. *New York Times,* May 30. http://www.nytimes.com/2018/05/30/us/politics/trade-talks-tariffs-trump.html (accessed 9/10/18).
Tarr, G. Alan. 2012. *Without Fear or Favor: Judicial Independence and Judicial Accountability in the States.* Stanford, CA: Stanford University Press.
Tate, C. Neal. 1987. Judicial Institutions in Cross-National Perspective: Toward Integrating Courts into the Comparative Study of Politics. In John R. Schmidhauser (ed.), *Comparative Judicial Systems: Challenging Frontiers in Conceptual Empirical Analysis.* London: Butterworths, 7–33.

———. 1994. The Judicialization of Politics in the Philippines and Southeast Asia. *International Political Science Review*, 15: 187–97.

———. 1995. Why the Expansion of Judicial Power? In C. Neal Tate and Torbjörn Vallinder (eds.), *The Global Expansion of Judicial Power*. New York: New York University Press, 27–38.

Tate, C. Neal, and Stacia L. Haynie. 1993. Authoritarianism and the Functions of Courts: A Time Series Analysis of the Philippine Supreme Court, 1961–1987. *Law & Society Review*, 27: 707–40.

Tate, C. Neal, and Torbjörn Vallinder. 1995. *The Global Expansion of Judicial Power*. New York: New York University Press.

Taylor, Matthew M. 2006. Veto and Voice in the Courts: Policy Implications of Institutional Design in the Brazilian Judiciary. *Comparative Politics*, 35: 337–55.

———. 2008. *Judging Policy: Courts and Policy Reform in Democratic Brazil*. Stanford, CA: Stanford University Press.

Terry, Laurel S. 2007. The Bologna Process and Its Implications for U.S. Legal Education. *Journal of Legal Education*, 57: 237–52.

———. 2010. The Bologna Process and Its Impact in Europe: It's So Much More Than Degree Changes. *Vanderbilt Journal of Transnational Law*, 41: 107–228.

Thio, Li-Ann. 2006. Taking Rights Seriously? Human Rights Law in Singapore. In Randall Peerenboom, Carole J. Petersen, and Albert H.Y. Chen (eds.), *Human Rights in Asia: A Comparative Legal Study of Twelve Asian Jurisdictions, France and the USA*. London: Routledge, 158–91.

Thomas, Landon, Liz Alderman, and Aureliean Breeden. 2016. I.M.F Stands by Christine Lagarde, Convicted of Negligence. *New York Times*, December 19. https://www.nytimes.com/2016/12/19/business/imf-trial-christine-lagarde-france-verdict.html (accessed 9/10/2018).

Thorson, Carla. 2004. Why Politicians Want Constitutional Courts: The Russian Case. *Communist and Post-Communist Studies*, 37: 187–211.

Thorton, John L. 2008. Long Time Coming: The Prospects for Democracy in China. *Foreign Affairs*, 87: 2–22.

Tiede, Lydia Brashear, and Aldo Fernando Ponce. 2014. Evaluating Theories of Decision-Making on the Peruvian Constitutional Tribunal. *Journal of Politics in Latin America*, 2: 139–64.

Toharia, José I. 1975. Judicial Independence in an Authoritarian Regime: The Case of Spain. *Law and Society Review*, 9: 475–96.

Tolley, Michael C. 2018. Courts in Developed Countries. In Robert M. Howard and Kirk A. Randazzo (eds.), *Routledge Handbook of Judicial Behavior*. New York: Routledge, 389–405.

Tomz, Michael. 2007. Domestic Audience Costs in International Relations: An Experimental Approach. *International Organization*, 61: 821–40.

Trochev, Alexei. 2004. Less Democracy, More Courts: A Puzzle of Judicial Review in Russia. *Law and Society Review*, 38: 513–48.

———. 2009. All Appeals Lead to Strasbourg? Unpacking the Impact of the European Court of Human Rights on Russia. *Demokratizatsiya*, 17: 145–78.

Tsebelis, George. 1995. Decision Making in Political Systems: Veto Players in Presidentialism, Parliamentarism, Multicameralism and Multipartyism. *British Journal of Political Science*, 25: 289–326.

———. 1999. Veto Players and Law Production in Parliamentary Democracies. *American Political Science Review*, 93: 591–607.

———. 2000. Veto Players and Institutional Analysis. *Governance*, 13: 441–74.

———. 2002. *Veto Players: How Political Institutions Work*. Princeton, NJ: Princeton University Press.

Tucker, Robert W. 2001. The International Criminal Court Controversy. *World Policy Journal*, 18: 71–81.

Tushnet, Mark V. 2007. *Out of Range: Why the Constitution Can't End the Battle over Guns*. Oxford: Oxford University Press.

———. 2008. *Weak Courts, Strong Rights*. Princeton, NJ: Princeton University Press.

———. 2014. *Comparative Constitutional Law*. Cheltenham, UK: Edward Elgar.

Tyler, Tom R. 2008. Psychology and the Law. In Keith E. Whittington, R. Daniel Kelemen, and Gregory Caldiera (eds.), *Oxford Handbook of Law and Politics*. Oxford: Oxford University Press, 711–22.

Uprimny, Rodrigo. 2003. The Constitutional Court and Control of Presidential Extraordinary Powers in Colombia. *Democratization*, 10: 46–69.

Uribe-Urán, Victor M. 2011. From Exception to Normalcy: Law, the Judiciary, Civil Rights, and Terrorism in Colombia. In Mary L. Volcansek and John F. Stack Jr. (eds.), *Courts and Terrorism: Nine Nations Balance Rights and Security*. Cambridge, UK: Cambridge University Press, 199–223.

Urribarri, Raul A. Sanchez. 2007. News from the Comparative Realm. *Law and Courts*, 17: 11–13.

Urribarri, Raul A. Sanchez, Susanne Scharpp, Kirk Randazzo, and Donald R. Songer. 2011. Explaining Changes to Rights Litigation. *Journal of Politics*, 73: 391–405.

Uvin, Peter, and Charles Mironko. 2003. Western and Local Approaches to Justice in Rwanda. *Global Governance*, 9: 219–31.

Vallinder, Torbjörn. 1995. When the Courts Go Marching In. In C. Neal Tate and Torbjörn Vallinder (eds.), *The Global Expansion of Judicial Power*. New York: New York University Press, 13–26.

Van Hees, Martin, and Bernard Steunenberg. 2000. The Choices Judges Make: Court Rulings, Personal Values and Legal Constraints. *Journal of Theoretical Politics*, 12: 305–23.

Vanberg, Georg. 1998. Abstract Judicial Review, Legislative Bargaining, and Policy Compromise. *Journal of Theoretical Politics*, 10: 299–326.
———. 2000. Establishing Judicial Independence in West Germany: The Impact of Opinion Leadership and the Separation of Powers. *Comparative Politics*, 32: 333–53.
———. 2001. Legislative-Judicial Relations: A Game-Theoretic Approach to Constitutional Review. *American Journal of Political Science*, 45: 346–61.
———. 2005. *The Politics of Constitutional Review in Germany*. Cambridge, UK: Cambridge University Press.
———. 2008. Establishing and Maintaining Judicial Independence. In Keith Whittington, R. Daniel Kelemen, and Gregory A. Caldeira (eds.), *Oxford Handbook of Law and Politics*. Oxford: Oxford University Press, 99–118.
Vermeule, Adrian. 2007. *Mechanisms of Democracy: Institutional Design Writ Small*. Oxford: Oxford University Press.
Vermeulen, Joan. 2016. Access to Justice in Latin America. http://digitalcommons.nyls.edu/impact_center/6 (accessed 9/10/2018).
Versteeg, Mila, and Emily Zackin. 2016. Constitutions Unentrenched: Toward an Alternative Theory of Constitutional Design. *American Political Science Review*, 110: 657–74.
Vibert, Frank. 2007. *The Rise of the Unelected: Democracy and the New Separation of Powers*. Cambridge, UK: Cambridge University Press.
Victor, Daniel. 2018. Suit over Oxford Comma Is Settled, for $5 Million and a Slew of Semicolons. *New York Times*, February 10, A-10.
Villamor, Felipe. 2018. Tribunal Will Investigate Duterte over Drug War. *New York Times*, February 9, A-4.
Volcansek, Mary L. 1990. The Judicial Role in Italy. *Judicature*, 73: 322–27.
———. 1993. *Judicial Impeachment: None Called for Justice*. Urbana: University of Illinois Press.
———. 2001. Constitutional Courts as Veto Players: Divorce and Decrees in Italy. *European Journal of Political Research*, 39: 347–72.
———. 2007. Appointing Judges the European Way. *Fordham Urban Law Journal*, 34: 363–85.
———. 2010. Bargaining Constitutional Design in Italy. *West European Politics*, 33: 280–96.
Volcansek, Mary L., and Jacqueline Lucienne Lafon. 1988. *Judicial Selection: The Cross-Evolution of French and American Practices*. New York: Greenwood Press.
Volcansek, Mary L., and Charles Lockhart. 2012. Explaining Support for Human Rights Protections: A Judicial Role? *Journal of Human Rights*, 11: 33–50.

Von Bogdandy, Armin, and Ingo Venzke. 2012. In Whose Name? An Investigation of International Courts' Public Authority and Its Democratic Justification. *European Journal of International Law*, 23: 7–41.

Vondoepp, Peter. 2005. The Problem of Judicial Control in Africa's Neopatrimonial Democracies: Malawi and Zambia. *Political Science Quarterly*, 120: 275–301.

Vose, Clement. 1959. *Caucasians Only*. Berkeley: University of California Press.

Wallace, Julia. 2017. Democracy Fades as Cambodia's Top Court Dissolves Main Opposition Party. *New York Times*, November 17, A-6.

Walsh, Declan. 2018. Sisi Critic Is Sentenced to 5 Years in Prison. *New York Times*, April 25, A-6.

Wasby, Stephen L. 1970. *The Impact of the United States Supreme Court*. Homewood, IL: Dorsey Press.

Weingast, Barry R. 1997. Political Foundations of Democracy and the Rule of Law. *American Political Science Review*, 91: 245–63.

Westerland, Chad, Jeffrey A. Segal, Lee Epstein, Charles M. Cameron, and Scott Comparato. 2010. Strategic Defiance and Compliance in the U.S. Courts of Appeal. *American Journal of Political Science*, 54: 891–905.

Wetstein, Matthew E., and C. Ostberg. 2017. *Value Change in the Supreme Court of Canada*. Toronto: University of Toronto Press.

Wheatley, Steven. 2010. *The Democratic Legitimacy of International Law*. Oxford: Oxford University Press.

Wheatstone, Richard. 2015. Woman to Be Stoned to Death for Adultery in Saudi Arabia—While Male Partner to Receive 100 Lashes. *Mirror*, November 27. http://www.mirror.co.uk/news/world-news/woman-stoned-death-adultery-saudi-6912835 (accessed 9/10/2018).

Wiarda, Howard J. 1993. *Introduction to Comparative Politics: Concepts and Processes*. Belmont, CA: Wadsworth Publishing Company.

Widner, Jennifer. 2001a. *Building the Rule of Law: Francis Nyalali and the Road to Judicial Independence in Africa*. New York: W. W. Norton & Company.

———. 2001b. Courts and Democracy in Post-Conflict Transitions: A Social Scientist's Perspective on the African Case. *American Journal of International Law*, 95: 64–75.

Widner, Jennifer, with Daniel Scher. 2008. Building Judicial Independence in Semi-Democracies: Uganda and Zimbabwe. In Tom Ginsburg and Tamir Moustafa (eds.), *Rule by Law: The Politics of Courts in Authoritarian Regimes*. Cambridge, UK: Cambridge University Press, 235–60.

Wilson, Richard J. 2009. Western Europe: Last Holdout in the Worldwide Acceptance of Clinical Legal Education. https://digitalcommons.osgoode.yorku.ca/clpe/143 (accessed 10/11/2017).

Winthrobe, Ronald. 2007. Dictatorship: Analytical Approaches. In Carles Boix and Susan C. Stokes (eds.). *Oxford Handbook of Comparative Politics*. Oxford: Oxford University Press, 363–96.

Woodman, Gordon R. 2011. A Survey of Customary Laws in Africa in Search of Lessons. In Jeanmarie Fenrich, Paolo Galizzi, and Tracy E. Higgins (eds.), *The Future of African Customary Law*. Cambridge, UK: Cambridge University Press, 9–30.

Woods, Patricia J. 2009. Ideational Foundations of Israel's Constitutional Revolution. *Political Research Quarterly*, 62: 811–24.

Woodward, Jennifer. 2015. Making Rights Work: Legal Mobilization at the Agency Level. *Law and Society Review*, 49: 691–723.

World Values Survey, 2010–2014. 2017. http://www.worldvaluessurvey.org/WVSOnline.jsp (accessed 9/10/18).

Zemans, Franes Kahn. 1983. Legal Mobilization: The Neglected Role of Law in the Political System. *American Political Science Review*, 77: 690–703.

Zheng, Chunyar, Jiahui Ai, and Sida Liu. 2017. The Elastic Ceiling: Gender and Professional Career in Chinese Courts. *Law and Society Review*, 51: 168–99.

Index

★ ★ ★

Page numbers in *italics* refer to boxes, figures, and tables.

abortion, 155, 157, 167–68
ACA. *See King v. Burwell*
access: in dispute resolution, 19–20, 63; lack of, 51–52, 61–62; lawyers and, 53–54
administrative courts, 45–46
adultery, 23–24
adversarial criminal proceedings, 24–25, 43–44
advisory opinions, 86–87, 97
Affordable Care Act (ACA). *See King v. Burwell*
Africa: access in, lack of, 51–52, 61–62; constitutional review in, 107; customary law in, 38–41, 62; legal education in, 57–58; legal mobilization in, 64, 66. *See also specific countries*
African Union, 6
Agreement on Trade-Related Aspects of Intellectual Property Rights (TRIPs Agreement), 13
Aldeen, Salam, *160*
Ali, Khaled, 72

Almond, Gabriel A., 16
Alpay, Sahin, *102*
Alter, Karen J., 145, 148
American Bar Association, 3, 56
amici curiae, 69
Anbang Insurance Group, 159
Anti-Federalists, 165
appointment commissions, judicial, 81
Arab Spring, 13
Argentina, 95; constitutional hardball in, *115*; constitutional review in, 107, 123; military rule in, 47–48, 85, 87
Arusha Peace and Reconciliation agreement (2000), 4–5
Asaram Bapu, 170
Asia: gay rights in, 65–66; legal education in, 58–59. *See also specific countries*
attitudinal model, 121–22
Australia, 83
Australian High Court, 116
authoritarian regimes: in Argentina, military, 47–48,

85, 87; in Chile, military, 17, 77, 85, 87, 109; extrajudicial execution in, 85; institutional design in, 91–92; judicial independence in, 8, 75, 77, 87, 91, 95; legal mobilization in, 65–66; legitimacy under, 8–9, 47–48, 179, *180*, 180–81; military courts under, 47–48, 87; veto players in, 92–93
authority, judicial: constitutional review and, 118–21; institutional design and, 74–75, 91; judicial independence and, 4, 20, 73, *74*, 76, 90–96, 100; veto players and, 92–96

backlash court model, 157–58
Baird, Vanessa, 176
barristers, 55–56, 61
Bashir, Omar Hassan al-, 59–60
Basuki Tjahaja Purnama, 89
Beard, Joshua, 151
Becker, Theodore, 154
Bermuda, *167*
Blackstone, William, 31
Bleak House (Dickens), 51–52
Bolivia, 80–81, 87, 90, 96, 120
Bologna Process, 56
Bosnia-Herzegovina, 120, 122
Brazil, 47, 100; extrajudicial executions in, 85; Federal Supreme Court of, 114, 116–17, 122; health care and litigation in, 64–65, 160–61, 163; judicial independence in, 86–87, 89, *90*, 122
Brinks, Daniel M., 163
Britain, 42, 45, 69; constitutional review in, 114–15; constitution of, 103; EU exit of, 186; Human Rights Act of, 114; JAC in, 81; legal education in, 55–56; legal profession in, 61; Norman conquest of, 26, 30–31, 55; precedent in, 31–32; in Sudan, law of, 33, 36; Supreme Court of, 21, 105–6; trials of, judge in, 44. *See also* Scotland
Buddhism, 15, 26
Bulgaria, 85, 183–84
Burma, 87
Burundi, 60; judicial independence in, 74, 85; Nkurunziza term limits case in, 1, 3, 5–6, 8–9, 19–21, 85, 116, 120; US compared with, 3–4, 16–17
Bush, George W., 88
Bush v. Gore, 21, 174

Caldeira, Gregory A., 176, 185
Cambodia, 58, 169–70
Canada, 158; constitutional review in, 114–16; enforcement in, 151–52; interest group litigation in, 68–70; Supreme Court of, 65
canon law, 26–27, 42
career judiciary, 78–79
case studies, 17–18
cassation, 43
causality, 154, 166
cause lawyers, 67
Central African Republic, 51–52
Chase, Samuel, 4
Chaudhry, Iftikhar Muhammad, *111*
Chavez, Hugo, *115*
Chile, 17, 77, 85, 87, 109
China, 159; cause lawyers in, 67; civil law tradition in, 29; executor judge in, 96–97, 183; ICJ, Philippines and, 22; intellectual property in,

13; Jiang case in, 67, 169; judiciary in, 79, 82, 85–87, 91–95; lawyers as barriers in, 65; legal aid in, 63; legal education in, 59, 62, 79; Supreme People's Court of, 105–7; women lawyers in, 63

civil law tradition, 26; administrative courts of, 45–46; in China, 29; common law convergence with, 30; constitutional review and, 107; French, 28–29; Germanic, 28–29, 43; globally, 27; hierarchy in, 42; investigatory form in, 44–45; Islamic law compared with, 33–34; judges in, 27–28, 94; legal education in, 54–55; public law and, 29

class action lawsuits, 67–68

codes, legal, 27

Coke, Edward, 31

Colombia, 84, 120, 163

colonization, 24

comma case, 152

common law tradition, 2, 26; adversarial form in, 43–44; amici curiae in, 69; as British, 30–32, 42, 44–45; in British colonies, 32–33; civil law convergence with, 30; globally, 27, 32–33; hierarchy and horizontality in, 42–43; Islamic law compared with, 33–34; judge in, 32, 80; legal education under, 55–57; precedent in, 31–32; in US, 3, 44–45

Constitution, US, 4, 95; constitutional review not granted by, 108; judicial power and, 165; Second Amendment of, 178

constitutional hardball, *115*

constitutional review, 89, 94, 183; abstract and concrete, 111–13; attitudinal model of, 121–22; in Britain, 114–15; in Canada, 114–16; constitutions and, 103–5, 107–8, 181–82; co-optation theory of, 109, 118; credibility theory of, 108–9; delegation theory of, 109–10, 118, 120; in France, 112, 117–19; in Germany, 112, 123, 125; human rights and, 104–5, 125, 182; impact and, 161–62, 165; insurance theory of, 110; in Italy, 112, 117, 123, 162–63; judicial empowerment and, 7, 9, 20–21, 104; judicial independence, authority and, 118–21; Kelsian model of, 105–6, *106*, 107, 111–12; legitimacy and, 177–78, 182; liberal democracy and, 186; in new democracies, 123–25; in Poland, 101–3, *125*, 163; political judges and, 121; in Russia, 108–9, 113, 122–23; strategic choice in, 122–23; strong and weak forms of, 113–14, *115*, 115–17, 126, 166; in Turkey, *102*, 102–3, 105, 109, 118, 122; in US, 7, 78, 103, 108, 113–14, 124–25; US model of, 105, 107, 111, 181–82; veto players and, 116–17, 119

constrained court model, 156–58, 166

Convention on the Prevention and Punishment of the Crime of Genocide, 134

co-optation theory, 109, 118

Costa Rica, 127

council, judicial, 79
Cour de Justice de la République, French, 25
credibility theory, 108–9
criminal proceedings: adversarial, 24–25, 43–44; investigatory, 24, 43–45
customary law, 62; in Burundi, 3; judicial selection in, 78; in Kenya, 14; with national law, hybrid formation of, 38–39, 48; reconciliation in, 40–41; in Togo, 26–27; women in, 39, 40–41; in Zimbabwe, 39, *39*

Dahl, Robert, 109
decision making, 96; formalistic, 97; identity and, 99; local influences on, 99–100; policy preferences motivating, 97
delegate courts, 120
delegate judge, 73, 74, 76, 78, 94, 183
delegation, 7–8, 109–10, 118, 120
democracy: Islamic law and, 36; liberal, constitutional review and, 186; new, constitutional review in, 123–25
Democracy in America (de Tocqueville), 16
Dentons, 61
desegregation, racial, 153, 158
de Tocqueville, Alexis, 16, 186–87
dialogue court model, 157–58, 166
Dickens, Charles, 51–52
dispute resolution, 16; access in, 19–20, 63; consent in, 10–11; economic, 12–13; impact of, 159–61; legitimacy and, 170–71; multiple legal systems and, 14–15; in Palestine, 9–10; triadic, 10, 38, 71–72, 129, 170–71
Dispute Settlement Body (DSB). *See* World Trade Organization
District of Columbia v. Heller, 69, 178
divorce, 11–12, 19
Druze, 46–47
DSB. *See* World Trade Organization
Duda, Andrzej, 101
Duterte, Rodrigo, 127
dynamic court model, 156–57, 166

East Africa Community, 6
ECJ. *See* European Court of Justice
economic development, 70
ECtHR. *See* European Court of Human Rights
Ecuador, 86
Egypt: high court of, 72–73, 108, 119; legal education in, 59; legal mobilization in, 66; trial courts in, 13–14
election, of judges, 80–81
Ely, John Hart, 182
empowerment, judicial, 6, 8; constitutional review and, 7, 9, 20–21, 104; legitimacy and, 171–72, 183
enemy combatants, 88
enforcement, 151–53
Epp, Charles, 66, 157
Erdogan, Recep Tayyip, 84, 92, 93, 102, *102*
Ersson, Svante, 114
EU. *See* European Union
European Court of Human Rights (ECtHR), *102*, 139–40;

Germany and, 127; Russia and, 141; Spain and, *140*
European Court of Justice (ECJ), 21, 138; cuisine and, *139*; effectiveness of, 139, 147–48; Germany and, 127; legitimacy of, 176; as politically constrained, 157–58; Switzerland and, 131
European Union (EU): British exit from, 186; constitutional review in, 107; Court of First Instance, 138; judicial independence and, 82–84; legal education in, 56; Visitors Information Program of, ix
euthanasia, 98–99
executor courts, 120
executor judge, 73, *74*, 76, 78; in China, 96–97, 183; identity and, 99
extrajudicial execution, 84

families, of law, 26
Federalist Papers, 165
Feeley, Malcolm M., 154
France: *cassation* in, 43; civil law tradition of, 28–29; constitutional review in, 112, 117–19; Court de Justice de la République of, 25; judges in, 79–80; legal education model of, 54–55
Franco, Francisco, 87
free speech, 164–65
French Civil Code, 28
French Constitutional Council, 117–19

Gacaca, 40
Gandhi, Indira, 84
Gauri, Varun, 163
gay rights, 65–66, *167*

Gaza Strip, 47–48, 88
gender discrimination. *See* sex discrimination
Geneina, Hisham, 151
Geneva Conventions, 141, 144
German Civil Code, 28
German National Democratic Party, 127
Germany: civil law tradition of, 28–29, 43; constitutional review in, 112, 123, 125; ECtHR, ECJ and, 127; Federal Constitutional Court of, 105–6, *106*, 119, 123, 125, 152–53; legal education model of, 54–55; specialized courts in, 45
Geyh, Charles Gardner, 124–25
Gibson, James, 182, 185
Ginsburg, Tom, 8
globalization, 128–29, 149
Gómez Murillo, Daniel Gerardo, 127
Greece, 55, *160*
Guantanamo Bay, Cuba, 47, 88
guardian courts, 120–21, 168
guardian judge, 73–74, *74*, 76–77, 94; identity and, 99; legitimacy and, 171–72, 183
Guarnieri, Carlo, 73, 75, 118
Guatemala, 100
gun control, 178
Guttiérrez, Lucio, 86

hadith, 33–34
Hajjar, Lisa, 48
hard law, 133–34, *134*, 136, 147
Al Hassan Ag Abdoul Aziz Ag Mohamed Ag Mahmoud, *137*
health care, 64–65, 160–61, 163
Henry VI, Part II (Shakespeare), 51

Hernandez, Juan Orlando, 120
hierarchy, 42–43, 48
Hirschl, Ran, 109
Holy See (Vatican City), 26
Honduras, 120
housing, right to, 161
human rights, 104–5, 125, 165, 182
Human Rights Act, British, 114
Hungarian Constitutional Court, 104–5
Hun Sen, 169
hyper-presidentialism, 94

IACtHR. *See* Inter-American Court of Human Rights
ICC. *See* International Criminal Court
ICJ. *See* International Court of Justice
ICTs. *See* international criminal tribunals
identity: of judge, 99; legal, 48–49
IMF. *See* International Monetary Fund
impact: causality and, 154, 166; constitutional review and, 161–62, 165; of dispute resolution, 159–61; of high court decisions, 152–53; implementing audiences and, 156, *156*; of international courts, 155–56; of *King v. Burwell*, 5–6; policy, models of, 156–58, 166; policy and institutional, 161–65; public opinion and, 163, 166, *167*; ripple effects of, 5–6, 155, 159, *160*, 161; strategic choice and, 167; unintended, 167–68
implementing audiences, 156, *156*
independence, judicial, 6, 90, 122; in authoritarian regimes, 8, 75, 77, 87, 91, 95; constitutional review and, 118–21; de facto, 20, 74, 82–88; de jure, 20, 74, 77–83, 91; judicial authority and, 4, 20, 73, 74, 76, 90–96, 100; judicial councils for, 79; legal mobilization and, 64; legitimacy and, 175–77; overt threats to, 83–85; political insurance and, 92–93; selection and, 78; structural threats to, 86–88; unfettered, 88–90; veiled threats to, 85–86
India, 170; constitutional review in, 103, 122; judicial independence threatened in, 84; legal education in, 58; legal mobilization in, 66, 69; religious and secular courts in, 46; women lawyers in, 63
Indonesia: access in, lack of, 52; Constitutional Court of, 125; divorce in, 11–12, 19; economic field in, courts and, 12–13, 20; Islamic law in, 11–12, 19, 36–37, 89–90, 99–100; legal mobilization in, 66
institutional design: in authoritarian regimes, 91–92; judicial authority and, 74–75, 91; veto players in, 92–95
intellectual property, 12–13
Inter-American Court of Human Rights (IACtHR), 127, 131, 165
interest group litigation, 66–70
International Chamber of Commerce, 143
International Court of Justice (ICJ), 21, 134; China, Philippines and, 22; ITLOS

and, 135–36; Mexico, US and, 144; Nicaragua, US and, 22
international courts, 132; actual, 130–31, 135–38; coercive mechanisms of, 129, 131, 133, 144–48; globalization and, 128–29, 149; hard and soft law in, 133–34, *134*; hybrid, 131, 141–42, 165; impact of, 155–56; overlapping jurisdictions of, 146; regional, 131, 138–41; sovereignty costs and, 145–46, *146*; specialized and administrative, 131, 142; transactions and, 130, 133, 142–43; of transnational arbitration, 131, 142–44
International Criminal Court (ICC), 21, 130–31, 136–37; Burundi and, 6; coercive mechanisms of, 129; ICTs and, 141–42; Mali and, *137*; Philippines and, 127
international criminal tribunals (ICTs), 141–42
International Military Tribunal. *See* Nuremberg Tribunal
International Monetary Fund (IMF), 12–13, 23
International Refugee Assistance Project v. Trump, 72–73, 97
International Tribunal for the Law of the Sea (ITLOS), 130–31, 135–36
intervenor, 69–70
investigatory criminal proceedings, 24, 43–45
Iraqi Constitution, 107
Irish Supreme Court, 122, 124
Islamic law, 27, 182; civil, common law compared with, 33–34; global distribution of, 27; hierarchy in, 42; history of, 26, 33–35; in Indonesia, 11–12, 19, 36–37, 89–90, 99–100; in Israel, 46; judicial selection in, 78; in Pakistan, 41; in Philippines, 41; secular law and, 35–36; in Sri Lanka, 37, 41; strains of, 36; in Sudan, 59–60; Western influence and, 36–38. *See also* religious courts
Israel: cause lawyers in, 67; common law in, 33; constitutional review in, 108–10; military courts of, 47–48, 88, 178–79; religious courts in, 46–47
Italy, 98; constitutional review in, 112, 117, 123, 162–63; criminal proceedings in, 24–25; judicial independence in, 86, 89
ITLOS. *See* International Tribunal for the Law of the Sea

JAC. *See* Judicial Appointments Commission, British
Jackson, Andrew, 80
Jackson, Robert, 68–69
Japan: court hierarchy in, 43; intellectual property in, 13; legal education in, 58–60; Liberal Democratic Party in, 93, 95
Jiang Tianyong, 67, 169
jirgas, 41
judges: in Burundi, 3–4; in civil law tradition, 27–28, 94; in common law tradition, 32, 80; constitutional review and, 121; delegate, 73, 74, 76, 78, 94, 183; election of, 80–81; executor, 73, 74, 76,

78, 96–97, 99, 183; in France, 79–80; guardian, 73–74, *74*, 76–77, 94, 99, 171–72, 183; identity of, 99; in investigatory criminal proceedings, 44–45; in Latin America, appointment of, 80; legitimacy of, 171–72, 183; political, 74, *74*, 76–77, 94, 121, 171–72, 183; removal of, 77–78, 81–82; resident, 27–28; under US Constitution, 4; of US Supreme Court, 3–4
Judicial Appointments Commission, British (JAC), 81
judicialization, 6
juridification, 6
jury, lay, 45

Kaczynski, Jaroslaw, 84, 92
Kafka, Franz, 51
Kelsen, Hans, 105
Kelsian model, 105–6, *106*, 107, 111–12
Kenya, 40–41; judicial independence in, threats to, 85; land cases in, 14, 19; 2017 presidential election in, 168
Kenyatta, Uhuru, 168
King v. Burwell, 1–2, 4, 9; impact of, 5–6; judicial authority, independence and, 20
Kono, Daniel Y., 133
kugara nhaka (wife inheritance), 39

Lagarde, Christine, 23, 25
land rights, 14–15, 19, 175
Lane, Jan-Erik, 114
Latin America: access in, lack of, 52, 61; common law tradition in, 33; constitutional review in, 107, 119; judicial appointment in, 80; legal education in, 56–57. *See also specific countries*
Lavery, Cecil, 124
law, rule of, 172–73, 186–87
Law and Justice Party, Polish (PiS), 84, 92, 101–2
law firms, multinational, 61
lawyers: access and, 53–54; cause, 67; in China, 63, 65; women as, 63
legal aid, 62–63
legal education, 58–60, 70, 77, 79; in civil law tradition, 54–55; clinical, 62; in common law tradition, 55–57
legalization, 6–7
legal mobilization, 63, 69, 157, 161; in authoritarian regimes, 65–66; judicial independence and, 64
legal profession, 60, 63; concentration in, 61–62; legitimacy of, 171
legitimacy, 22; under authoritarian regimes, 8–9, 47–48, 179, *180*, 180–81; constitutional review and, 177–78, 182; diffuse support and, 173–74, 176, 178; dispute resolution and, 170–71; goodwill and, 174–75, 178, 185; judicial empowerment and, 171–72, 183; judicial independence and, 175–77; of legal profession, 171; political, courts and, 178–79, 184; political judges and, 171–72, 183; public opinion and, 176–77; rule of law and, 172–73, 186–87; World Values Survey of, 179, *180*, 180–81, 183–84, 186
lex mercatoria (market law), 143–44

Liberal Democratic Party, Japanese, 93, 95
Lijphart, Arend, 114
Lipset, Seymour Martin, 170, 173
Lula da Silva, Luiz Inácio (Lula), 89, *90*

Madison, James, 95
Maduro, Nicolás, 47
Mali, *137*
Marbury v. Madison, 113–14
market law (*lex mercatoria*), 143
Marriage Law, Indonesian, 11–12
Menem, Carlos, 85
Mexico, 17, 95, 119, 144, 158, 163
military courts: under authoritarian regimes, 47–48, 87; Israeli, 47–48, 88, 178–79; in US, 45–47, 88; in Venezuela, 47
Misihairabwi-Mushonga, Priscilla, *39*
Montesquieu, 28
Morales, Evo, 120
Moustafa, Tamir, 8, 66
Mozambique, 87
Muhammad (prophet), 26, 33–34
Musharraf, Pervez, *111*
Muslim travel ban, in US, 72–73, 97

NAACP. *See* National Association for the Advancement of Colored People
Napoleon, 26, 35
National Association for the Advancement of Colored People (NAACP), 68

National Organization for Women, 65
national sovereignty, 145–46, *146*
Netherlands, 79, 98–99, 105, 141
Nicaragua, 22
Nigeria, 66, 87
Nimpagaritse, Sylvere, 3
Nkurunziza, Pierre. *See* Burundi
Norman conquest, 26, 30–31, 55
norm compliance, 145
Nuremberg Tribunal, 134, 141
Nyalali, Francis, 124

OAS. *See* Organization of American States
O'Donnell, Guillermo, 187
Organization of American States (OAS), 131
Ottoman Empire, 35, 42

Pakistan: adultery in, 24; customary and Islamic law in, 41; Supreme Court in, *111*
Palestinians: dispute resolution of, 9–10; military courts and, 47–48, 88, 178–79
Paraguay, 80
party capability theory, 67
PCIJ. *See* Permanent Court of International Justice
Pederzoli, Patrizia, 73, 75, 118
Permanent Court of Arbitration, 143
Permanent Court of International Justice (PCIJ), 133–34
Perón, Juan, *115*
Peruvian Constitutional Tribunal, 123
Phan, Pamela, 62
Philippines, 22, 26, 41, 127
Pinochet, Augusto, 77, 85

PiS. *See* Law and Justice Party, Polish
pluralism, legal, 24–26, *37*, 47
pluralism, political, 184–85
Poland, 92, 183; constitutional review in, 101–3, 125, 163; populism in, 84, 102, 163, 184
political insurance, 92–95
political judges, 74, *74*, 76–77, 94; constitutional review and, 121; legitimacy and, 171–72, 183
populism, 80; in Poland, 84, 102, 163, 184; rise of, 16, 186
Powell, G. Bingham, Jr., 16
precedent, in common law, 31–32
prisoner's dilemma, 93
procedure, in common law, 32
promotion, judicial, 77–79
public law, civil law tradition and, 29
public opinion, *164*; impact and, 163, 166, *167*; legitimacy and, 176–77; in Poland, courts and, 163; US Supreme Court and, 163, 176, 185

qingshi, 86–87, 97
quota systems, 118
Quran, 33–34, 89

rabbinical courts, 46
Ramseyer, Mark, 82
rape, *164*
reconciliation, 40–41
recruitment, judicial, 77, 79–80, 82
religious courts, 46–47
removal, judicial, 77–78, 81–82
resident judges, 27–28
Riina, Salvatore (Totò), *98*
Ríos-Figueroa, Julio, 118

ripple effects, 5–6, 154, 159, *160*, 161
Roberts, John, 1–2
Roe v. Wade, 155, 157, 167–68
Romania, 82–83
Roman law, 26–27, 42
Rosenberg, Gerald, 161
Russia, 95; constitutional review in, 108–9, 113, 122–23; ECtHR and, 141; enforcement in, 152
Rwanda, 3, 6, 21, 40, 141–42

same-sex marriage, *167*
Sandholtz, Wayne, 129
Sarbah, John Mensah, 38
Saudi Arabia, 10, 23
Scotland, 61, *139*
Second Amendment, 178
selection, judicial, 78, 80–81
Serbian Constitutional Court, 110, 113
sex discrimination, 65, 69
Shakespeare, William, 51
Shany, Yuval, 145
Shapiro, Martin, ix, 38, 71–72
Shar'ia (way to water), 34
Shar'ia law. *See* Islamic law
Shelley v. Kraemer, 68
Sierra Leone, 131, 141–42
Singapore, 65–66, 77, 105
Sisi, Abdel-Fattah al, 72
Sitali, Alice, 52
soft law, 133, *134*, 147
solicitors, 55, 61
Sorbonne Declaration, 56
South Africa, 69, 77, 163; Constitutional Court in, legitimacy of, 174; constitutional review in, 112–13; customary law in, 40–41; housing in, right to, 161; Lands Claim Court in, 175;

lawyers in, 53; legal education in, 58; legal profession in, 61–62; reconciliation in, 40; Supreme Court of, dialogue theory and, 158
sovereignty costs, 145–46, *146*
Spain, 87, *140*, *164*
specialized courts, 47–48; in Germany, 45; international, 131, 142; in US, 45–46
Sri Lanka, 23, *37*, 41
stare decisis, 31–32
Stewart, Potter, 173
Stone Sweet, Alec, 129–30
Sudan, 33, 36, 59–60
Süleyman (sultan), 35
sunna, 34
Supreme Court, British, 21, 105–6
Supreme Court, US, 103, 124–25; *Bush v. Gore* decision of, 21, 174; as comparative framework, 18; as constrained, 158; desegregation ordered by, 153, 158; *District of Columbia v. Heller* decision of, 69, 178; judges of, 3–4; *King v. Burwell* decision of, 1–2, 4–6, 9, 20; on legislative veto, 153; *Marbury v. Madison* decision of, 113–14; military commissions and, 88; on Muslim travel ban, 72–73; nominations to, 119; previous decisions overruled by, 32; public opinion and, 163, 176, 185; *Roe v. Wade* decision of, 155, 157, 167–68; *Shelley v. Kraemer* decision of, 68; on student free speech, 164–65
Switzerland, 9, 131
Syrian refugee crisis, *160*

Tanzania, 57, 64–65
Team Humanity, *160*
Telegram, 152
Temer, Michel, *90*
tenure, judicial, 77–78
Thailand, 15, 19
Togo, 26–27
Tokyo Tribunal, 134, 141
Totò. *See* Riina, Salvatore
traditions, of law, 19; global distribution of, 27; legal identity offered by, 48–49; mixed, 26–27, *27*; pluralism of, 24–26, 47
transactions, 130, 133, 142–43
triad, legal, 10, 38, 71–72
The Trial (Kafka), 51
trial courts: criminal, in civil and common law, 43–45; dispute resolution and, 11, 13–16; military rule and, 47, 85; Muslim travel ban opposed in, 97; ripple effects of, 21, 159, *160*
TRIPs Agreement. *See* Agreement on Trade-Related Aspects of Intellectual Property Rights
Trump, Donald, 72, 97, 127–28, 186
Tsebelis, George, 92, 94, 116
Turkey: constitutional referendum in, 84, 92, 102–3; constitutional review in, *102*, 102–3, 105, 109, 118, 122; Erdogan in, 84, 92, *93*, 102, *102*
Tushnet, Mark, 113–14, 178

Uganda, 40, 48, 77
UK. *See* Britain
Ukraine, 95
UN. *See* United Nations

UN Convention on the Law of the Sea, 135–36
United Nations (UN), 6, 134
United Nations Charter of Human Rights, 165
United Nations Universal Declaration of Human Rights, 182
United States (US): abortion in, 155, 157, 167–68; Burundi compared with, 3–4, 16–17; comma case in, 152; common law tradition in, 3, 32, 44–45; as comparative framework, 18; constitutional review in, 7, 78, 103, 108, 113–14, 124–25; constitutional review model of, 105, 107, 111, 181–82; constitution of, 4, 95, 108, 165, 178; desegregation in, 153, 158; de Tocqueville on, 186–87; enforcement in, 152–53; IACtHR and, 131; ICJ and, 22, 144; institutional veto players in, 92; interest group litigation in, 67–69; international courts and, 144–45; judicial appointments in, 80; judicial elections in, 80–81; judicial independence in, 74, 78; judicial selection in, 78; legal education in, 56; military courts in, 45–47, 88; Muslim travel ban of, 72–73, 97; precedent in, 32; specialized courts in, 45–46; state judges in, 99; student free speech in, 164–65; WTO and, 144–45. *See also* Supreme Court, US
Urribarri, Raul A. Sanchez, 66
US. *See* United States

Vallinder, Torbjörn, 6

Vatican City (Holy See), 26
Venezuela, *47, 79, 115,* 144–45
veto players: constitutional review and, 116–17, 119; judicial authority and, 92–96; partisan, 92, 94–96
Vienna Convention on the Law of Treaties, 135
Vietnam, 14–15, 19, 58
Vose, Clement, 68

Wasby, Stephen L., 154
way to water (*Shar'ia*), 34
Wen Jiabao, 82
West Bank, 9–10, 48, 88
Westphalian system, 132, 145, 149
Wheeler, Russell, ix
wife inheritance (*kugara nhaka*), 39
women: in customary law, 39, 40–41; as lawyers, 63. *See also* sex discrimination
World Trade Organization (WTO), 13, 58; Appellate Body of, 136; coercive mechanisms of, 129; dispute settlement of, 21, 128–31, 136, 144–45; hard law and, 136
World War II, 134, 141
WTO. *See* World Trade Organization
Wu Xiaohui, 159

Yeltsin, Boris, 123
Yugoslavia, civil war in, 141–42, 165

Zambia, 52, 57, 62, 103
Zimbabwe, 39, 39, 51, 77